THE LIBRARY
ST. MARY'S COLLEGE OF MARYLAND
ST. MARY'S CITY, MARYLAND 20686

P9-AOW-826

THE CIVILIZATION OF THE AMERICAN INDIAN SERIES

(Complete list on page 255)

The Southern Indians

THE STORY OF
THE CIVILIZED TRIBES
BEFORE REMOVAL

THE
SOUTHERN
INDIANS

THE STORY OF
THE CIVILIZED TRIBES
BEFORE REMOVAL

BY R. S. COTTERILL

NORMAN

UNIVERSITY OF OKLAHOMA PRESS

BY R. S. COTTERILL

The Southern Indians: The Story of the Civilized Tribes
before Removal (Norman, 1954)
A Short History of the Americas (New York, 1945)
The Old South (Glendale, California, 1935)
History of Pioneer Kentucky (Cincinnati, 1917)

The Southern Indians is Volume 38 in
The Civilization of the American Indian Series.

INTERNATIONAL STANDARD BOOK NUMBER: 0–8061–0286–1

LIBRARY OF CONGRESS CATALOG CARD NUMBER: 54–5931

COPYRIGHT 1954 BY THE UNIVERSITY OF OKLAHOMA PRESS
PUBLISHING DIVISION OF THE UNIVERSITY
MANUFACTURED IN THE U.S.A.
FIRST EDITION, 1954
SECOND PRINTING, 1963
THIRD PRINTING, 1966
FOURTH PRINTING, 1971

DUOBUS FRATRIBUS MEIS

PREFACE

This book has been written in self-defense. The writer on beginning his teaching of Southern history found that he needed a knowledge of Southern Indians and failed to find it in the books then in print. He was forced, therefore, into an investigation of source material which, before it was completed, spread out over some twenty-five years and carried him into practically all Southern states as well as into several in the North.

The Southern Indians, with the exception of Alexander Mc-Gillivray, were singularly inarticulate; the records of their history are records by white men. They deal chiefly with the relations of Indians and whites and are marred by prejudices and misunderstanding. Anyone attempting, as in this case, to write a history of the Indians, as distinguished from a history of their foreign relations, will find his labors multiplied by these characteristics of his sources. The writer finishes his task with no boast that his portrayal has been precise or his account complete. He hopes he has moved at least a little toward the goal of depicting Indian history as it was.

There are several schools of thought concerning plurals of Indian tribal names; in this book, plurals have been formed in accordance with the policy of the University of Oklahoma Press.

In the course of his investigation the author has received undue aid and courtesies from so many people that it would be impossible even to enumerate them here. To Miss Louise Richardson and her staff of the Florida State University Library, to the Lawson McGee Library, the Filson Club, the Manuscript Division of the Library of Congress, the United States Archives, the Georgia, Alabama, and Mississippi departments of archives and history, the state historical societies of Wisconsin, Kentucky, and Florida, the writer can make only this blanket expression of gratitude for manifold favors received.

Finally, the writer is grateful to President Doak S. Campbell and to Dean Edwin Walker for release from teaching duties at Florida State University so that he could complete this book.

R. S. Cotterill

Tallahassee, Florida

CONTENTS

ILLUSTRATIONS

MAPS

The Southern Indians

THE STORY OF

THE CIVILIZED TRIBES

BEFORE REMOVAL

I

The Southern Indians

THE INDIANS who at the close of the American Revolution occupied those regions of the South then claimed and partially possessed by the United States were comparatively late comers to the land. Preceding them had been a branch of those people who were called Siouan by their unadmiring neighbors and who in some remote, pre-Columbian period had broken from their Northern brethren in the neighborhood of the Great Lakes to become (as far as ethnology knows) the oldest inhabitants of the South. About the time of the discovery of America they were wandering out again, but the first explorers of the South found some of them lingering in broken tribes between the James and the Cooper and traces of their long-continued stay in the Piedmont of Virginia and in the valley of the upper Ohio. Their migration went down the Ohio to divide at its mouth, sending one group up the Mississippi to rejoin the parent stock and a second one down the river to become the Quapaw and Osage; little Siouan fragments, such as the Ofo in northern Mississippi and the Biloxi on the Gulf of Mexico, at this time perhaps became detached from the main current and were left in isolation. The migration was apparently a mass movement under pressure from Indians recently arrived whose enmity later destroyed such Siouan groups as now rejected emigration or escaped expulsion. For the other Indians of the South regarded the Sioux not with the routine intertribal animosity, but with a loathing not to be appeased short of extermination. The Siouan characteristics of head-flattening, tattooing, long hair, and professional prostitution impressed the other Indians as heathenish and even as sub-human.[1]

The Siouans seem to have occupied principally the perimeter of the South: the Algonquian family penetrated only into Maryland and Virginia, where they were entirely underfoot by the time of the American Revolution. An eccentric and isolated bit of Algonquian penetration that broke loose from the Sac in Illinois flanked the mountains to the west and reached so far south as to gain the name Shawnee. Settling on the Cumberland at a place later called French Lick and now Nashville, these Indians became thoroughly identified with the river which bore their name for eighty years until 1749, when Dr. Thomas Walker, with more regard for current events than for native tradition (of which he may have been ignorant), renamed it. From the Cumberland some of the Shawnees went, perhaps on Cherokee invitation, to the Savannah River, on which they settled and to which they gave their name. Encountering, and probably provoking, the hostility of their Siouan neighbors and the enmity of the Carolinians, a part of the Savannah band joined the Creeks in Alabama, while the main portion migrated to Pennsylvania to rejoin their brethren who had fled thither from French Lick under the compulsion of Chickasaw attack. In 1747 the Shawnee element among the Creeks was increased by the coming of certain of their Pennsylvania brethren who had tried to settle near Muscle Shoals and had been driven out by the unrelenting Chickasaws. The Shawnees among the Creeks were few but influential; until the War of 1812 they served as liaison agents between Northern and Southern Indians and frequently brought them into combination.[2]

[1] The definitive account of the southern Siouan tribes is James Mooney's *The Siouan Tribes of the East*, Bureau of American Ethnology (hereafter cited as B. A. E.) *Bulletin No. 22*. Chapman J. Milling, in *Red Carolinians*, chapters XII and XIII, discusses the culture and history of the various Siouan tribes of the Carolinas. James B. Griffin, "On the Historic Location of the Totero and the Mohetan in the Ohio Valley," *American Anthropologist*, New Series, Vol. XLIV, 275–80, and John R. Swanton, "Siouan Tribes in the Ohio Valley," *ibid.*, XLV, 49–66, deal with the location and migrations of the Siouans of the upper Ohio.

[2] Charles A. Hanna's *The Wilderness Trail* contains the fullest account of

The incorporation, expulsion, and destruction of the Siouan and Algonquian families left the Indian South in the stronger hands of Cherokees, Creeks, Choctaws, and Chickasaws, the first belonging to the Iroquoian, the last three comprising the Muskhogean family. The Cherokees were the mountaineers of the South; their villages clung to the four slopes of that high hip roof which forms the four corners of Tennessee, Georgia, and the Carolinas. Their forty towns, with a population (in 1775) somewhat in excess of fifteen thousand, were grouped by the Carolina traders as Lower (on the Savannah waters), Middle (on the Tuckaseegee and headwaters of the Little Tennessee), and Upper, comprising the valley towns (on the Hiwassee) and Overhills (on the lower reaches of the Little Tennessee). Between the Lower and the others there was a difference of dialect sufficient to distinguish but not to separate them. From their villages in the extreme southeastern corner of their domains, the territorial claims of the Cherokees ran from the northward-flowing Tennessee on the west to the Kanawha, Broad, and Edisto on the east; from the Chattahoochee, Coosa, and Black Warrior on the south to the Ohio on the north. Although none of these boundaries was conceded by their neighbors, the Cherokees succeeded in transmitting their claims thereto into an ownership sufficient for sale.

The Cherokees (as practically every Indian tribe) were given their name not by themselves but by their neighbors. Their name Cherokee (people of the cave country) was given by the Choctaws, whose estimate of them was far less flattering than that the Cherokees themselves expressed in Aniyunwiya, "the principal people." Their language revealed their Iroquoian ancestry; their dialect, an ancient separation from the parent stock. Their Algonquin-given name, Allegewi, points to Pennsylvania as their former home, while Delaware traditions picture their movement to the South as a tribal expulsion punishing a treacherous attack on a Delaware ally. Several generations of warfare were probab-

the Shawnee wanderings. More local detail is given in Lucien Beckner, "Eskippakithiki: The Last Indian Town in Kentucky," *The Filson Club History Quarterly*, Vol. VI, 355–82. John R. Swanton, in *Early History of the Creek Indians and Their Neighbors*, B. A. E. *Bulletin No. 73*, gives considerable data on the Shawnees among the Creeks.

ly required to effect their migration until they finally halted in North Carolina around their foundation town, Cuttawa (Bryson City). Although this occurred (so far as it occurred at all) in remote pre-Columbian times, the Cherokees continued until 1768 to feel, through continuous Iroquois raids, the effects of the ancient family quarrel. At the time of their earliest white contacts the political center of the tribe was at Echota on the Little Tennessee.[3]

The three main members of the Muskhogean family had a common migration legend of a removal from some indefinite trans-Mississippi region to new homes in the Southeast. There are many indications to suggest, although insufficient evidence to prove, that the Choctaws and Chickasaws, then united as a single tribe, formed the van of this migration and spread themselves thinly over the South from the Tennessee to Tampa. It was possibly this early wide dispersion of the Choctaws that caused their language to become the basis of that Mobilian trade language known to all the Southern tribes. From this overextension the Choctaws contracted until, at the time when the first Europeans found them, they were living on the waters of the Pearl, the Chickasawhay, and the Pascagoula in the present Mississippi where their sixty or seventy towns, containing some twenty thousand people, were grouped in a southern, a western, and an eastern district. The southern district, composed of towns on the waters of the Chickasawhay and the Pascagoula rivers and having as its nucleus a group called the Six Towns, contained a large element of Siouan people whom the Choctaws had incorporated and whose dialect they found difficult to understand. The western district, with a thin population, faced the Mississippi; the eastern district contained most of the towns and the Choctaw "capital" at Koweh Chito. The name Choctaw is derived from the Creek word *cate* or *chate*, red; their Indian neighbors called them, de-

[3] For the early Cherokees there is nothing else that approaches in value James Mooney's *Myths of the Cherokee*, B. A. E. *Nineteenth Annual Report.* Cyrus Thomas, in *The Cherokees in Pre-Columbian Times*, traces the origin of the Cherokees and their enforced migration to the South. James Adair, in *History of the American Indians*, gives a description of the Cherokees at the beginning of their relations with the United States. It is most available in *Adair's History of the American Indians*, edited by S. C. Williams.

risively no doubt, Pansfalaya (long-haired people), from a Siouan custom they had adopted. Their modest territorial claims ran only from the Mississippi and the Gulf to the Cahaba and the Oktibbeha.[4]

The separation of the Chickasaws from the Choctaws is the first recorded instance of secession in Southern history, but in historic time neither tribe could say either when or why it occurred. It might be not implausibly conjectured that the schism came after they had entered the South and as a result of Chickasaw contempt for the Choctaw adoption of such heathenish Siouan customs as wearing their hair long, flattening the heads of their infants, and picking the flesh from the bones of their dead. The antiquity of the separation is suggested by the development of different dialects by the two adjacent and often intermingling peoples, although they seem to have retained a common ceremonial language. The Chickasaws possessed the fewest towns, the smallest population, and, proportionately, the most extensive territory in the Indian South. Their four or five towns were located on the Yazoo-Tombigbee divide in north central Mississippi, but their territorial claims extended from the Oktibbeha to the Ohio and from the Mississippi eastward to the Tennessee-Cumberland divide; the existence of a Chickasaw Old Fields on the Tennessee east of Muscle Shoals attested their former residence there before they retired, probably as a result of Cherokee pressure, to the safer ground of Mississippi. Their population, never more than five thousand in their palmiest days, was probably small at the time of their secession from the Choctaws and was maintained only by a policy of constant adoption of alien people. So extensive was this assimilation that by 1775 it would have been difficult to find in the tribe any "native" Chickasaw; the realistic traders in colonial days called them bluntly "The Breeds," as they did their

[4] John R. Swanton's *Source Material for the Social and Ceremonial Life of the Choctaw Indians*, B. A. E. *Bulletin No. 103* gives practically all that is known of Choctaw culture and customs. In the *Publications* of the Mississippi Historical Society are several articles by Henry S. Halbert: "Nanih Waiya, the sacred mound of the Choctaws," Vol. II, 223–34; "Funeral Customs of the Mississippi Choctaws," Vol. III, 353–66; and "The Choctaw Creation Legend," Vol. IV, 267–70. His "District Divisions of the Choctaw Nation," *Publications* of the Alabama Historical Society, Misc. Colls. I, 375–85 is very detailed.

Choctaw kinsmen the "Flat Heads." The undoubted Chickasaw courage, so often noted in history, was the result of accretion and not of native spirit.[5]

The Creeks were not a tribe, but a confederacy in which the dominant element was the Muscogee. Neither the word Muscogee nor the word Creek is Muskhogean; the latter term, of doubtful meaning, was apparently coined by the Shawnees as a labor-saving device for designating their friends who seemed to lack a collective name, and the former name was given by the South Carolina traders because the Indians to which it applied were then living on Ocheesee (Ocmulgee) Creek in Georgia. The frail testimony of place names tentatively suggests that the Muscogees preceded the Cherokees and followed the Choctaws into the South; that their inland drive forced the main body of the Choctaws westward to their historic homes in Mississippi; and that one Choctaw fragment, the Alabamas, became by force or persuasion united with them. To these two elements of the confederacy was added in time by conquests or guile the Hitchitee people who, before the coming of the Muscogees, had occupied southern Georgia and at least that part of Florida between the Apalachicola and the Aucilla rivers. To the Hitchitees in Florida the Creeks gave the name Seminole, which means, roughly, "frontiersmen." The fourth, and last, people to be incorporated in the Creek confederacy were the Euchees, who were known to their Algonquian enemies as Tohogalega and gave a corrupted form of their name, Hogaloge, to the Tennessee River, on which they had their earliest-known homes. In the seventeenth and early eighteenth century the Euchees, perhaps an isolated Siouan fragment, drifted south in several bands to settle on the Savannah and the Choctawhatchee. Incorporated, traditionally by fraud, into the Creek confederacy, they moved their towns to the Chattahoochee.

[5] John R. Swanton's *Social Beliefs and Usages of the Chickasaw Indians,* B. A. E. *Forty-fourth Annual Report,* is the most comprehensive account of Chickasaw life. *Adair's History of the American Indians* is chiefly concerned with the Chickasaws, but a considerable part of its firsthand information is made suspect by the author's obsession with the idea that the Chickasaws were descended from the Lost Tribes of Israel.

The English traders, ignoring although not ignorant of these ethnic distinctions, divided the confederacy into two geographical groups which they called the Lower Creeks and the Upper Creeks. The Lower Creeks, comprising all the Euchee and Hitchitee towns as well as a minority of the Muscogee, lived on the Flint and the Chattahoochee; the Upper Creeks, made up of the majority of the Muscogee towns, and all the Alabamas (who were Muskhogean) lived on the Coosa, Tallapoosa, and Alabama rivers. The Seminoles were sometimes counted as a part of the Lower Creeks, but generally considered as a third division. The confederacy contained fifty or sixty towns with a population of fifteen to eighteen thousand. Their towns were located roughly in the center of their claimed territory, which ran from the Gulf to the Tennessee and from the Tombigbee to the Savannah.[6]

Notwithstanding their differences of ancestry, language, and environment, the Southern Indians possessed an extensive community of culture and custom and a great similarity of social and economic patterns. A primitive distaste for isolation made them all town dwellers, with only their outcasts and pariahs living their lives alone. Their towns, located invariably on the banks of a stream or, if inland, close to a spring, commonly straggled prodigiously over areas wholly disproportionate to the population thereof. The dwellings, widely scattered and haphazardly placed, centered, socially rather than geographically, around a "square," on the sides of which were such buildings for government and public utility as the town possessed. The dwelling places of the people, after the introduction of axes, were log cabins with makeshift roofs, without floors, bunks doing double duty as beds and chairs, and a fireplace in the center, from which the smoke (and most of the heat) ascended through a hole in the roof. There was no kitchen, for cooking was done whenever possible in the open. The houses were dirty, flea-ridden, uncomfortable, and unsightly

[6] The definitive account of the Creeks is given in two works by John R. Swanton: *Early History of the Creek Indians and Their Neighbors,* and *Social Organization and Social Usages of the Indians of the Creek Confederacy,* B. A. E. *Forty-second Annual Report.* Because of liberal quotations from contemporary accounts, both are practically source books. Benjamin Hawkins, in *A Sketch of the Creek Country in the Years 1798 and 1799,* gives much earlier history in connection with a contemporary description.

but they served their purpose as points of departure. The Southern Indian, being both Southern and Indian, regarded his house as a place in which to sleep at night and to find haven from inclement weather; he lived out of doors. But each family tried to possess a "hot-house," in which it could live during cold weather in warm but unventilated comfort.

From these towns, of no typical size or shape, the Indians went out to their work in field and forest. All Southern Indians depended for their subsistence on agriculture, and every town and village had around it its cultivated fields from which it drew its food supply. The favorite crop, and the largest, was everywhere corn, the importance of which to them was shown by their custom of timing their festivals and councils to its appearing and ripening grain. They raised melons for current consumption, and beans, potatoes (Irish and sweet), squash, and pumpkins for deferred as well as immediate use. Their fields were, in fact, "truck patches," and their agriculture limited to subsistence farming: only the sedentary and thrifty Choctaws ever had a surplus stock for sale. Planting and harvesting were communal enterprises in which both men and women participated; cultivation was scanty, not, it is to be supposed, because it was done by the women but because of the crude implements in use. Returns were generally as scanty as the cultivation, but as a rule each family raised enough, when supplemented by hunting, to feed itself and to place some portion in the public storehouse on the square for common use in emergencies. When a field wore out, as it eventually did even under the lenient and undemanding Indian cultivation, there was no recourse but to abandon it and move the town to another location. The Creeks called an abandoned town site a *tallahassee*, and the name, modified sometimes to *talassie* or *tulsa*, is common in the South; one of these tallahassees has become a state capital.

Before the coming of the white trader, the Indians hunted, as they farmed, only for subsistence. Hunting was a species of work, and, although it is not to be supposed that it was unenjoyable, the Indians seemed rarely to have indulged in it as a sport. They killed apologetically only what they needed, not so much in a provident preserving of their game supply as in superstitious awe of the departed animal spirits. Hunting on foot with bow and arrow and rarely using even the dog as an accessory, the hunters served materially to replenish the domestic larder but little to diminish the game supply. Not until the white trader came among them did hunting become a source of profit and hunting grounds a subject of contention.

There is much to suggest that previous to their contact with white men the Southern Indians were ardent neither for hunting nor for war. The frantic mourning in an Indian town over the death of a warrior reveals their high regard for human life and suggests that they would not lightly risk in war what they so highly valued. There were few occasions for intertribal quarrels: boundaries were matters of indifference when hunting grounds were so wide, game so plentiful, and hunters so few; there were no conflicting economic interests because there were no economic interests to conflict; there was no struggle for power because there was no use to which power could be put; and the Southern Indians no more considered war a sport than they considered hunting a pastime. Even if it is not admitted that the inclination for war was lacking, it must be conceded that the means for it were few. Because their food supply was always scanty, Indian war parties were rarely able to enlist large numbers or to take them far afield; as long as they fought with bow and arrow, they were unable because of a lack of supplies either to long sustain a battle or to bring it to a quick conclusion. Their ordnance and commissary arrangements were always defective. Scalping, if not unknown, was rare before the white men brought the steel knife; prisoners experienced adoption more often than torture; and burnings at the stake occurred among the Indians about as frequently as lynchings among the white men and, like lynchings, were indulged in when passions were high. Since even in colonial days the Indian tribes rarely fought each other except in wars fomented by white allies, it may be doubted whether there ever existed among them any of those "hereditary feuds" to which reference is often made. The Chickasaws and Choctaws seem to have separated in peace and to have agreed on a dividing line (the only one in the South really needed because of the nearness of their respective towns) so early that both tribes had forgotten the date and only remembered the fact. The "feud" between Creeks and Choctaws permitted them to trade, to interchange ceremonial visits, to engage in ball games against each other, and occasionally to ally themselves against a common foe. Creeks and Cherokees, Cherokees and Chickasaws met each other often in amity, infrequently in war.

Certainly at home among his own people the Indian was orderly (as the Indian estimated order) and peaceable, but not as a result of legislation, of which he had little, or of restraint, of which he had still less. The Southern Indians (and other Indians as well) had managed to reconcile a system of economic communism with a retention of individual liberty—a combination that no modern society has been able to effect. They did this by reducing their government so nearly to anarchy that it operated only by practically unanimous consent and, consequently, had no dissident minorities to restrain. In all four nations, if it be proper so to refer to them, the unit of government was the town with its elective, permanent civil chief and elective, temporary war chief. The town chiefs composed the national council, which met generally twice a year, in May (when vegetables were plenty) and in September (when the grain was harvested). Then, with elaborate ceremony and prolific oratory, it declared the national policy and occasionally made a law. There is little evidence that prior to contact with the Europeans any Southern Indian tribe had a head chief or even regional chiefs. These positions seem to have been instituted by the French and English in order to secure responsible agents with whom they might deal. Among the Chickasaws the head chieftanship, perhaps by English suggestion, took the odd, un-Indian turn of becoming hereditary, being handed down, according to Indian custom, from ruler to brother or nephew. Englishmen and Americans always called the Chickasaw head chief the king. Hereditary or elective, the head chief's authority was legally little and actually only what his influence and ability could make it. The decisions of the national council did not bind any town which chose to dissent; even the decrees of the town councils bound no individual who wished to disobey. Notwithstanding this virtual absence of authority, life among the Indians was perhaps as tranquil as among the white people. Civil wars were almost unknown; the abnormality of murder is shown by the horror in which it was held; civil disputes were settled by arbitration; lesser crimes were compounded rather than punished. The paradox of anarchy and order is, of course, to be explained by the strength of custom which regulated conduct and disregard of which made the Indian a pariah.

Communism, therefore, among the Indians represented not the will of the rulers (of whom they had none), but the unity of the tribe. By combining it with anarchy the Indians kept it free from those encroachments on individual liberty which seem inseparable from all its modern expressions and practiced it purely as an economic device. The Indians did not have, and have never willingly accepted, any conception of private ownership of land. They insisted that the land belonged to the tribe as a whole and could not be engrossed by individuals, towns, or districts. Custom permitted or recognized the control of each town over the adjacent fields and over their annual allotment to families for cultivation. It permitted private ownership of the crops raised by private effort subject to a reserve for public use. Private ownership of personal property was recognized but hampered by the scarcity of personal property to own. War and hunting equipment, houses, dogs, horses, and clothing about completed the list of things available to the Southern Indians in 1775.

Communism freed the Indian from ambition to acquire wealth as anarchy freed him from temptation to seek power. It made him improvident of the future, minimized class distinctions, re-emphasized co-operation, promoted tribal solidarity. It may be that the hospitality for which the Indian was noted sprang from his inability to store up wealth; his generosity, from the inutility of saving; his idleness, from a lack of incentive to thrift. His large amount of uncensured leisure gave him an opportunity to visit and entertain and to lounge in the sun in the square, where he listened with respect to the admonitions of the old men and with pleasure to the talk of the young. Ordinarily he was as garrulous as he was gregarious, inveterate in gossip, and much given to the telling of jokes which depended on neither subtlety nor refinement for their appeal. Taciturnity he reserved for state occasions, for meetings with suspected strangers, and for negotiations with known enemies, at all which times he could remain silent with dignity and decorum. He was neither sad nor sadistic. His release from the bonds of ambition and his sense of security made him cheerful and tolerant; his cruelty resulted from temporary passion and not from innate disposition. He had a primitive talent for domestic life, deferred prudently to his wife (to whom by Indian custom the home and household furnishings belonged), and was devoted to his children, over whom he had no control and whose lineage he traced, realistically, through their maternal forebears. He painted himself artistically for personal adornment, sparingly for identification, horribly for war, grotesquely for amusement, and seasonally as a kind of mosquito control. Both as spectator and participant, he delighted in games and gambling, the combination of which frequently sent him home, bereft of all worldly goods, to his family, for the same reason equally bereft. What religion he had was private, unorganized for public expression, without missionary duties, and wholly unrelated to his morality, which he drew from tribal custom. He held women in high esteem, admitting them to share his private labors as well as his public counsels, imparting to them secrets which they frequently, unpenalized and apparently uncriticized, revealed, and conceding to them a freedom of action and an immunity to regulation such as modern women have nowhere obtained.

Finally, the Southern Indian was a child of the forests whom the open country filled with great uneasiness. Through these unbroken forests he was accustomed to travel on private visiting and on public business, in war parties and hunting groups, as trader and even as tourist. So doing, he made innumerable paths leading from town to town, from home to hunting camp, and from tribe to tribe. These paths were literally "highways," since to avoid jungles and swamps and low lands made impassable by overflowing streams, the Indians journeyed, whenever possible, along the divides. The narrowness of the paths was a laborsaving device which resulted in the Indian custom of traveling single file. So numerous were the paths and so intricate the network with its variants and detours that no Indian, whatever his native instinct or acquired woodcraft, could, without direction, long keep his course. Therefore the Indian roads, as distinguished from the animal trails, were commonly marked; a painted tree, a cabalistic sign on a rock, a pattern of small mounds, and other signs guided the traveler as he journeyed through the forests. Many of these roads, adapted from buffalo trails, graduated into traces for white traders, evolved into the pioneer dirt roads, and finally became the paved highways for modern traffic. Such has been the history of the great Warrior's Path through Kentucky, the Occaneechee Path through the Siouan tribes of North Carolina, the Natchez Trace through the Choctaw and Chickasaw country of Mississippi and Tennessee, and many others.[7]

There was (what is often overlooked) a considerable amount of trade over these roads and a professional class of Indian traders who carried it on. They peddled salt from the many "licks," pipes from the Cherokee country, farm products from the Choctaw, shells from the seacoast for wampum and decoration, flint for arrows, and a variety of other objects. The Shawnees were avid traders, whose Eskippakithiki town in central Kentucky, where the Warrior's Path entered, or emerged from, the mountains, had many of the features of a "fair" town resorted to by Indians from north and south seeking an interchange of goods. The professional traders were professional neutrals whose activities were so valued that they could continue them practically unhampered in the midst of war. Like most professionals they had a peculiar jargon (called Mobilian), a sort of "pidgin" Indian, employing words from every Southern Indian language, especially the Choctaw, and everywhere well enough understood to make trade possible. It was the Indian's familiarity with the benefits of trade that made them accept the white trader so avidly as to affect their development and to alter their destiny.

[7] W. E. Myer's "Indian Trails of the Southeast," B. A. E. *Forty-second Annual Report*, describes the Indian roads in detail, with a helpful accompanying map. This article and John R. Swanton's "Aboriginal Culture of the Southeast," in the same volume, are indispensable for any understanding of the Southern Indians.

II

The Colonial Background

T HE FIRST of the Southern Indians
to come into continued contact with the English settlers were
those of the Muscogee towns near the falls of the Chattahoochee.
To these in 1685 came the traders from Charleston, bringing a
wealth of commodities that the Creeks had never known to exchange for things for which the Creeks had hitherto had no market. When the Spanish mission, Santa Cruz at the junction of the
Flint and the Chattahoochee, after a vain effort to prevent, by
oral exhortation, its prospective spiritual charges from falling under the secular influence of the English, prepared to temper its
ineffective spiritual appeal with a seasoning of military argument,
the Creeks, preferring the role of English customers to that of
Spanish converts, moved their towns to new sites on Ocheese
Creek (Ocmulgee River).[1] To these new locations, having (for
the Creeks) the double charm of proximity to English trade and
remoteness from Spanish reproaches, came the Carolina traders
bringing their novel wares of hardware and clothing to exchange
for peltry. Probably the (Ocheesee) Creek Indians lost no time in
carrying to their brethren on the Coosa and Tallapoosa the glad
tidings of their new commercial blessedness; whether as a result
of these suggestions or the promptings of commercial enterprise,
the Indians of Alabama were, by 1696, welcoming the Carolina

[1] Verner W. Crane, "The Origin of the Name of the Creek Indians," *Mississippi Valley Historical Review*, Vol. V, 339-42.

traders. Two years later the rustic Chickasaws were receiving them in a spirit of appreciation destined to be permanent. Because of the long transportation and difficult approach to them, the Cherokees received only the crumbs that fell from the Charleston table; for the time being the Choctaws, because of remoteness or the neighborly enmity of Chickasaws and Creeks, remained unvisited and unsupplied.[2]

No Indian indifference to this trade is indicated by their policy of waiting in their towns for the wares to be brought to them on English initiative. It brought them comforts and conveniences they had never known: guns and ammunition which increased the tempo of both their hunting and hostility; cutting tools such as hatchets, knives, axes, and hoes, which enabled them to build better houses and more easily cultivate their fields; creature comforts such as pipes, scissors, beads, kettles, pots and pans, mirrors, salt, vermilion (for paint), and rum; and clothing in the form of blankets, shirts, coats, and hats, as well as staples like strouds and calico, which they could use as their fancy suggested. For these they bartered chiefly two things—deerskins and slaves. The demand for the former elevated, or at least changed, hunting from a supplementary means of subsistence to the dignity of a business and intensified, if, indeed, it did not create, tribal competition for hunting grounds with an accompanying increase of hostilities. Increasing wars resulted also from the demand for slaves (to be sold to the West Indies), which could be, legitimately, met only by the sale of captives. A Chickasaw-Choctaw war, beginning apparently about 1690, by 1702 (according to later French statistics) had augmented the Chickasaw trading facilities by five hundred Choctaw captives and had accumulated a by-product of eighteen hundred Choctaw and eight hundred Chickasaw dead before the

---

[2] The rapid advance of the Carolina traders through the Creek and Chickasaw country is described by Verner W. Crane in *The Southern Frontier, 1670–1732*. The Cherokees had been visited by the Virginians, Arthur and Needham, in 1673, and after the obstructing Occaneechee had been removed by Nathaniel Bacon in 1676, Virginia traders had been reaching the Cherokee towns over the Occaneechee Path; this trading path was long and hazardous, and the trade, therefore, intermittent. Both trade and road are well described by Neil Franklin, "Virginia and the Cherokee Indian Trade, 1673–1752," East Tennessee Historical Society *Publications*, Vol. IV, 3–21.

French, lately established at Mobile, were able by triple promises of protection (against Illinois Indians), merchandise, and missionaries to induce them, in March, 1702, to make peace.[3]

With the opening of Queen Anne's War in 1702, the four great tribes of the South found themselves the apparently enviable recipients of solicitations for support from the English, Spanish, and French. So great was the lure of English trade that both Creeks and Chickasaws aligned themselves with Carolina, their native recognition of self-interest being powerfully reinforced by the arguments of the traders and a timely adjustment of prices. In the summer of 1702 the Creeks furnished the Carolinians a force of five hundred warriors to scuttle a Spanish advance on the Flint River; in January, 1704, they sent an army of one thousand into Florida to the almost total destruction of Apalachee province; and, in the same year, massacred a French diplomatic mission. These scattered manifestations of good will were followed in August, 1705, by a formal alliance with Carolina.[4]

The Chickasaws, not less ardent than the Creeks in perpetuating their source of supplies, revived in 1704, in order to secure an even flow of captives, the Choctaw war, which two years before had been "forever" closed. In such an emergency the Choctaws could do nothing less than ask for French aid, and the French could do nothing more than promise it. The protective qualities of French assurances were made clear in the autumn of 1705, when the Choctaw country was invaded and laid waste by a force of Chickasaws and Creeks numbering three thousand or three hundred, according as one adopts French or English reports. In 1708 the weary Choctaws, thoroughly convinced of the superiority of English guns over Choctaw bows, made peace. But the English traders, finding that a Chickasaw-Choctaw peace only opened a competing supply line from Mobile, renewed their pressure, with the result that the war reopened in May, 1711, with such hearty

---

[3] Peter J. Hamilton, *Colonial Mobile*, 43.

[4] Verner W. Crane, "The Southern Frontier in Queen Anne's War," *American Historical Review*, Vol. XXIV, 379–95, Swanton, *Early Creek Indians*, 121–23. Dunbar Rowland and Albert G. Sanders, eds., *Mississippi Provincial Archives, French Dominion*, III, 19–22 (hereafter cited as *Miss. Prov. Ar., French Dominion*).

good will that before the year ended the Choctaws increased their casualties by 160 dead and 260 prisoners. Completely dissatisfied with such progress, all the Choctaw towns but three allied themselves with the English; the other three removed in loyalty and fear to the vicinity of Mobile.[5]

Shortly after the close of Queen Anne's War it became evident that the outward co-operation of the Creeks with the English had not been the reflection of a complete spiritual accord. Disharmony between the two had resulted when the traders, unsatisfied by the number of commercial captives created by the normal operations of intertribal war, had supplemented their supply of slaves by kidnapping the Creeks themselves. To this act (which the primitive Creeks suspected was a violation of business ethics), the traders had added the uncommendable practices of cheating in trade, of defrauding their hosts while hampered by intoxication superinduced by the traders themselves, of arrogance toward the men and lewdness toward the women. Creek protests against these imported forms of misconduct had brought no improvement until in 1707 Carolina's extremity forced an attempted reform. The colony at that time took control of the trade, required traders to have licenses, provided for resident agents, and forbade the sale of rum to friendly Indians. When this plan (which was the model for all future, local or central, regulation of Indian trade) broke down because the traders refused to take out licenses, observe the regulations, or discontinue their criticized conduct, the exasperated Creeks proceeded to apply their own remedy.

The extremely logical plan of the Creeks was to reform the Carolina system by annihilating the Carolinians, to follow the murder of the traders with a destruction of the colony from which the traders came, and to fill the resulting commercial vacuum by trading with the French and Spaniards. This plan had all the earmarks of domestic manufacture, and there is no reason to believe that the prospective French and Spanish beneficiaries had any part in formulating it. The Creeks, having successfully inaugurated the reform movement by murdering all the traders they

[5] Crane, "The Southern Frontier in Queen Anne's War," *loc. cit.*; *Miss. Prov. Ar., French Dominion*, I, 156–57; III, 34, 183.

could find, entrusted the next step to the sympathizing Yemassee in southern South Carolina, and for the prosecution of the ensuing "Yemassee War" attempted to enlist the co-operation of the Choctaws and Cherokees. Bienville, the French governor at Mobile, aided the attempt (with or without Creek suggestion) by securing in 1715 the murder of Conchak Emike, who was violently pro-British and "the most distinguished man of the Choctaws"; by appointing his murderer, Chickacha Oulacta, as head chief; and by permitting, when perhaps he could not prevent, the killing of the Carolina traders who had swarmed in after Queen Anne's War. Among the Cherokees the antagonism to the Creeks was currently so strong that neither their remembrance of trading iniquities nor the opportunity of destroying white men could bring them into the conflict. Instead, in August, 1715, they made an alliance with the Carolinians and promised for use against the Creeks a force which they failed to supply. When shortly after this the Lower Cherokees received simultaneously the visit of a small Creek embassy and the diplomatic mission of three hundred Carolina militia, they resolved their embarrassment by murdering the Creeks and combining with the Carolinians to chase back to the Creek country a force of five hundred warriors who had come to add weight to the Creek suggestions. The Yemassee War, which after a fair beginning had been proceeding more and more falteringly for the Indians, virtually came to an end with this decided Cherokee action. During the course of the war distance had prevented the Choctaws from attacking, and the Chickasaws from aiding, the Carolina settlements.[6]

The failure of the Creek movement (which, since it failed, is entitled to the label "conspiracy") was followed by a shifting of Creek towns, a change of Creek policy, and a long Creek-Cherokee war. In 1716 the Creeks moved their Ocmulgee towns, now menaced by a Cherokee flanking attack, back to their old positions on the Chattahoochee in supporting nearness to the main

---

[6] *Miss. Prov. Ar., French Dominion*, I, 157–58; III, 187; Crane, *The Southern Frontier*, 179–82; Milling, *op. cit.*, 148–50. When Bienville learned that the Creeks were killing the traders, he sent a French mission to them "to get out of their hands the Englishmen whom they had not yet killed." Chichacha Oulacta was apparently the first head chief the Choctaws ever had.

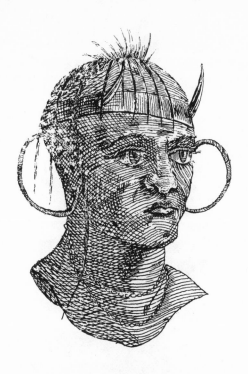

Characteristic head of a Creek war chief
From Bernard Romans' *A Concise
Natural History
of East and West Florida*

*Smithsonian Office of Anthropology
Bureau of American Ethnology Collection*

Bust of a Chickasaw warrior
From Bernard Romans' *A Concise
Natural History
of East and West Florida*

*Smithsonian Office of Anthropology
Bureau of American Ethnology Collection*

Muscogee body in Alabama. Gathering around them there and on the Flint the Hitchitee people of southern Georgia and the Euchee people who had moved down from the Tennessee, they perfected from these discordant elements in combination with the Choctaw Alabamas, and the Upper Muscogees that union thereafter called the Creek Confederation. Its leading town was the Muscogee Coweta under the astute direction of a chief whom the Carolinians called Old Brim.[7]

The attitude of the confederation toward the French and British reflected, if it did not result from, a division of sentiment. The Alabamas, from proximity and Choctaw influence, favored the French, while the Upper Muscogees, perhaps because of Chickasaw influence, preferred the British: the former in 1717 went to the extreme of permitting, and perhaps of soliciting, the building of a French fort in the heart of their country.[8] Under these conditions the Creek policy dictated by Old Brim anticipated the Jeffersonian formula of peace and friendship with all nations, entangling alliances with none. Between the bickering French and British, Old Brim wished the Creeks to hold the balance of power and so be forever wooed and never won. In November, 1717, he negotiated, on Carolina invitation, a peace which named the Savannah as the Creek-Carolina boundary and provided for a resumption of trade on such favorable terms that even the Alabamas, after being suitably softened with presents, accepted it. Although the Creeks admitted a Carolina factor to permanent residence, they received for several years few British supplies, because in 1715 Carolina had disciplined the private traders by forbidding private trade and had substituted for it a system of

[7] Crane, in *The Southern Frontier*, 254, says that the Yemassee War promoted a further amalgamation into Creek confederation; Swanton, in *Early Creek Indians*, 257, gives reasons for believing that the confederation existed in the time of DeSoto. The Hitchitees and Euchees spoke languages unintelligible to the Muscogees. The Alabamas took practically no part in the confederation councils.

[8] The fort, officially christened Fort Toulouse but commonly called the Alabama Fort, was on the Tallapoosa near its junction with the Coosa. It became the center of French influence and French trade, but it is not apparent from the records that it served to influence Creek policy. Too far from Mobile to be effectively supported, its garrison was, in effect, hostages held by the Alabama division of the Creeks.

public stores on the Savannah, to which the Indians were invited to bring their peltry for exchange. Accustomed to having their trade brought to them, the Creeks showed, by continued absence, such an antipathy to the new arrangement that after three years of progressive failure it was abolished and private trade restored.[9] Thereafter the Creeks traded with both Charleston and Mobile, but no British forts were permitted in the Creek country; a French request for a Lower Creek fort was skillfully evaded; and Spanish appeals for the expulsion of English traders were refused, although in 1717 a Creek delegation is said to have visited the viceroy of New Spain and to have courteously taken the oath of allegiance to Spain.

The twelve-year Creek-Cherokee war, resulting from the mass murder of the Creek mission at Tugalo in 1715, owed its duration to the absence of peacemaking machinery among the Indians. The Cherokees had leisure for a Creek war, since they had in 1712, in conjunction with Carolina, expelled their inimical Tuscarora kinsmen, and in 1715, with Chickasaw aid, had driven the Shawnees back from the Cumberland to a new location on Red River in Kentucky, from which their occasional raids constituted more a nuisance than a danger.[10] In 1721 they increased their content thus created by signing at Congaree with Francis Nicholson, the first royal governor of South Carolina, a treaty providing for certain trading reforms and a common boundary. As a by-product of this treaty they created, on Nicholson's suggestion, the new office of principal chief, elevating thereto a chief whom the Carolina writers have effectively disguised as Wrosetasatow.[11] From this treaty, however, the Cherokees received no aid from the Carolinians, whose ambition was to see both tribes

[9] The Carolina experiment with the factory system is described in Crane, *The Southern Frontier*, 193-99.

[10] Samuel Cole Williams, *Dawn of Tennessee Valley and Tennessee History*, 75-78. The Shawnees seem to have fortified at least one of their Cumberland towns. From a French trading post there the location was generally known as French Lick. The final blow in the expulsion of the Shawnees was given apparently by the Chickasaws alone.

[11] Milling, *op. cit.*, 273-74. It has been conjectured that this name is a form of Outacite, "man killer." At this time Chorite Haygi was chief of the Lower towns, and Caesar of the Middle towns.

weakened by a long war to a condition of mutual impotence. As usual, the neutral pleased neither; and when their displeasure became so great as apparently to presage a joint attack on South Carolina, that province in January, 1727, arranged, with some difficulty, an uneasy end to their mutually satisfactory war.[12]

While the British were clandestinely encouraging the Cherokees and Creeks in a policy of mutual destruction, the French had been openly promoting a revival of the Choctaw-Chickasaw "hereditary" feud. The eagerness of the Choctaws to promote this enterprise grew out of the necessity of delivering to the French a constant supply of slaves and scalps, for which alone they could secure guns and ammunition from that friendly but impecunious colony. The Alabamas, solicited to join their Choctaw kinsmen against the French foe, decided (with an eye to continued English supplies) on a neutrality, the benevolence of which prompted them in August, 1721, to assist the officers at Fort Toulouse in suppressing a mutiny by massacring the garrison. For three years the martial ardor of the Choctaws expended itself more in pledging devotion than in inflicting casualties, until in January, 1723, they responded to French appeals by invading the country of their minuscule adversary, from whom they secured four hundred scalps and one hundred prisoners.[13] Although the French account of this affair is subject to the discount usual in evaluating war dispatches, there can be no doubt that the Chickasaws were grievously hurt. One band of them went to live with the Cherokees, another among the Upper Creeks, and a third settled on the Savannah under Carolina protection. But the remainder succeeded so completely in cutting the Mississippi life line between New Orleans and Illinois that in December, 1724, Bienville, on a joint Chickasaw and Choctaw application, reluctantly arranged a peace, which he knew would be followed by an infiltration of Carolina traders into the Choctaw country.

Knowing that Indian affections followed the trade routes, the French exerted themselves to keep the Choctaws supplied and even built a storehouse for their goods at Koweh Chito the resi-

[12] Crane, *The Southern Frontier*, 269–70.
[13] *Miss. Prov. Ar., French Dominion*, III, 343.

dence of the head chief. Since, however, there were practically no stores to be stored in the storehouse, the destitute Choctaws turned to the British and, in response to Chickasaw promptings, even joined in a conspiracy to destroy the Louisiana colony. The spearhead of this Chickasaw anti-French conspiracy was the Natchez tribe, as the Yemassee had been of the Creek anti-British movement. A premature Natchez attack on French Fort Rosalie (Natchez) induced the Choctaws to substitute for their projected attack on Mobile a resort to Fort Rosalie to share the spoils. Dissatisfied with the distribution and suspected by the French, they took what seemed to them the logical course of joining the French in punishing the Natchez. When the Chickasaws refused to surrender the Natchez, who, after defeat, fled to them for refuge, the French in January, 1730, declared war, and the Choctaws, inspired by renewed loyalty, went on the warpath.[14] For this war both the Chickasaws and the Choctaws evolved new techniques of fighting, the former, under British tutelage, fortifying their towns, and the latter, by French teaching, substituting siege tactics for their former raids.[15] Against the fortified towns the Choctaws could do nothing, but with vastly superior man power they swarmed over the Chickasaw fields, destroying crops, preventing the planting of new ones, and cutting off small Chickasaw parties venturing out to hunt or to defend their fields. In their efforts the Choctaws were aided by Illinois Indians whom the French had incited, but their assistance was counterbalanced by the help the Chickasaws received from the Cherokees, inspired by the Carolinians, by the Natchez, who had taken refuge with them, and by the Cherokees' antipathy to the Illinois Indians.

The Cherokee war party, centering at Tellico, was greatly strengthened by a visit in 1730 from Sir Alexander Cuming, who interrupted a tour of the Cherokee country to assemble the Chero-

14 John R. Swanton, *Indian Tribes of the Lower Mississippi Valley and Adjacent Coast of the Gulf of Mexico*, B. A. E. *Bulletin No. 43*, 217–47, gives a detailed description of this war with copious quotations from the sources. The official French accounts make up the bulk of the first 136 pages of the *Miss. Prov. Ar., French Dominion*, I.

15 For the Chickasaw fortifications see *Miss. Prov. Ar., French Dominion*, I, 307–308.

kees at Nequassee, where with dramatic showmanship he crowned Moytoy as head chief, secured an acknowledgment of British sovereignty, and took six Cherokees back with him on a visit to England. The net result of this diplomatic whirlwind was to confirm the dazed Cherokees in their war against the French Indians.[16] Within their fortified towns, the Chickasaws received such an abundance of supplies from the Carolina traders as to excite a continuous envy in the minds of the conquering but hungry Choctaws. Their consequent negotiations with the enemy convinced Bienville that the Chickasaws must be destroyed and that French soldiers must do it. In 1736 the long-suffering Chickasaws had to defend their towns against a double attack from Mobile and the Illinois. Fortunately for them, the two attacking forces did not arrive at the same time and were consequently beaten one at a time. The disgruntled Choctaws fully realized that Fort Tombecbe, which the departing Bienville had left in their territory, was not so much to discourage Chickasaw raids as to prevent English trade.[17] Nevertheless, they continued the war until in 1740 Bienville moved up the Mississippi to their support. Unable to move his artillery inland, he made an inglorious treaty of peace which, however, did not include the Choctaws.[18]

While the Choctaw-Chickasaw war went wearily on, the stage of Indian drama shifted to the East, where Creeks and Cherokees were playing the principal parts. In 1733 the Creeks had found themselves compelled to shift the focus of their diplomatic and commercial attention from South Carolina to the newly founded Georgia. In May, 1733, they met Oglethorpe in their own Coweta, agreed on rates of exchange, and gave him title to a restricted tract of land on the lower Savannah. The increased British trade resulting from the competition of Carolinians and Georgians enabled the Alabamas to exact from the French a lowering of prices and encouraged the Upper Creeks to promote an anti-French public opinion which resulted in a two-year Creek-Choctaw war,

[16] The Journal of Sir Alexander Cuming is given in S. C. Williams, ed., *Early Travels in the Tennessee Country, 1540–1800,* 128ff.
[17] The official French reports of this campaign are in *Miss. Prov. Ar., French Dominion,* III, 297–332.
[18] *Ibid.,* III, 419–69.

1739–41. Neither the interests nor the sentiments of the distant Cherokees were affected by the founding of Georgia, but the arrival among them of Christian Gottlieb Priber in 1736 intensified the bewilderment engendered by Sir Alexander Cuming six years before.

Priber was a Saxon communist, who, after his neighbors had turned resentful ears to his teaching, had come through South Carolina to the Cherokee country, where he hoped to evoke a more favorable response from the primitive and unpolluted Indians. He settled down in Tellico, adopted what there was of Cherokee dress, learned the Cherokee language, and began to instruct these Indians in the theory of communism, which they had hitherto known only through the imperfect medium of practice. His reorganization of their government by the crowning of their head chief and his self-appointment as "His Cherokee Majesty's Secretary of State" appealed to their innate love of pageantry, and his doctrine of communal marriage seems not to have aroused antagonism in either sex, although the Cherokee mind was perhaps too untutored to accept the logical corollary of state care for children. All these teachings were considered by the British traders among the Cherokees as the harmless outpourings of an amiable lunatic; but when he began to insist on honest yardsticks, they began to suspect that he was a French agent; and when he went so far as to urge the Cherokees to make peace with the Northern Indians and to trade with both French and British, they became convinced that he was a Jesuit. In 1743, Priber set out on a visit to Fort Toulouse; and as he was passing through the Upper Creek country, he was seized by the traders there and taken to Frederica, where he soon died in what was euphemistically termed confinement.[19] The arguments of Priber against intertribal warfare were powerfully supplemented by a smallpox epidemic that struck the Cherokees in 1738 and is said to have killed half the population before the tribe could be rescued from the local physicians.[20]

In 1738, when Great Britain and Spain drifted into a display of mutual impotence that history has dignified as the War of

[19] Williams, *Dawn of Tennessee Valley and Tennessee History*, 101–13.
[20] Williams, *Adair's History*, 231–34.

Jenkins's Ear, the Cherokees and Creeks became the objects of affectionate attention from both South Carolina and Georgia. In return for a small cession of land (1739), which they had probably never owned and certainly did not then possess, the Creeks received from Oglethorpe a new and lower schedule of prices. The Cherokees, perhaps feeling that reports of Priber's teachings made desirable some further affirmation of loyalty, came down to Augusta, where the General, on the eve of conflict, "received them with all tenderness" as well as with presents of a more tangible nature. As a result of these interchanges, both tribes in the ensuing war gave Georgia an unlimited moral support adulterated by a slight tincture of military assistance. As the War of Jenkins' Ear widened into King George's War, the spotlight shifted to the Choctaws and Chickasaws. The latter, although grievously hurt by the Choctaw siege tactics and wasted by smallpox (doubtless a Cherokee importation), resisted the pleas of the British and disappointed French hopes that they remove eastward. Fortunately for the Chickasaws, the eastern and western divisions of the Choctaws chose, with rare acumen, at this precise moment to engage in a civil war stirred up by John Adair, the talented Chickasaw agent of South Carolina.[21]

While the Choctaws were directing their energies to self-immolation, the Chickasaws had an opportunity to dispose of a new threat from the north. A band of the Pennsylvania Shawnees, led by the French half-blood, Peter Chartier, and undoubtedly instigated by the French, moved down to the Eskippakithiki town in Kentucky, from which as a base they proceeded by way of the Tennessee and Bear Creek to an attack on the Chickasaws. This was a part of a pincers movement designed to eliminate the Chickasaws, but that tribe, which invariably reacted unfavorably to plans for its elimination, beat off the initial Shawnee attack, and then with the assistance, and perhaps at the suggestion, of Adair and other British traders, attacked Chartier in his Bear Creek camp, with the result that the Shawnees dispersed among the Cherokees and the Upper Creeks, where their activities grave-

[21] *Ibid.*, 345ff. The Choctaw eastern division wanted peace and English trade; the backwoods western division was thoroughly under French influence.

ly disturbed the precarious balance of interracial and intertribal relations.[22] They persuaded the Cherokees to make peace with the French Indians in the Northwest and to approve, if not actively to assist, their own raids on the British-allied Catawbas, which occasionally extended to attacks on South Carolina settlements receiving the refugee Catawbas. They also, by the murder of some Creek-dwelling Chickasaws, provoked a Cherokee-Creek war, which, in the absence of intertribal peacemaking machinery, might have gone on indefinitely had not Governor Glenn of South Carolina—disturbed, it was charged, by the dwindling dividends from his private trading ventures—intervened in 1753 to make peace. The close of the Creek war left the Cherokees free to take aid to the beleaguered Chickasaws, who were being subjected to a final attack by a combined French and Choctaw force up the Tombigbee. The relieving Cherokees, although having lost their guns in running the Muscle Shoals ("they came into this nation in a manner naked"), so heartened the Chickasaws that they easily beat off Vaudreuil's uninspired attack on their fortified towns.

From the close of King George's War in 1748 until the ending of the French and Indian War in 1763, the Cherokees held the center of the Indian stage, while the French-English rivalry shifted to the upper Ohio Valley. Most of the towns were pro-British, with French interests centering at Tellico, where Priber had resided and where his influence was still strong. Amascossite, the head chief, was apparently a fairly complete nonentity, the real authority resting in the chief of the Upper division, whose Indian name was Connecorte and whom the British in subtle allusion to his lameness called Old Hop. The chief warrior was Oconostota, while Attakullaculla had been a power in the tribe ever since his trip to England with Sir Alexander Cuming in 1730.

Hard beset by disease at home and enemies abroad, the Cherokees were planning to follow the Chickasaw example of concentration by removing the Lower towns to a new Overhill location. South Carolina, reluctant to have the Lower Cherokees out of reach, prevented this move by building for their protection Fort

[22] *Ibid.*, 4, note.

Prince George on the Keowee, where its protective capacity was hampered by its distance from the Overhills, who needed it. The envious Overhills carried their request for a fort with such persistency to Virginia and North Carolina that the former in August, 1756, in return for promised Cherokee aid, built a fort on the north bank of the Little Tennessee near Echota, the Cherokee capital. Never named and never garrisoned during its brief existence, it was called the Virginia Fort.[23] From South Carolina, which had no need of Indian assistance, the Upper Cherokees could obtain a fort only by a land cession (1755), which, since it was necessarily taken exclusively from the Lower Cherokee country, probably did not promote intertribal harmony. The South Carolina fort finished in March, 1767, at the junction of the Little Tennessee and Tellico rivers was named Fort Loudon in honor of the British commander in chief.[24]

Despite, or because of, these forts, Cherokee-English relations steadily grew worse, owing to the misconduct of the traders, mistreatment of Cherokee auxiliaries, and French intrigue. The Cherokees, from long contact with the Carolina traders, were well versed in such commercial rudiments as unbalanced steelyards and variable yardsticks but were entirely unfamiliar with the higher forms of chicanery practiced by the Virginians. The consequent criticism of their professional ethics aroused the wrath of the Virginians, who proceeded to assert their integrity by the simple and direct method of chastising the critics, including the "Emperor." Such time as they had free from commerce and brawling, the traders seem to have devoted liberally to drunkenness, arson, grand larceny, and the ravishing of Indian women on a scale hitherto unknown to Cherokee society. The embarrassment of the Cherokees caused by the manifestations of the high spirits of the traders was increased by the proneness of the Virginia frontiersmen to massacre Cherokee auxiliaries returning from assisting them on expeditions against the French. Such treatment the Cherokees always resented, generally reciprocated, and occasionally avenged before it occurred.

[23] Williams, *Dawn of Tennessee Valley and Tennessee History*, 171–83.
[24] *Ibid.*, 184–95.

In this atmosphere French propaganda found ideal working conditions. Lantagnac, who had once lived among the Cherokees in the guise of a Carolina trader, directed from Fort Toulouse an intrigue for the execution of which he depended on Outacite of Tellico and Great Mortar chief of the Upper Creek Oxchai town.[25] In March, 1757, Lantagnac sent to Outacite two hundred pack-horse loads of presents, presumably designed to inculcate in the Cherokees a spirit of hospitality toward a proposed French fort on the Hiwassee for the protection of the Cherokees against their British oppressors. Since their oppressor anticipated this provision for Cherokee comfort by building the Virginia Fort and Fort Loudon, Lantagnac could only spread reports, readily believed by the exasperated Cherokees, that the British forts were placed not for the security but the enslavement of the tribe. As a result of a personally conducted evangelical campaign by Great Mortar among the Cherokees in 1759, Moytoy, chief of Tellico, defying both the tribal chief warrior and his division chief, went on the warpath, from which he presently returned with twenty-two scalps that he had detached from the heads of certain Carolinians on the Yadkin River. To Governor Lyttleton of South Carolina this accomplishment seemed to be so considerably in excess of routine Cherokee mayhem as to threaten their peaceful relations with the British and to necessitate an invasion from South Carolina in order to renew the ancient ties. A placating Cherokee delegation, including Oconostota, was refused a hearing by the irate governor, ordered home, and, presumably in order to facilitate its return, imprisoned at Fort Prince George. This fortress became the terminal of Lyttleton's punitive expedition because smallpox invaded his camp, whereupon his army rapidly and informally disintegrated. Before returning to Charleston to receive the plaudits of his people, Lyttleton demanded from Attakullaculla, as a compensation for his good will in abandoning the campaign, that the Cherokees surrender twenty-four of their number to be executed. Until this was done, the imprisoned delegates were to stay in prison, although they were to enjoy the more elevated social status of hostages.

[25] Williams, *Early Travels in the Tennessee Country*, 177ff.

Any chance peace-loving Attakullaculla may have had of influencing the Cherokees to accept these unpalatable terms was negatived by the death in January, 1760, of the imperious Old Hop, whose passing removed the one Cherokee force inclined and able to restrain them. His successor, Standing Turkey, was unable to dominate the tribe; and Oconostota, released from prison but burning with resentment, on February 15 invested Fort Prince George, ambushing some of the garrison and indirectly contributing to the massacre of the hostages, who had, during the firing, committed the error of shouting encouragement to the assaulting Cherokees. Solidarity restored by the fate of the hostages, the three Cherokee divisions, audibly aided by a Creek contingent under Great Mortar, invested Fort Loudon.

Officially the Creeks maintained a neutrality owing, in some measure at least, to the recently appointed superintendent of Southern Indians, Edmund Atkins, who in the spring of 1759 had come among them accompanied, from pride or precaution, by an imposing force. From the Creeks, with an additional guard, he had gone on to the Choctaws, where on July 18 he made a treaty of trade and friendship with those whose loyalty to the French had not survived the war-caused dearth of supplies. In a conference at Cusseta on his return, the Creeks in October reaffirmed their devotion to peace. One result of Atkins' tour among the Creeks was the hasty departure of Chartier's Shawnees, who set out northward in evident anticipation of chastisement long overdue. Reoccupying their old village sites at French Lick, they were promptly discovered, attacked, and driven into Kentucky by the watchful Chickasaws.[26]

Neither Prince George nor Loudon was endangered by the bucolic siege tactics of the Cherokees. But Loudon, unable to be reached by a relieving force, as Prince George had been, in August, 1760, preferred surrender to starvation. The subsequent massacre of the retiring garrison developed, perhaps, from a resisted attempt to take hostages and certainly was neither designed nor approved by Oconostota or Standing Turkey. These two chiefs were now thinking only of peace, realizing that the French

[26] Swanton, *Early Creek Indians*, 416.

could not and the Creeks would not aid them, that Iroquois and Chickasaws were at their throats, that their Middle and Lower towns had been destroyed, and that they were helpless without British supplies. One would like to think that the readiness with which South Carolina met their peace overtures sprang from an uneasy conscience; the war ended in a peace without reprisals.[27]

Of the Southern Indians only the devoted Chickasaws could rejoice over the outcome of the French and Indian War. The Cherokees had lost five thousand of their people, including half their warriors, and faced the continuing resentment of Iroquois and Chickasaws even after their British peace. The Upper Creeks had gone so far in aiding the Cherokees that they had good reason to expect British reprisals; the Alabamas, in fact, in 1763 removed their towns to the Tombigbee valley.[28] The Choctaw allies of the fallen French could have presentiments only of evil. Neither the Creeks nor the Cherokees could draw comfort from the royal proclamation of 1763 that left much of their land within the line, nor the Choctaws, from the shifting of the western Florida line northward to 32 degrees, 30 minutes the following year. The substitution of imperial for colonial control of Indian affairs promised a greater supply of trade goods, a better regulation of trade, and perhaps a cessation of tribal wars. The Indians perhaps did not yet realize that they could not have British commerce without British control and that they could gain security only by surrendering sovereignty.

In November, 1763, the Southern tribes liquidated the war in a peace conference at Augusta with the governors of Virginia, the Carolinas, and Georgia, and the new superintendent, John Stuart. At this conference the Creeks, mostly from the Lower Towns, ceded to the British their lands east of a line beginning on the lower Savannah and running obliquely across the Ogeechee

[27] Thirty men and women were killed in the massacre at Fort Loudon, and many wounded died later. In the first fury there seems to have been considerable mistreatment of prisoners, but later they were treated kindly and many of them continued to live among the Cherokees after peace was made.

[28] Williams, *Adair's History*, 267. Homesickness overcame these refugee Alabamas and after the Upper Creeks made peace with the British, they moved back to their old homes.

to the Altamaha.[29] Following this conference the Lower Creeks preserved an appearance of friendliness that was not wholly pretense. But the Great Mortar among the Upper Creeks and the Choctaw head chief, the aged Alibamo Mingo, were openly encouraging their people to murder Englishmen, in which endeavor they were meeting with a fair measure of success. Even if these chiefs were not in communication with Pontiac, Superintendent Stuart had the astuteness to realize the danger of the situation and the prudence to mollify the Indians. Isolating the malcontents by confirming the ancient Chickasaw alliance and forging a new alliance with the Cherokees, he summoned the Creeks and Choctaws and, as a precautionary measure, invited the Chickasaws to meet him in the spring of 1765. In a March conference at Mobile, he greeted the Chickasaws as allies and received the Choctaws as erring, penitent, and forgiven children.[30] Peace was confirmed, trade restored, and, after some plain hints from Stuart, the Choctaws made a cession of their West Florida lands for twelve leagues back from the coast as well as a small tract north and west of Mobile Bay. Both tribes agreed to furnish escorts for Farmer's expedition up the Mississippi to the Illinois country. In May at Pensacola, Stuart conferred with the Creeks led by the Great Mortar and Emistesigo, who had resolved their rivalry in a compromise by which the latter attained his policy and the former secured his position. The Great Mortar, styling himself "king of the Creeks," made peace, accepted a British medal, and ceded a small tract around the Bay.[31] The Choctaws and Creeks compensated themselves for their British peace by starting a war with each other in 1766.

[29] J. R. Alden, *John Stuart and the Southern Colonial Frontier*, 176–91.

[30] Stuart's address to the Chickasaws has the ring of deep sincerity: "You generous friends of the Chickasaw nation, who have so long adhered to the interests of the English, whom neither dangers could startle nor promises seduce from our interest. I hope there is little more necessary with you than to renew our ancient alliance, which as it has continued for many ages to the mutual advantage of both nations, so I hope it will continue until this earth is dissolved and the great day of Judgment shall come when God will pronounce on the actions of men."

[31] The official records of these two conferences are in *Mississippi Provincial Archives, English Dominion*, edited by Dunbar Rowland, I, 188–255. At the March meeting the Choctaws were led by Alibamo Mingo, and the Chickasaws by Opoia Mataha, later known as Piomingo, their war chief.

After the Choctaws and Creeks had been successfully introduced to the *pax Britannica*, the Cherokees, owing to their current
indulgence in the sport of murdering trespassers on their unceded
land east of the line, demanded the attention of the busy superintendent. Stuart's suggestion that if they would cede the land, the
trespassers would no longer be trespassing impressed the Cherokees as being so reasonable that in October they made the cession
and restored the broken peace.[32] Cherokee sensibilities were not
appreciably damaged either by this cession or by the arrangement
with North Carolina the following year for a new line running
from the northern boundary of South Carolina to Chiswell's mine
in Virginia. But they were so irked by the illogical continuance
of Iroquois raids that in March, 1768, they sent Oconostota and
Attakullaculla to New York, where, with the reluctant assistance
of Superintendent Johnson, they finally ended what was probably the most prolonged family quarrel in Indian history.[33]

From 1768 to 1775 the history of the Southern Indians except
that of the Chickasaws is little more than a record of misfortune.
In 1768 the control of trade was returned to the colonies and the
royal commissaries were withdrawn temporarily from the tribes.[34]
North Carolina and Virginia were trespassing on Cherokee land
in northeastern Tennessee and even building a fort on the Watauga; the Creek-Choctaw war widened with the intervention, perhaps at British suggestion, of the Chickasaws in favor of the Choctaws; and the Iroquois at Fort Stanwix celebrated the recent
family reconciliation by ceding to Superintendent Johnson all the
Cherokee land north of the Tennessee. The Cherokees, sufficiently acquainted with frontier psychology and British irresolution
to realize that the land was, although illegally, lost, disregarded
Shawnee importunities to re-establish joint ownership by war
and proceeded to salvage what they could by selling it themselves.
Fortunately their claim to the land had been confirmed by Stuart
at Hard Labor in 1768, upon the completion of the Cherokee
boundary from Chiswell's mine to the mouth of the Kanawha.

[32] Alden, *op. cit.*, 215–19.
[33] *Ibid.*, 222–24.
[34] Helen Louise Shaw, *British Administration of the Southern Indians,
1756–1783*, 175–76; Alden, *op. cit.*, 260–61.

Attakullaculla, at the far right, and six other Cherokees

British Museum and Bureau of American Ethnology

I Alexander McGillivray, Agent to the Creek nation of Indians, and Brigadier General in the service of the United States, do solemnly swear to bear true allegiance to the said United States of America; And to serve them honestly and faithfully against all their enemies or opposers whomsoever; and to observe and obey the orders of the President of the United States of america, And the orders of the officers appointed over me, according to the articles of war; and the true intent and meaning of the secret articles of the treaty of peace, made and concluded between the united States of america, and the Creek nation of Indians, On the seventh day of the Present month of August —

Alexr. McGill

Sworn before me in the City of New York
This Fourteenth day of August in the year
of our Lord One thousand Seven hundred and
Ninety. —

John Blair an associate judge of the supreme
Court of the United States —

In presence of
Knox Secy of War

McGillivray's oath of allegiance before Justice John Blair

Courtesy Massachusetts Historical Society

At Lochaber in 1770, they ceded to Superintendent Stuart the part of the land ceded by the Iroquois to Superintendent Johnson that lay east of a line from the mouth of the Kanawha to the vicinity of Long Island in the Holston. This grant was enormously enlarged the next year when the Virginia surveyor, John Donelson, at Cherokee suggestion (so he reported), ran its western boundary not to the mouth of the Kanawha but to the mouth of the "Louisa," which Virginia later identified as the Kentucky.[35] Not only did the Cherokees acquiesce in this action, but they followed it most amazingly in 1775 with a cession at Sycamore Shoals on the Holston to Richard Henderson and his partners of the Transylvania Company of all their remaining land between the Ohio and the Cumberland-Tennessee divide.[36] Neither of these cessions, by which the Cherokees alienated the greater part of their domain, was made under British pressure, although it is legitimate to suspect local bribery: the Donelson extension was made without Stuart's knowledge and the Sycamore Shoals cession denounced by him as contrary to the proclamation of 1763 and to previous treaties.

Had the swift approach of the American Revolution not prevented, Stuart might have been able to nullify the Sycamore Shoals cession as he had previously nullified certain private cessions of the Cherokees and Creeks. Partly as a result of high-pressure salesmanship by the traders, more numerous and more competitive after the abolition in 1768 of the trade regulations, and partly because the Creek-Choctaw war and other restrictions made it impossible for the Indians to gather exports sufficient to balance imports, both the Cherokees and the Creeks had fallen deeply in debt to the traders among them. In 1771, at the suggestion of the traders, the Cherokees liquidated their debt by ceding to them a tract of land on the upper Savannah, including in it a considerable territory claimed by the Creeks; the latter promptly retaliated by paying their own debts with a cession of Cherokee

[35] The most militant, if not the most convincing, argument for the Kentucky is by Alden in *op. cit.*, 283ff. and 344–50. Dr. Thomas Walker on his exploration of 1750 had given the name Louisa to a branch of the Big Sandy.
[36] The Sycamore Shoals sale is discussed most fully by W. S. Lester, *The Transylvania Company*, 28–47.

territory. When Stuart refused to recognize either of these private cessions, he was directed to take a joint cession from the two tribes and himself to compensate the traders. This he did at Augusto in May, 1773, with a "new purchase" of land between the Savannah and Ogeechee extending from Little Creek on the south to beyond the Broad on the north.[37]

[37] Alden, *op. cit.*, 294–305.

III

The American Revolution

1775-1783

THE OUTBREAK of the American Revolution gave the Southern Indians their first opportunity since the French and Indian War of watching their white neighbors destroy each other. Since none of the tribes had a desire to mar by any premature participation the complete attainments of these pleasing prospects, their general inclinations were toward neutrality in the struggle. This ambition coincided with both American and British policy, since neutrality was the most favorable attitude the Americans could expect from people whom they had consistently wronged, while the British feared that Indian allies in war would be unable to discriminate between loyalists and rebels. The two contestants, then, from different motives, adopting a common policy at the beginning of the Revolution, urged Cherokees, Creeks, and Chickasaws to refrain from hostilities. The Choctaws had no rebel neighbors, since the Floridas, from lack of grievances or lack of inhabitants, failed to revolt.

Both Emistesigo, head chief of the Creeks since the death of Mortar in the Choctaw war, and Oconostota, the aged, weary, and infirm "emperor" of the Cherokees, were devoted to peace, the former from temperament and the latter from experience. They received the first American overtures in the summer and early fall of 1775 from agents of the South Carolina and Georgia provincial congresses, who demanded that the tribes should remain neutral and give proof of their neutrality by expelling Depu-

37

ty Superintendent Cameron from the Cherokees and Commissary Taitt from the Creeks. These astonishing diplomatic gambols, supplemented by the seizure of British supplies for the Creeks and by attempts to assassinate Cameron, left the Creeks unimpressed, although they seem to have inclined the timid Oconostota toward a policy of appeasement. In the midst of them the two tribes received in November from Salisbury, North Carolina, letters from commissioners appointed by the Continental Congress proposing conferences the next spring—with the Cherokees at Fort Charlotte, April 16, and with the Creeks at Augusta, May 1.[1] Cameron, although sorely tried by the American policy of peace through elimination, continued to urge on the Cherokees the British advice of neutrality and loyalty, warning them that the abandonment of the former would bring a loss of British support, and of the latter, a forfeit of British trade. Notwithstanding the inept wooing by the Americans, the warnings of the British, and the inclination of Oconostota, there was a faction of the Cherokees that wanted war with the Americans. The anti-Americanism of this faction had no connection with the issues of the Revolution but was due to resentment over the encroachment on Cherokee land as represented by the Watauga settlement. The most outspoken member of the war faction was a young chieftain named Dragging Canoe.[2]

[1] The first step by Congress in the management of Indian affairs was taken in June, 1775, with the appointment of a committee on Indian affairs. In accordance with a recommendation made by this committee on July 11, Congress set up three Indian departments, of which the Southern Department comprised all the tribes south of the Ohio River. The Southern Department was placed under a board of five commissioners, two of whom—John Walker, of Virginia, and Willie Jones, of North Carolina—were appointed by Congress, and three—George Galphin, Robert Rae, and Edward Wilkerson—named by the South Carolina Council of Safety. The Southern commissioners met at Salisbury, N. C., November 13, 1775, and fixed the dates and places for meeting the Indians. George Galphin, Leroy Hammond, and David Tubly were the Georgia and South Carolina agents among the Creeks. Galphin, the Georgia agent, had been an Indian trader for thirty years, and had great influence among the Lower Creeks. W. C. Ford and Gaillard Hunt, eds., *Journals of the Continental Congress, 1774-1789*, II, 1741; William L. Saunders, ed., *The Colonial Records of North Carolina*, X, 329-31.

[2] Dragging Canoe was the chief of Mialoquo (Big Island Town). His Indian name, variously spelled, was Chincohacina and he was the son of Ookoonekah (White Owl). He had opposed the sale of lands to Henderson as well as the

Early in 1776, Superintendent John Stuart, in furtherance of his delicate task of keeping the Southern Indians both loyal and quiescent, started his brother Henry from Pensacola as a special envoy on a tour of the four tribes. At Mobile, Henry was met by Dragging Canoe, who told him that South Carolina had cut off trade with the Cherokees and that war was imminent. In view of these developments Henry took along with him thirty pack horses laden with supplies for the Cherokees and, deferring his Creek visit, went directly to the Cherokees to urge peace; on account of the slimness of his pack train and the necessity of conferring with Choctaws and Chickasaws, he did not reach Echota until April 24.

The attack by Northern Indians on the caravan as it was moving up the Tennessee, resulting in a loss of nine pack horses, was probably directed less against the British than against the Chickasaws, with whom the Illinois Indians were then at war.[3] Arriving at Echota, Stuart joined his representations to those of Cameron, with the result that the war party agreed to defer direct action while Stuart and Oconostota attempted by diplomatic means to induce the Wataugans to withdraw at least into the limits of their alleged purchase in order to avoid war. Both sent letters to the Wataugans, and Stuart suggested that they move to Florida where, he said (with apparent sincerity), they would find it easier to make a living. To these overtures the Wataugans made an evasive reply, stayed where they were, and proceeded to solidify their ethical position by circulating a forged letter from Stuart urging the loyalists to join the Cherokees in a war against the frontier rebels. Nevertheless, the peace party among the Cherokees would probably have prevailed but for the arrival of a delegation of Northern Indians—Iroquois, Shawnees, Delawares, Ottawas, and "Nantucas"—to urge a united war against the Americans. The Lower Cherokees, most heavily and most recently mistreated by

lease and later sale of territory to the Wataugans. A. V. Goodpasture, "Indian Wars and Warriors of the Old Southwest, 1720-1807," *Tennessee Historical Magazine*, Vol. IV, 23.

[3] The chief source for this journey is Henry Stuart's report in Saunder's *Colonial Records of North Carolina*, X, 763-83. Commissary James Colbert accompanied Stuart from the Chickasaw country to the Cherokee, and Dragging Canoe, who had returned from Mobile through the Creek country, met him at Bear Creek.

the Americans, were so aroused by the oratory of the visitors that immediately after returning home from the council they began to attack the frontier, thus precipitating the war that Stuart and Oconostota had so earnestly opposed and that the peace chiefs at Fort Charlotte were then promising to prevent.[4] Stuart, having prolonged his stay among the Cherokees until July 15, set out in company of Dragging Canoe and Attakullaculla to the Creeks, meeting on his way a Cherokee delegation that had taken the Shawnee "talks" to the Creeks and was returning with Emistesigo's refusal to act without Cameron's approval.[5]

The outbreak of the Cherokee war forced Superintendent Stuart to the enlistment of the Southern Indians as active and immediate allies, thereby carrying out his instructions, the spirit if not the letter of which he had disregarded in his previous recommendations of neutrality. The Americans, hopeless of assistance, devoted their efforts to thwarting the British efforts among the Creeks and Chickasaws: the remoteness of the Choctaws gave them immunity from American pressure, while their lethargy and former loyalties made them unresponsive to British importunities. Among the Creeks, Emistesigo was reluctant to become involved in the war because he was doubtful if the British could supply the trade that hitherto the Americans had monopolized, because the Creeks were still engaged in war with the Choctaws, and because a considerable element, especially of the Lower Creeks, was so well disposed toward the Georgians and South Carolinians that any pro-British tribal policy might bring civil war. On May 1, 1776, some two hundred Creeks, consisting not only of Lower Creeks, but also of delegations from Tallassie and from Okfuskee

---

[4] The only reliable account of these preliminaries is P. M. Hamer, "The Wataugans and the Cherokee Indians in 1776," East Tennessee Historical Society *Publications*, Vol. III, 108–26, and "John Stuart's Indian Policy During the Early Months of the American Revolution," *Mississippi Valley Historical Review,* Vol. XVII, 351–67 (December, 1930).

[5] The Shawnee delegation on its return to Ohio was accompanied by three Cherokees. It was this party which went by Boonesborough and carried off Jemima Boone and Frances Calloway. After a four-day pursuit they were overtaken by a rescue party from Boonesborough, which recovered the captives and killed three of the Shawnee chiefs. The three Cherokees escaped. Colonial Office Records, Series 5, Vol. 78, p. 11 (hereafter cited as C. O. R.), Cameron to Stuart, August 31, 1776.

(the largest town in the nation), met the American commissioners at Augusta, where they were importuned by George Galphin to stay out of the war, to rely on the Americans for trade, and to expel the British agents from the nation.[6] The Americans, as a matter of fact, had no trade goods, as Taitt pointed out to the Creeks, but they were able to secure them in such large quantities from the French islands that their trade with the friendly towns continued despite British opposition throughout the Revolution.[7] Stuart, indeed, found the question of trade very embarrassing since it became necessary to organize new routes of supply as substitutes for the routes from Georgia and Carolina. New traders also had to be engaged because many of the old ones (like Galphin himself) were rabidly American and, consequently, subversive agents.

Galphin's exhortation to the Creeks to expel the British agents was beyond the power, as it was beyond the inclination, of the friendly towns to accomplish. Taitt, the commissary, to be sure, was unpopular, not because he was British, but because he was trying to suppress the sale of liquor. The British secured the safety and even the influence of their organization when, in 1776, they appointed Alexander McGillivray as assistant commissary. McGillivray not only was the head of the powerful Wind clan and, as chief of Little Tallassie, an intimate of Emistesigo, but he had returned to the Creeks with a burning hatred for the Georgians because of their confiscation of his father's estate.[8] Even in 1776 no Creek dared to lift a hand against one with such powerful connections as McGillivray. All this, of course, was known by the

---

[6] C. O. R., Series 5, Vol. 77, pp. 387–90. This is the report of the American commissioners at Augusta.

[7] *Ibid.*, Series 5, Vol. 78, p. 231. Stuart to Knox, March 10, 1777.

[8] For a sketch of this great Creek see A. P. Whitaker, "Alexander McGillivray, 1783–89," *North Carolina Historical Review*, Vol. V (1928), 181–203, 289–309. J. W. Caughey's *McGillivray of the Creeks* is a source book composed chiefly of letters to and from McGillivray until his death in 1793. The exact date of McGillivray's return to the Creeks is unknown. Louis (Le Clerc) Milfort, in *Mémoire ou coup d'oeil rapide sur mes différens voyages et mon séjour dans la nation Crèck*, says that McGillivray was living among the Creeks in May, 1776, and was then a chief of Little Tallassie (which was Emistesigo's town). It is likely that McGillivray's appointment as assistant commissary was due to the influence of Commissary David Taitt, who had married McGillivray's sister (1768).

astute superintendent, who, from the beginning, seems to have centered his hopes on the young chief.[9]

The Revolution, which brought so much embarrassment to Emistesigo, also brought one beneficence—an escape from the long-continued and disastrous war with the Choctaws. The many applications of the weary Creeks to Stuart to mediate this struggle had hitherto been refused on the ostensible ground that British policy precluded any interference with tribal activities not endangering British interests. But British interests were now endangered, since the preoccupation of Creeks and Choctaws with mutual destruction would prevent them from dedicating their energies to the destruction of the Americans. Consequently, Stuart, acting on an appeal from the second man of Little Tallassie (undoubtedly representing Emistesigo himself), called the two tribes to Pensacola, where on October 26, after ten days of ceremony, peace was made.[10] For Emistesigo this was merely the exchanging of an old war for a new, since Stuart had set as his price of mediation the immediate dispatch of Creek assistance to the Cherokees. Accordingly, on November 19, he notified Cameron at Little Tallassie that he was preparing for war.[11]

The Cherokees were greatly in need of help. It is doubtful whether Dragging Canoe had envisioned a general war; his objective had been limited, apparently, to the ending of Wataugan trespassing by the direct, if somewhat primitive, method of disembodying the trespassers. But the war did not long remain confined to South Carolina, where it began, but spread inevitably to the frontiers of Georgia, North Carolina, and Virginia, where, as Stuart had foreseen, the Indians fell without discrimination on both loyalists and rebels, forcing them into an unnatural union for protection and revenge. When the inevitable retaliation came from the Carolinas (with incidental help from Georgia) the

---

[9] C. O. R., Series 5, Vol. 79, p. 57, Stuart to Germain, October 6, 1777.

[10] *Ibid.*, Series 5, Vol. 78, p. 30, Stuart to Germain, October 16, 1776. The letter from Neaha Thloco, of Little Tallassie, to Stuart, asking for peace with the Choctaws, was written October 29, 1775. *Ibid.*, Series 5, Vol. 77, p. 95. In July, 1777, Franchimastabe (described as a small-medal chief of Yazoo) led a Choctaw delegation to the Creeks to confirm the peace.

[11] *Ibid.*, Series 5, Vol. 78, p. 161.

Cherokees were unable to resist, partly because the great majority of the Cherokees remained at peace, and perhaps chiefly because, as in their previous war, their supplies and ammunition were inadequate. Stuart made strenuous efforts to keep them supplied, but the route was so long and so exposed to American interception that he was unable to deliver adequate supplies.[12] At the time Emistesigo was making peace with the Choctaws, practically all the Lower, Middle, and Valley towns of the Cherokees had been destroyed, and the homeless Cherokees were seeking refuge among the Creeks and with the British in West Florida: there were, in fact, two hundred destitute Cherokees at Pensacola when the treaty was made.[13] Consequently, when Emistesigo finally marched in February, 1777, with three or four hundred men to co-operate with the Cherokees, the Cherokees had ceased to operate.[14]

The location of the Choctaws and Chickasaws, remote from the seat of war, rendered their co-operation with the British less vital and more difficult than that of the Cherokees and Creeks. The traditional friendship of the Chickasaws for the British would have made their choice of allies in the Revolution almost automatic—even without the powerful influence of James Colbert, the British commissary.[15] The only evident opposition to the British came from the American traders who were well established in the tribe and could not easily be dislodged. The Choctaws did not have the Chickasaws' enthusiasm for the British, and their notorious lethargy made them slow to espouse any cause, even their own. Moreover, the Six Towns at the end of the French and

[12] The details of this war can be found in J. G. M. Ramsey, *Annals of Tennessee to the End of the Eighteenth Century;* Theodore Roosevelt, *Winning of the West;* Mooney, *Myths of the Cherokee;* J. P. Browne, *Old Frontiers;* and many other places. Colonel Samuel Jack with a force of 200 Georgians destroyed in July the towns on the Tugalo and Chattahoochee: Colonel Williamson with 1,100 South Carolinians destroyed the Lower towns in September and then joined with General Rutherford and his 2,000 North Carolinians (who had just finished the Middle towns) to destroy the Valley towns. Colonel Christian with 1,800 Virginians penetrated to the Overhill towns without a battle.

[13] C. O. R., Series 5, Vol. 78, p. 143, Stuart to Germain, November 24, 1776.

[14] *Ibid.*, Series 5, Vol. 78, p. 65, Stuart to Germain, March 10, 1777.

[15] For the Colbert family among the Chickasaws, see Harry Warren, "Some Chickasaw Chiefs and Prominent Men," *Publications* of the Mississippi Historical Society, Vol. VIII, 555–70.

Indian War had transferred not to the British but to the Spanish the loyalty they had previously given to the French.[16] In May, 1777, the two tribes sent delegations to Mobile to confer with Stuart. The forty Chickasaws included the Chickasaw king (Mingo Homa) and the chief warrior (Piomingo), whom the Americans and British called by his translated name, the Mountain Leader. It may be assumed that the presence of 2,800 Choctaws indicated chiefly an enthusiasm for presents. Both tribes declared their loyalty to the king and accepted their war assignment, which was to keep watch on the Mississippi against any attempt of the Americans. This meant for the time being the harassing of communication between the Americans and the Spaniards at New Orleans.[17]

While busy in arranging for the co-operation of Creeks, Chickasaws, and Choctaws, Stuart did what he could to salvage the Cherokees. The war party of the Cherokees had begun hostilities in defiance of British advice and in indifference to Revolutionary issues: the course of the war, in which they secured supplies only from the British and aid only from the loyalists, made them British partisans as well as enemies of the Americans. Since the rebuilding of their ruined towns in their ancient locations would have exposed them to American domination, they decided with Cameron's approval, and perhaps at his suggestion, to remove beyond the reach of the Americans. Accordingly, in March, 1777, the homeless inhabitants of Big Island, Settico, Tellico, Toquo, and Chilhowee moved westward to Chickamauga Creek, where they built new homes—of the same names—centering around the home of the British commissary, John McDonald. This group was henceforth called the Chickamaugas, and their removal has been generally considered a secession. As a matter of fact, Oconostota appears to have connived at the removal, which relieved him of the need of delivering Dragging Canoe to Ameri-

---

[16] C. O. R., Series 5, Vol. 79, p. 271, Stuart to Germain, May 2, 1778.

[17] Ibid., Series 5, Vol. 78, p. 285, Stuart to Germain, June 14, 1777. At this conference the Choctaws ceded to the British a strip of land lying on the Mississippi south of the mouth of the Yazoo and extending eastward along the border of their 1765 cession to the Pascagoula. The triangular section of this cession on the Mississippi was later made into Bourbon County by Georgia.

can punishment. Dragging Canoe's subsequent denial of Oconostota's authority relieved Oconostota of responsibility for future Chickamauga misconduct—misconduct that Dragging Canoe meant to make occur as frequently as possible.

With the Chickamaugas safely removed, Oconostota pressed his overtures for peace, which resulted in treaties with the South Carolinians and Georgians at Dewitt's Corner on May 20 and with the Virginians and North Carolinians at Long Island on July 20. Knowing from experience that with the Americans the word "treaty" was a euphemism for land cession, the Cherokees showed little hesitation in surrendering to the Carolinas at these treaties the land demanded by these two states.[18] It is possible, too, that Cherokee amiability in the transactions was due in part to the fact that the ceders were Overhills while the owners were the Middle Towns and Lower Towns. For her war effort, which had been limited to viewing the remains, Virginia received no territorial compensation inasmuch as the Cherokees had already been separated from practically all their lands north of 36 degrees, 30 minutes. Before leaving Long Island, the North Carolina commissioners named James Robertson as agent for North Carolina among the Cherokees; and in the following November, Virginia appointed Joseph Martin as Virginian agent and superintendent for the same tribe. Robertson was to reside at Echota, the Cherokee "capital," while Martin kept his agency at Long Island, which was erroneously thought to be in Virginia.[19] In view of the conspicuous failure of Congressional diplomacy to prevent the war, it is not surprising that the two states decided to rely on their own management of Indian affairs.

[18] The proceedings of the Long Island conference and the text of the Long Island and DeWitt's Corner treaties are given in Archibald Henderson, "The Treaty of Long Island of Holston, July, 1777," *North Carolina Historical Review*, Vol. VIII, 55-116. DeWitt's Corner is now called Due West. The land cession made at this place included the present counties of Greenville, Anderson, Pickens, and Oconee, South Carolina. The boundary line agreed upon at Long Island ran from Cumberland Gap to the junction of Cloud's Creek and the Holston, then to Chimney Top Mountain and on to Camp Creek on the south bank of the Nolichucky. Thence it ran southwest through the mountains to the Georgia line.

[19] S. B. Weeks, "General Joseph Martin and the War of the Revolution in the West," American Historical Association, *Annual Report* (1893), 426ff.

A considerable portion of the Lower and Middle Cherokees, now by their friends actually dispossessed of the land that their enemies had only devastated, moved their towns to new locations on the headwaters of the Coosa, affiliating with the Chickamaugas and becoming British partisans.[20] These Cherokees, the Chickamaugas, the Creeks, and the refugees in Florida, Stuart in the summer of 1777 was attempting to weld into an army to co-operate with a British force which General Prevost was planning to lead from St. Augustine into Georgia. A movement among the Creeks wrecked the plans and would have resulted in the expulsion of the British had it not been for the steadfastness of McGillivray. A small delegation from Cusseta and Okfuskee had, at Galphin's invitation, visited Augusta and Charleston, where they were royally entertained and, as a corollary, copiously exhorted to assit, by murdering the British agents among them, the inevitable triumph of American liberty. The Okfuskees on their return tried to carry out the inspiration thus communicated to them by attempting to kill Taitt and Cameron, who were visiting McGillivray at Little Tallassie. Both escaped assassination by a flight to Pensacola so hurried that they had only time to direct McGillivray to suppress the movement. McGillivray went at once to meet the Okfuskees, tongue-lashed the malcontents into submission, and coolly took possession of the effects of Cameron and Taitt, which the Okfuskees were attempting to plunder. Following this action, he called a meeting of the national council, in which he so berated the offenders that the Okfuskees sent him to Pensacola to apologize for them; and in January, 1778, ten town chiefs of the Upper Creeks journeyed to Pensacola to deplore the action of the Okfuskees. In the same month six hundred of the Lower Creeks came to Pensacola to disavow the action of Cusseta in chasing Commissary McIntosh out of the nation. The Creek consciousness of wrongdoing had perhaps been materially intensified by the immediate embargo that Stuart placed on British supplies. The direct result of this movement was the resumption of Creek raids on the

[20] Milling, *op. cit.*, 319, calls attention to the fact that the Lower Cherokees rebuilt many of their towns in Oconee County, South Carolina, and by "political indulgence" continued to live in the ceded territory.

Georgia frontier, the return of the Cherokee refugees to their Chickamauga brethren, a great decline in the influence of the American faction among the Creeks, and a marked increase in the already great prestige of Alexander McGillivray, who from this time on, notwithstanding the resumption of their posts by Taitt and Cameron, was the acknowledged leader of both Creeks and Chickamaugas.[21]

While the Creeks were rebelling, confessing their sins, and promising to bring forth fruit meet for repentance, the Chickasaws and Choctaws were not only quiet but apparently sleeping. Only a hypothesis of deep somnolence can explain their failure to intercept, or at least to detect, the Willing expedition down the Mississippi to Natchez in February, 1778.[22] The alertness of the Chickasaws was directed more against the Illinois Indians, with whom they were at war, than against the Americans, who were only the enemies of their allies. Moreover, Piomingo, who as chief warrior had charge of all military operations, was reluctant to kill Americans and, it is to be supposed, for that reason none too vigilant against them. As it was, if Willing had been as intent on aiding the American cause as he was on plundering for private gain, his expedition might well have been a disaster and not merely a nuisance .The net result of the episode was that Superintendent Stuart tightened his organization among the two tribes, with Commissary Colbert apparently taking over the task of guarding the Mississippi.

To the superintendent, in his overestimate of the American threat on the Mississippi, it must have seemed providential that the peace party of the Cherokees was now inclining to unite with Dragging Canoe against the Americans. In no other way can one interpret the visit of Attakullaculla to Pensacola in February, 1778, and the promise he then made to Stuart to lead the Cherokees northwards to guard the Ohio.[23] Attakullaculla was an inti-

[21] The best account of the Creek meeting is in C. O. R., Series 5, Vol. 79, pp. 65-68, McGillivray to Stuart, September 21, 1777; *ibid.*, p. 57, Stuart to Germain, October 6, 1777; and *ibid.*, p. 127, Stuart to Germain, January 23, 1778.

[22] J. W. Caughey, "Willing's Expedition down the Mississippi," *Louisiana Historical Quarterly*, Vol. XV, 5-36.

[23] C. O. R., Series 5, Vol. 79, p. 223, Stuart to Germain, March 5, 1778.

mate of Oconostota, belonged to the ruling group of the Cherokees, and had been the heart and soul of the peace policy. But the
Cherokees were finding that their most earnest appeasement had
been without profit, for the Wataugans continued their encroachments after the treaty of Long Island even more avidly than they
had done before, apparently considering that the Long Island
boundary had been fixed primarily as a base for further advance.
These encroachments carried the Watauga settlers so close to the
Overhill towns that in April, 1778, the Raven of Echota, who, since
the war, had been administering the Cherokee government in the
name of Oconostota, protested to Governor Caswell that the Wataugans were "marking trees all over the country," even "near
the place I live." The only result of this protest was an urbane
assurance from the Governor that he had warned the Wataugans
not to damage the trees.[24] When the governors of Virginia and
South Carolina also protested against the encroachments which
they feared might bring on another war, Caswell appointed a commission to make a treaty with the Cherokees. The commissioners
declined with the pointed comment that it was not a new treaty the
Governor needed but the observance of the one he already had.[25]

To the mental anguish of the Cherokees over the encroachments on their land, there was added an acute physical distress
caused by the lack of trade. Stuart saw to it that British supplies
reached the Chickamaugas and their allies on the Coosa, but
rigorously interdicted any dealings with the Overhills and other
elements of the peace party. Since the Americans were entirely
unable to furnish the requisite supplies, the peace party soon found
themselves paying in penury for their indulgence in appeasement.
So extreme became the sufferings of the Cherokees that in February, 1778, Joseph Martin, their Virginia agent, took the extraordinary step of writing to Stuart that the Cherokees were all in
favor of the British and were only prevented by fear of the Americans from openly expressing themselves. He asked Stuart, therefore, to restore trade, adding that he himself had no sympathy
with the American (Wataugan) actions and would come to

[24] Walter Clark, ed., *North Carolina State Records*, XIII, 90 and 117.
[25] *Ibid.*, XIII, 203.

Pensacola if Stuart desired.[26] It can hardly be doubted that the Cherokee towns, ostensibly friendly to the Americans and therefore caught between the upper and nether millstones of encroachment and penury, looked upon the raiding expeditions of the Chickamaugas with a large degree of benevolence.

The intensified border raids of the Creeks and Cherokees in 1778, although testifying to an increase of British influence, were for the most part unco-ordinated with any specific British objective. But in 1779, Stuart was able at last to put into practice his long-cherished ambition of using Indian troops as auxiliaries to British armies. The Cherokees in early spring were assigned the task of raiding the upper Holston Valley in order to distract to home defense the militia that might otherwise be sent to reinforce Clark in the Illinois country. The excessive gusto with which the Cherokees carried out this assignment gave Governor Henry of Virginia the opportunity of disguising as a punitive expedition the force of three hundred militia under Evan Shelby, which he sent down the Tennessee in April against the Chickamauga towns. The martial success of Shelby in burning some Chickamauga towns and confiscating their supplies was achieved over the opposition of women and children only, since the warriors were away from home congenially employed on the frontiers of Georgia and South Carolina.[27]

In the spring and summer of 1779, Cherokees and Creeks were given a better opportunity to help the British cause when they were called on by Cameron and Taitt to co-operate with Prevost, who was invading Georgia from Florida. Stuart had died on March 26, but his agents acted vigorously, enlisting some three hundred Cherokees and five hundred Creeks. The Cherokee force in August marched to the border of South Carolina, where, finding itself confronted by a force of fifteen hundred South Carolinians, it promptly dissolved into its constituent elements and

[26] C. O. R., Series 5, Vol. 79, p. 279, Joseph Martin to Stuart, February 20, 1778.

[27] Governor Henry in a letter to Governor Caswell, January 8, 1779, said that it was necessary to keep the Tennessee open as a highway to the Illinois country. He suggested that Cherokee affairs be divided among North Carolina, South Carolina, and Virginia, the last named taking the Overhills (and presumably the Chickamaugas).

went home. The Creeks, meanwhile, had held together long enough to capture an American fort on the Ogeechee (May), after the capture of which, on the strength of a convenient report of British defeat, all but about a hundred scattered to their homes. These co-ordinated fiascos, however, kept a large force of American militia immobilized and thus indirectly aided Prevost.[28]

The promotion of Cameron to a superintendency after the death of Stuart indicated that the British were satisfied with Cherokee conduct during the war; the limitation of his authority to the Choctaws and Chickasaws is evidence of the increased importance of these two tribes resulting from the entrance of Spain into the war. After Shelby's expedition the cautious Overhills and Valley towns of the Cherokees apparently resumed their neutrality, and the Raven was superseded by Old Tassel, who was one of the leading advocates of appeasement. Robertson had resigned as Cherokee agent for North Carolina, January 14, 1779, and had been succeeded by Ellis Harling, whose appointment the Raven had requested on the ground that he was a man who wouldn't lie.[29] To the disillusioned chief such a disinclination in an American marked him as outstanding, but the scantiness of the records makes it impossible to judge whether or not the Raven underestimated Harling's capacity. Robertson, after leaving the Cherokees, had led a party of Wataugans to French Lick on the Cumberland, where on New Year's Day, 1780, he had established a settlement for Richard Henderson on the North Carolina portion of his Cherokee purchase of five years before. Whatever this meant to Robertson, Henderson, and Caswell, to the Chickamaugas it appeared as an act of a benevolent providence intent on making their prospective victims more accessible. Dragging Canoe was not so inhospitable as to refuse an attack so openly invited. He was un-

[28] The activities of Creeks and Cherokees in the spring and summer of 1779 are summarized in Helen Louise Shaw, *British Administration of the Southern Indians, 1756–1783*, 128–35.

[29] Clark, *op. cit.*, XIII, 500. Talk by the Raven in council, December 22, 1778; *ibid.*, XIII, 566; *ibid.*, XIV, 246, Robertson to Caswell, January 14, 1779. Robertson left Echota, December 24, 1778, and formally resigned in his letter to Caswell, January 14, 1779. Harling was appointed January 29, 1779. The Raven, after being superseded by Old Tassel, went to Georgia, where he continued to seek British supplies for the Cherokees.

William McIntosh, Creek chief
From a painting by Washington Alston

Courtesy Alabama Department of Archives and History

William Augustus Bowles, adventurer, who founded and headed the Indian state of Muscogee   *From a painting by Thomas Hardy*

Photograph courtesy Dr. Mark Boyd

able to prevent Donelson from bringing reinforcements down the Tennessee, but he kept the Cumberland settlements under constant attack, being aided and abetted by the Upper Creeks, whose road of communication with the Northern Indians the Cumberland settlement blocked.[30]

The same stimulation that had been imparted to the Chickamaugas and Upper Creeks by the settling of French Lick in January was furnished the Chickasaws by the erection of Fort Jefferson in April. The failure of the Chickasaws to oppose the Spanish attack on the lower Mississippi posts in September or their capture of Mobile in March (1780) may be attributed more to the confusion incident to a change of superintendents than to tribal indifference. Certainly they had displayed zeal of a high order in the harassing of Spanish travel and traffic on the Mississippi.[31] A half-century of assiduous practice against the French enabled them to impart a high degree of polish to their operations of this nature, in which they became so engrossed that they seem to have remained unconscious of their conquest by a Spanish proclamation. Neither the Virginians trading with the Spaniards of New Orleans nor those consorting with Indian enemies of the Chickasaws in the Illinois country could expect any discriminating treatment from the Chickasaws; but the tribe, from distance, indifference, or preoccupation, seems to have refrained from attacking the frontier. There is no clear evidence that they joined in the attack on French Lick, apparently considering that, since it was not on Chickasaw territory, it was not a matter for Chickasaw concern. But when Virginia decided to erect a fort on Chickasaw territory, reports of Chickasaw hostilities necessary to justify the act were readily forthcoming. Since the fort was on the Mississippi, it was the business of Colbert, as guardian of that stream, to deal with it.[32] During the summer and fall of 1780 he led repeated

[30] Donelson's Journal of this adventurous voyage is to be found in Ramsey, op. cit., 197-203.

[31] D. C. Corbitt, "James Colbert and the Spanish claims to the East Bank of the Mississippi," The Mississippi Valley Historical Review, Vol. XXIV, 457-72.

[32] Fort Jefferson was located in the present Ballard County, Kentucky, about five miles below the junction of the Ohio and Mississippi. It was on Mayfield Creek but not immediately on the Mississippi and, therefore, could be surrounded by a besieging force. Its siege and assault by the Chickasaws is described

forays against it, but not until January, 1781, could he gather sufficient force and supplies for an attempt to take it by storm. Although the attack failed, it was so evident that the fort could not be maintained against Chickasaw resentment that Virginia abandoned it in June.

The liquidation of Fort Jefferson was accomplished by the Chickasaws not so much to aid the British cause as to preserve the integrity of their tribal lands. But both Dragging Canoe and Emistesigo co-operated with the British advance through the Carolinas by their incessant raids on the frontier. Thomas Browne, who after the death of Stuart became superintendent of the Cherokees and Creeks, entrusted the business of supplying the Indians to his close friend, William Panton, with the result that Creeks and Cherokees were better armed and equipped than ever before but were still feeling the effects of a smallpox epidemic that had killed 2,500 Cherokees.[33] As Cornwallis advanced northward, the Creek co-operation inevitably became less effective, but the Chickamauga raids became so frequent and deadly as to call forth another joint retaliation of Virginia and North Carolina against what Jefferson called the "seceders."[34] Their militia, however, after a diversion to King's Mountain marched in December, 1780, not against the Chickamaugas but against the villages on the Hiwassee and Little Tennessee. The pacific conduct of these Valley and Overhill towns was so offset by their accessibility that practically all of them, Echota included, were destroyed before the astonished and unresisting Indians could find an opportunity to beg for peace. Following these Christmas activities, Governor Jefferson, who had initiated the war, appointed commissioners to arrange a peace, but withdrew their commissions upon learning

in Lewis and Richard Collins, *History of Kentucky*, II, 39-40, and in A. V. Goodpasture, "Indian Wars and Warriors of the Old Southwest 1720-1807," *loc. cit.*

33 For Panton's introduction into the Indian trade by Browne see *American State Papers, Indian Affairs*, I, 458 (hereafter cited as *Indian Affairs*), Blount to ———, August 13, 1793. The Chickamaugas are supposed to have contracted smallpox from their victims on the Donelson expedition of 1780, but it is evident from C. O. R., Series 5, Vol. 8, p. 322, that the disease had been raging among the Cherokees the preceding year.

34 Clark, *op. cit.*, Vol. XV, 47, Jefferson to Nash, August 12, 1780.

that General Greene, then resting in Virginia after his strategic, although hurried, retreat across the Carolinas, was preparing for treaty making under the authority of Congress. Greene appointed eight commissioners from Virginia and North Carolina to meet the Cherokees to arrange for a suspension of hostilities, a settlement of the boundary, an exchange of prisoners, and to do anything else they thought best—the last instruction being an oblique reference to a land cession. Martin, in his double capacity as Virginia superintendent and United States commissioner, exchanged preliminary talks in April with Oconostota, as a result of which a large delegation from the friendly towns came to Long Island on July 31, Old Tassel acting as spokesman for the absent Oconostota. The failure of the North Carolina commissioners to attend made it impossible for the Cherokees to obtain even a promise of relief from encroachment, but at least it relieved them from making the land cession by which North Carolina hoped to compensate herself for the expenses of the late "war." The only thing possible was to exchange speeches, to blame the British for the war, and to make peace.[35]

When the Spaniards finally launched their attack on Pensacola in March, 1781, there were present only some five hundred Indians to help in the defense. Practically all of these were Choctaws; the scarcity of Chickasaws may be attributed to distance and to their obsession with Fort Jefferson; the Creeks, whom McGillivray and McIntosh had led down, had been dismissed by an inept and parsimonious British commander. The fall of Pensacola was the end of the war for the Choctaws, since it was from Pensacola that they had drawn their supplies after the capture of Mobile. The Choctaws, accepting their fate with characteristic stolidity, arranged a *modus vivendi* with the Spaniards, but the Chickasaws

[35] Papers of the Continental Congress, No. 155, Letters of General Nathanael Greene, Folios 255, 259, 263, and 289; Draper MS, LXXX, 49. Greene appointed as commissioners William Christian, William Preston, Arthur Campbell, Joseph Martin, Robert and John Sevier, Evan Shelby, and Joseph Williams; only Christian and Martin attended. From 1776 to 1779, Congress had a standing committee on Indian affairs, but in the latter year it gave its functions to the Board of War. In March, 1781, the Board voted that the commanding general in the field should act as Indian superintendent of his department. It was under this authority that Greene acted.

entered on the most vigorous phase of their war. The Chickasaw recalcitrance was due to the influence of several score of British refugees who had fled to the Chickasaw country when Natchez was captured and the additional refugees who had come in after the failure of the insurrection there in June, 1781. These refugees and an even greater number from Georgia and the Carolinas enlisted under James Colbert to harry the Spaniards from the Mississippi. This they continued to do with considerable success for the remaining years of the war, their energy and hatred of Spain compensating for their lack of discipline. In May, 1782, they captured a Spanish boat on which was the wife of the Spanish commander at St. Louis.

Colbert did not cease his ministrations even when the treaty of peace was signed; in April, 1783, he led his motley force of refugees and Indians across the Mississippi and besieged (unsuccessfully) the Spanish Fort Carlos on the Arkansas.[36] It was Colbert's hatred of the Spanish that induced him, when he saw the downfall of the British impending, to make overtures to the Americans; with Great Britain gone, the Chickasaws would have to depend on either Americans or Spaniards for trade, and Colbert preferred even Americans to Spaniards. It was not, however, until the spring of 1782 that the Chickasaws, at Colbert's suggestion, took their first step toward peace by sending a message to Joseph Martin at Long Island. This being unanswered (probably because of nondelivery), they again in July sent out a message, this time addressed to George Rogers Clark at the Falls of the Ohio. In due season the message was forwarded to Governor Harrison at Richmond, who appointed Martin and John Donelson to conduct the treaty making. But the Revolution ended before the treaty could be made, thus leaving the apprehensive Chickasaws still nominally at war.

But the martial ardor of Cherokees and Creeks was apparently undiminished by the fall of Pensacola or the surrender at Yorktown. Dragging Canoe, indeed, had no intention of making peace since he was at war not so much because of loyalty to the British as because of hatred of the Americans. The continued encroach-

[36] J. W. Caughey, *Bernardo de Gálvez in Louisiana, 1776–1783*, 215–42.

ments on Cherokee land, which evoked from Old Tassel only a series of pathetic remonstrances, were answered by Dragging Canoe with burning and slaughter until, in the fall of 1782, Governor Martin of North Carolina was provoked into sending another punitive expedition against him. In this campaign Sevier and McDowell apparently attempted to discriminate between friendly and hostile towns, with the result that a number of the latter on Chickamauga Creek and the headwaters of Coosa River were destroyed.[37] After this episode Superintendent Browne, foreseeing that the recalcitrant chief would soon be left unaided to face the Americans, advised him to remove his towns further out of the American reach. This Dragging Canoe did, establishing new towns lower down on the Tennessee that became known as the Five Lower Towns.[38]

The devotion of Emistesigo to the British seemed to increase in direct proportion to the decline of their fortunes. With the Creek nation united behind him (except for Cusseta and Tallassie), he kept his war bands constantly on the frontier to harass the operations of Greene's army as it gradually drove to the recovery of Georgia. In the fall of 1782, he led a large Creek force to the relief of the British in Savannah and was himself killed in cutting his way through Wayne's besieging force.[39] This practically ended the fighting, for Wayne proffered the Creeks a suspension of hostilities, which McGillivray accepted.[40] There was perhaps a renewed flickering of the war spirit; and the first week in January, 1783, when a deputation of Northern Indians and

---

[37] It was Governor Martin's plan to exact a cession of all Cherokee land in North Carolina at the end of this campaign. Then the Cherokees were to receive a payment and be assigned a reservation in the angle of the French Broad and Tennessee. The plan failed because the state could not secure the goods for payment. Clark, *op. cit.*, XVI, 710, Martin to Cherokee Treaty Commissioners, September 20, 1782.

[38] C. O. R., Series 5, Vol. 82, p. 695, Browne to Townshend, January 12, 1783. The Five Lower Towns were Lookout Mountain Town, Crow Town, Long Island Town, Nickajack, and Running Water—the last being the residence of Dragging Canoe. Some of these towns are located and described in O. D. Street, "Cherokee Towns and Villages in Alabama," *Publications* of the Alabama Historical Society, Vol. I, 416–21.

[39] *Ibid.*, p. 711, Browne to Townshend, June 1, 1783.

[40] Indian Office Records, McGillivray to Houston, June 30, 1784.

Cherokees came to St. Augustine to propose a confederation, Browne gave his approval. In April a general meeting of the four Southern tribes was held at Tuckabatchee.[41]

The movement was too late, for, on June 1, Browne received orders to withdraw all British officials and traders from the Indian country and at once proceeded to carry out his instructions, which action was equivalent to notifying the Indians that the war was over as far as Great Britain was concerned. When McGillivray on August 30 sent a written protest against the British abandonment, he was acting no longer as British commissary but in his new capacity as chief and head warrior of the Creek Nation, to which position he had been elected as successor of Emistesigo by the Creek National Council in May, 1783.[42]

[41] C. O. R., Series 5, Vol. 82, p. 695, Browne to Townshend, January 12, 1783; *ibid.*, p. 749, McGillivray to Browne, April 10, 1783.

[42] *Ibid.*, p. 711, Browne to Townshend, June 1, 1783; *ibid.*, p. 801, Browne to North, October 24, 1783. This statement of Browne definitely disposes of the question when McGillivray became head chief. It also disposes of Milfort's statement that the Creeks in 1780 made McGillivray chief and himself principal warrior.

Alexander McGillivray

1783-1793

Fᴿᴏᴍ ᴛʜᴇ American Revolution the Southern Indians emerged with their territory theoretically undiminished since the enforced Cherokee cessions of 1777; the encroachments on Cherokee land after the treaty of Long Island had been the acts of individuals eliciting from the North Carolina government as little of approval as of opposition. But with the return of peace the expropriation of Indian land became an official North Carolina policy directed at both Cherokees and Chickasaws. In May, 1783, North Carolina, by legislative act, confiscated the entire Indian domain within her limits except the land in the angle of the French Broad and Tennessee, which the Cherokees were permitted to retain. For the Chickasaws no reservation at all was provided, whether because North Carolina knew the tribe lived outside the state or was unaware that it claimed land within. The expropriated lands were opened to entry, and in the summer and fall of 1783, the two bewildered and exasperated tribes saw their domain overrun by a host of white men locating claims.[1]

The example of grand larceny set by North Carolina was one

[1] It is only fair in judging this act of May 17, 1783, to note that it was the expressed intention of North Carolina to follow this confiscation with treaties in which provision would be made for compensating the Indians for the land taken. Such treaties were not held, partly because North Carolina could not secure the necessary supplies and partly because of the rise of Franklin. For the overrunning of Chickasaw lands after the passing of the act see Samuel C. Williams' *Beginnings of West Tennessee in the Land of the Chickasaws, 1541–1841*, 40–46.

that Georgia could wholly approve but was unable to follow; since the Indians within her borders were too strong to be dispossessed by legislation, the state could only essay piecemeal spoliations by treaty. A beginning was made with the Cherokees, from whom Georgia demanded a land cession in compensation for Chickamauga ravages in 1782. This venerable stratagem of exacting from the peaceful Cherokees a payment of debts due from the hostile Chickamaugas was countered by the Cherokees with a cession of lands belonging to the Creeks. The land between the Tugalo and the Apalachee rivers was ceded on May 31, 1783, at Augusta, by a delegation of Overhill Cherokees led by the Terrapin, son of the deceased Oconostota.[2] The beguiled Georgians, forced to the conclusion that a Creek cession of the same land was a prerequisite to peaceful possession, invited that tribe to meet them at Augusta, November 1, 1783. This invitation the tribe as a whole ignored but the civil chiefs of Cusseta and Tallassie—the Fat King and the Tame King—who had defiantly remained friendly to the Americans during the Revolution and were now smarting under their recent demotion by McGillivray, attended the conference and made the cession which Georgia desired. On their return home, the two chiefs justified themselves to their outraged neighbors by alleging that they had been forced by the Georgians to make the cession in spite of their protest that their act could not bind the tribe.[3]

The third American inroad on Indian lands in 1783 was initiated at Long Island on July 9, 1783, when Joseph Martin, now Cherokee agent of North Carolina (since the spring of 1783) as

---

[2] Milling, *op. cit.*, 322–23. Oconostota had died in 1782 after an abortive attempt to resign in favor of his son Tuckasee, but the Cherokee council elected Old Tassel (Corn Tassel or Tassel) as head chief (*Calendar of Virginia State Papers*, III, 234; *ibid.*, IV, 176, 341).

[3] The Georgia account of this treaty is given in *Indian Affairs* I, 23; the Creek version is set forth in letters by McGillivray in May, 1786, to Miró and O'Neill in J. W. Caughey's *McGillivray of the Creeks*, 105–107. It can not be said with any degree of positiveness whether the right to alienate land lay in the tribe as a whole or in that portion which had occupied it. In a later treaty the tribal chieftain pleaded inability to cede because the portion of the tribe owning the land was absent. In view of the previous and future conduct of the Fat King and the Tame King, one must conclude that coercion was unnecessary to secure their signatures at Augusta.

well as of Virginia, and John Donelson, acting for a group of North Carolina speculators, bought for a promised $5,000 in merchandise from a group of Indians, whom they called Chickamaugas, the Muscle Shoals region north of the Tennessee River. Only the high reputation for integrity which Martin deservedly enjoyed prevents the suspicion that he here employed the hoary frontier legerdemain of buying from one set of Indians the property belonging to another. For it is by no means clear that the Indians with whom he dealt were really Chickamaugas, since the Indian spokesman in the Virginia treaty immediately preceding the land deal was the Raven. Moreover, the prospect of free rations and presents, which ordinarily made an Indian treaty delegation approximate in numbers the tribal population, attracted to Long Island on this occasion only twenty-two Indians, of whom six were women. Whether or not the twenty-two were Chickamaugas they certainly did not represent the Five Lower Towns, the inhabitants of which were the Indians nearest the Muscle Shoals region. Moreover, any settlement there would certainly be opposed by the Chickasaws, who claimed part of the region, and by the Creeks, who claimed it all.[4]

Against the rapacity of North Carolina, the sly nibbling of Georgia, and the infiltration of the speculators, the Southern Indians reacted in various ways. The Chickasaws made treaties with Virginia and Spain; the Choctaws made overtures to Georgia and a treaty with Spain; the Creeks allied themselves to Spain; the Chickamaugas went on fighting. The Chickasaws had addressed their overtures in 1782 to Virginia partly because they considered Virginia and the United States to be synonymous. These overtures finally bore fruit in the summer of 1783, when an agent sent by Joseph Martin reached the Chickasaw towns and arranged for a conference to be held at French Lick in November. In this conference on November 5 and 6 with Martin and Donelson, the Red King (Mingo Homa) and Piomingo asserted the Chickasaw own-

---

[4] No record of the proceedings at this purchase seems to be extant. The only record of the Virginia-Chickamauga treaty (which Martin negotiated, in his public capacity, immediately before making the purchase in his private capacity) is in Draper MSS, IXX, 55. This is an invoice of the presents given at the treaty; they went to four chiefs, twelve young men, and six women.

ership of the territory west of a line running along the Cumberland-Tennessee divide from the Ohio to Duck Creek and thence up Duck Creek to its source. Undoubtedly their emphasis on this matter was a notification to all and sundry that they meant to oppose the Carolina confiscation act of the preceding May.[5]

Since it became evident to the Chickasaws that while Virginia could grant peace it could not supply trade, they were forced in their desire for the latter commodity to have recourse to Spain. On this question of friendship, public opinion among the Chickasaws was divided, with Piomingo and the Colberts leading an American faction, while Mingo Homa (the "king") with the younger men favored the Spaniards. But on the necessity for trade there could be no difference of opinion, and the delegation that went to Mobile to treat with the Spaniards (at their invitation) in June, 1784, seems to have been representative of the nation. The resulting treaty, made on June 22 and 23, confirmed peace and bound the Spaniards to provide an adequate trade. In return, the Chickasaws promised to prohibit traders other than those with Spanish licenses, to report all strangers in their country to the Spanish authorities, and to maintain peaceful relations with all Indian nations except the Kickapoos, with whom the Chickasaws were nourishing an ancient feud.[6]

The Chickasaws had turned to the Spaniards only after applying to the Americans, but the Choctaws, dealt with them both at the same time. In June, 1783, Franchimastabe, the head chief, with the approval of the Choctaw council started a delegation to Savannah to solicit peace and trade from the Georgians. On July 17 the Governor of Georgia answered their request by professing friendship and promising trade provided the Choctaws should induce the Creeks to permit the Georgia traders to go through their territory.[7] While this delegation was on its way to Savannah, the

[5] For this treaty and its preliminaries see R. S. Cotterill's "The Virginia-Chickasaw Treaty of 1783," *The Journal of Southern History*, Vol. VIII, 483–96.

[6] The proceedings of this conference and the text of the treaty have been consulted in the Mississippi Provincial Archives, Spanish Dominion, II, 162–70 (hereafter cited as Miss. Prov. Ar., Spanish Dominion). The treaty was signed by the Chickasaw king (Mingo Homa or his successor), Piomingo, and about ten other chiefs. For the Kickapoo war see Papers of the Continental Congress, III, 56.

hungry Choctaws at home went in mass formation to Mobile to confer with the Spaniards. The resulting treaty on June 14 was practically the same as that made a few days later between Spaniards and Chickasaws except for the omission of the Kickapoo clause.[8]

The position of Alexander McGillivray at the close of the Revolution was eminent and unenviable. He was head chief and principal warrior of the Creek confederacy, thus uniting in himself the power of peace and war, but he was "deserted by the British, without pay, without money, without friends, and without property, saving a few negroes, and he and his nation threatened with destruction by the Georgians, unless they agreed to cede them the better part of their country." To this catalog of woes it may be added that the collapse of the British deprived the Creeks of the trade on which their power and perhaps even their existence depended. Future trade could be secured only from the Spaniards, whose ability and disposition to supply it McGillivray distrusted, or from the Georgians, against whom he felt a bitter and unabating resentment because of their confiscation of his father's estate. While pondering this dilemma, McGillivray put his house in order against his two recent foes and now unfriendly neighbors by a governmental reform which subordinated the town civil chiefs to the war chiefs. This measure, which had the effect of placing the nation on a permanent war footing, was bitterly opposed by some of the civil chiefs, notably by Opothle Mico (the Tame King), of Tallassie, and Neah Mico (the Fat King), of Cusseta, both of whom had clashed repeatedly with McGillivray because of their pro-Americanism during the Revolution. Tribal custom made it impossible for McGillivray to punish the chiefs themselves, but he had the satisfaction of executing several of their white followers.[9]

[7] Archives of Georgia, Creek Indian Letters, 1705–1793, pt. I, 56, 58, 59–60. The Choctaw delegation to Georgia was led by Mingohoopa, second chief of the Choctaws. It is probable that at this meeting the Georgians laid the foundations for their later Bourbon County venture.

[8] The text of this treaty, with the names of the signers, has been published in Manuel Serrano y Sanz, *España y Los Indios Cherokis y Choctas en la Segunda Mitad del Siglo XVIII*, 82–85.

[9] McGillivray's reforms are briefly alluded to in Caleb Swan, "Position and

From the difficulties that were besetting him, McGillivray found relief through the counsel of his father's old friend and neighbor, William Panton, head of the firm of Panton, Leslie and Company. Panton advised him to make an alliance with the Spaniards by which the latter would guarantee the Creek lands against Georgia in return for a monopoly of Creek trade to be supplied through Panton, Leslie and Company, of which McGillivray should become a partner, and to be controlled by McGillivray as Spanish commissary.[10] Accepting this sage, although not disinterested, advice, McGillivray wrote to O'Neill, the Spanish commander at Pensacola, soliciting protection and trade for the Creeks, and for himself an appointment as commissary.[11] The result of his overtures was a Creek-Spanish treaty at Pensacola, June 1, 1784, by which Spain guaranteed the Creek territory within her limits and pledged a permanent trade in return for a Creek promise to refrain from dealing with Americans and to honor only Spanish passports. After the signing of the treaty, McGillivray was appointed commissary.[12]

The territorial guarantee contained elements of imperfection, since a considerable portion of the Creek lands (including the Augusta cession) lay east of the Flint and therefore beyond the limits of the Spanish claims. For the firm of Panton, Leslie and Company, in which he had a silent, although unconcealed, part-

State of Manners and Arts in the Creek or Muscogee Nation in 1791" in Henry R. Schoolcraft's *Historical and Statistical Information Regarding the History, Condition and the Prospects of the Indian Tribes of the United States*, V, 251–83.

[10] Panton's responsibility for McGillivray's decision to deal with the Spaniards is evident in Panton's letter to Lachlan McGillivray, April 10, 1794 (Caughey, *McGillivray*, 362–63). The Florida Historical Society possesses an unrivaled collection of material on Panton, Leslie and Company, of which students of the period have up to now made little use.

[11] This letter, written January 1, 1784, from Little Tallassie, is given in Caughey, *McGillivray*, 64. This book is the chief printed source on McGillivray, and the account of McGillivray's activities here given is drawn from it unless other reference is cited. R. C. Downes, in "Creek-American Relations, 1782–1790," *Georgia Historical Quarterly*, Vol. XXI, 142–184, deals fully with this period.

[12] The salient provisions of this treaty are given in Caughey, *McGillivray*, 75–76. The full text is in *American State Papers, Foreign Relations*, I, 278–79. McGillivray negotiated this treaty for the Upper Creeks, Lower Creeks, and Seminoles. The Spaniards made a treaty later at Mobile with the Alabamas, at the same time as with the Choctaws.

nership, McGillivray was able to secure from the Spaniards neither entrance into Pensacola for the Creek trade nor a share of the Choctaw-Chickasaw trade, but only permission to continue its store established near St. Marks in the last year of the war.[13] Accepting the half-loaf then possible of attainment in these two respects, McGillivray after the treaty set himself to the twin tasks of inducing (by an unceasing epistolary bombardment) the Spaniards to grant Panton entrance into Pensacola and persuading the Choctaws and Chickasaws to place themselves under Spanish protection. In both endeavors he used all his prestige as chief of the Creeks and as "principal in the late general confederacy of the Indian Nations in favor of the English." In the former objective his success was immediate; in the latter, delayed. Having done what he could to put the Creeks on a war footing, to secure Spanish protection, and to promote intertribal co-operation, McGillivray was in a position to undertake the recovery of the Augusta cession. But the Governor of Georgia, apparently impressed by these measures, heeded the official Creek repudiation of the cession and in November, 1784, notified McGillivray that the Georgians would not attempt to settle the disputed lands. This assurance McGillivray professed to, and perhaps did, accept, and so, for the time being, the Creeks kept the peace.

The Cherokees escaped the effects of the confiscation act not by virtue of their own opposition, but by the confusion of the spoilers. For when North Carolina in the spring of 1784, by the cession of her western land, threw on the United States the burden of protecting her satiated land speculators, rival speculators initiated the state of Franklin with such enthusiasm that even a repeal of the cession failed to impress them. The ensuing "war" between North Carolina and Franklin made white settlement of the confiscated land so impossible that both Cherokees and Chickasaws remained undispossessed. Dragging Canoe and the Chickamaugas remained relatively quiet through 1784, partly because their British ammunition was exhausted and partly because the Muscle Shoals speculation had not yet reached the stage of attempted

[13] The Spaniards entrusted the Chickasaw-Choctaw trade to the firm of Mather and Strother, in which McGillivray accepted a one-sixth share.

settlement. The speculators, after buying the land from Indians who did not own it, solicited a grant of it from a state whose title was in dispute. Selecting Georgia over South Carolina as their prospective benefactor, they presented through William Blount, in February, 1784, a petition, to which the legislature of that state responded inadequately, not by a grant, but by the appointment of commissioners to organize a district of the Tennessee and to survey the region for sale. Since three of the commissioners were members of the speculating group and the other four complaisant, the disappointed but persevering speculators still hoped by individual warrants to engross the land which Georgia had refused to grant. In July, 1784, four of the commissioners (including the three speculators) met and justified the trust placed in them by appointing members of the land company colonel, lieutenant colonel, major, Indian agent, and surveyor. To further the settling of this Carolina-manned Georgia District of the Tennessee the commissioners decreed the opening of a land office at Muscle Shoals in March, 1785. But the interest of the Franklin people, the only prospective settlers, in the land venture was so overshadowed by the attraction of their "war" against North Carolina that the opening failed to materialize.[14]

To the United States in congress assembled, the menace to peace inherent in the discontent of the Southern Indians was evident at the very close of the Revolution. But since its "sole and exclusive right and power of regulating the trade and managing all affairs with the Indians" was limited to those Indians who were "not members of any of the States," it could not constitutionally intervene in the South, where all the Indians were indubitably state members.[15] Until the North Carolina cession of 1784, Con-

[14] A. P. Whitaker, "The Muscle Shoals Speculation, 1783–1789," *Mississippi Valley Historical Review*, Vol. XIII, 365–86; Oliver D. Street, "Houston County in the Great Bend of the Tennessee," *Alabama Historical Quarterly*, Vol. VI, 50–59.

[15] According to the decision of the United States Supreme Court, *Harcourt v. Gaillard*, 12 Wheaton 716, the United States in 1783 contained no land other than that belonging to the individual states. The relative power of the states and United States over Indian affairs under the Articles of Confederation is discussed *ex parte* in a report of the Committee on Southern Indians, Continental Congress Papers, II, 311.

gress could only view with alarm a situation it was powerless to improve. While Congress hesitated, North Carolina rescinded its cession, the state of Franklin was organized, the Creeks, Choctaws, and Chickasaws placed themselves under the protection of Spain, and Georgia appointed commissioners to set up a government in the Muscle Shoals country. Perhaps assisted in making up its mind by the impact of these events, Congress on March 15, 1785, decided to appoint commissioners to treat with the Southern Indians.[16]

With none of the Southern Indians could the United States constitutionally treat except with a portion of the Cherokees, and even with them only on the doubtful theory that the North Carolina repeal of cession was invalid. Yet all four tribes received invitations to meet the commissioners, the Creeks at Galphinton in Georgia, October 24, and the others later at Hopewell in South Carolina. McGillivray's acceptance of the invitation to the Creeks was inspired partly by a hope of having the Augusta cession repudiated and partly by his regard for Pickens, from whom he had received a personal appeal supplementing the formal invitation to the "Kings, Headmen and Warriors of the Creeks." Since the conclusion of the Spanish treaty he had had the satisfaction of seeing the Spaniards forced by their own necessities to admit Panton, Leslie and Company into Pensacola (1785) and of holding (in July) a conference with the other Southern tribes as a further step in reforging an Indian confederacy. It is possible that his plan of using the United States to curb Georgia might have succeeded, since the commissioners, as their later actions revealed, were sincerely intent on checking encroachment on Indian land. But deciding, probably because of the strenuous objections of O'Neill, to absent himself from the Galphinton meeting, he sent

[16] In October, 1783, Congress appointed a committee to consider Indian affairs in the South, and this committee on April 19, 1784, recommended that conferences be held with the Southern tribes to fix boundaries without regard to state treaties and private purchases. On January 17, 1785, Congress appointed a committee to draw up an ordinance on Indian trade. The commissioners appointed in March were Benjamin Hawkins of North Carolina, Lachlan McIntosh of Georgia, Governor Pickens of South Carolina, Joseph Martin, and W. Perry. Acting on instructions from Congress, Hawkins, Pickens, and Martin held a preliminary meeting in Charleston to perfect their arrangements.

as his deputies two chiefs each from the Upper and Lower Creeks under definite instructions to have the Augusta cession nullified and the boundary fixed as it was in 1773. With these deputies the commissioners refused to treat, allegedly because they were too few, actually, perhaps, because the commissioners were intimidated by the Georgia agents, who had come to Galphinton determined to prevent any treaty between the United States and the Creek Indian "members" of Georgia. After the departure of the timid, or at least prudent, commissioners, the Georgia officials made a treaty of their own, not with the accredited Creek representative, but with the Tame King and Fat King, who had put in their appearance presumably as a mark of defiance to McGillivray. The two chiefs not only reaffirmed the Augusta cession, but made an additional cession of the territory east of the Oconee and of a line from the mouth of the Oconee to the headwaters of the St. Mary's.[17]

After the futile experiments at Galphinton, the disgruntled commissioners went on to Hopewell, on the Keowee, where 918 Cherokees including thirty-six chiefs from nearly as many towns, set siege to their inadequate commissary. This representative attendance from all the nation, except the Five Lower Towns, was attracted not solely, perhaps, by the culinary prospects but also by the hope of securing from the United States a redress of their grievances against North Carolina and Franklin. The latter community, appropriating the practices as well as the territory of North Carolina, had forced a faction of the Overhills into a treaty on Dumplin Creek in June, whereby the Indians surrendered that part of their reserved land which lay between the French Broad and the Little Tennessee divide. To the browbeaten Cherokees, the commissioners' opening announcement that no land cession was desired came as a surprise; but when they were called on to state their boundaries, they had recovered sufficiently to reassert

[17] McGillivray's account of the Galphinton meeting is in Caughey, *McGillivray*, 107. The Georgia treaty at Galphinton is given in *Indian Affairs*, I, 17. The treaty was signed November 12, 1785, by seventeen Creeks (*Colonial Records of Georgia*, XXXIX, 506–509). Navarro's decree admitting McGillivray to Pensacola was dated September 16, 1785 (D. C. Corbitt, ed. and trans., "Papers Relating to the Georgia-Florida Frontier, 1784–1800," *Georgia Historical Quarterly*, Vol. XXI, 77).

their claim to Transylvania colony. This claim they philosophically withdrew when the commissioners produced Henderson's deed signed by Oconostota and Attakullaculla. The boundary as finally agreed upon followed the southern boundary of Transylvania (so the commissioners thought), the treaty line of 1777 (with minor variations), and the Augusta line of 1783. To Old Tassel's plea for the removal of the trespassers on their land, the commissioners replied, in the classical formula for nonaction, that they would lay the matter before Congress. The treaty was signed on November 28, 1785, by thirty-six chiefs, including Old Tassel, of Toquo, the head chief, and Hanging Maw, of Echota, the chief warrior.[18]

The tardiness of the Choctaws in arriving at Hopewell nearly a month after the Cherokees made the treaty was likely because the Creeks, as a mark of displeasure or as a matter of routine, had stolen all the Choctaw horses as the latter passed through the Creek country, with the result that they had to finish their journey on foot. From the biographical details available, it is impossible to determine whether or not the Colonel Wood who led them in was the "intelligent, honest man" whom the commissioners had sent to the Choctaws with an invitation to treat. At any rate, he had been named by Georgia as one of her commissioners to set up Bourbon county in the Natchez country and, since the failure of that fantastic enterprise, had been living furtively among the Choctaws, styling himself Georgia Indian agent and seducing them into ceding him vast tracts of their land.[19] His ability to se-

[18] For the Dumplin Creek treaty see S. C. Williams, *The Lost State of Franklin*, 77-78. The proceedings at the Hopewell meetings are given in *Indian Affairs*, I, 40-52; the text of the three treaties made at Hopewell are in Charles J. Kappler's *Indian Affairs, Laws and Treaties*, II, 8-16. For all Indian land cessions and treaty lines the maps in Charles C. Royce's *Indian Land Cessions in the United States*, B. A. E. *Eighteenth Annual Report*, pt. 2, are indispensable. By the Cherokee treaty there was a small land cession in North Carolina. In the description of the Cherokee northern boundary the treaty text contained an ambiguity of which the Americans later took full advantage. For a discussion of this point see Charles C. Royce, in *The Cherokee Nation of Indians*, B. A. E. *Fifth Annual Report*, 153-54.

[19] For Bourbon County see E. C. Burnett, ed., "Documents Relating to Bourbon County," *American Historical Review*, Vol. XV, 66. The Choctaws always denied that they had made any cession to Wood (Miss. Prov. Ar., Spanish Dominion, IV, 437).

cure a Choctaw delegation to Hopewell was due to Choctaw discontent with trade conditions. The firm of Mathers and Strothers, to which the Spaniards had given a monopoly of Choctaw and Chickasaw commerce, had been unable to furnish an adequate supply of goods, and, because of a glut of Indian products on the market, had been compelled to lower their prices on peltry. To the Indians, innocent of any knowledge of economic laws, the explanation of their lowered income lay simply in Spanish perfidy, which they now proceeded to counter by turning to the Americans. Under the Spanish regime, the Choctaws had continued their ancient organization of three divisions, which the Spaniards called the Big District, Little District, and the Six Towns. Franchimastabe was head chief, and it was he who sent the Choctaw delegation to Hopewell, selecting men marked by their former loyalty to the British.

When the Choctaws arrived at Hopewell on December 26, their Mississippi clothing, at best inadequate for a Carolina winter, was so shredded and torn from their long overland journey that their wardrobes had to be replenished before the negotiations could proceed. The treaty signed January 3, 1786, contained a guarantee of Choctaw territory as it was on the last day of British rule, an acknowledgement by the Choctaws of American sovereignty, and a recognition of American control of their trade. The Choctaws ceded to the United States two six-square-mile tracts for trading posts, the location of which was to be determined later. In gratitude, perhaps, to Wood for leading them to new clothes and two weeks of free meals, the Choctaws asked that he be appointed their superintendent; the commissioners tempered their refusal of the request, which was beyond their authority to grant, by appointing John Pitchlynn as official interpreter for the tribe. This completed the farcical treaty, which was signed by thirty-one Choctaws (so they later explained to the accusing Spaniards) only after they had been so saturated with liquor by the Americans as to be insensible.[20]

[20] Trade conditions among the Choctaws and Chickasaws at this time are discussed in Serrano y Sanz, *op. cit.*, 31ff. The Choctaw version of the Hopewell proceedings is given in a letter by McGillivray to Miró, May 1, 1786, in D. C. and Roberta Corbitt, eds., "Papers from the Spanish Archives Relating to Ten-

The ethical scruples that had prevented the commissioners from treating with the four Creeks at Galphinton did not now embarrass them in dealing with the three Chickasaws who arrived as the Choctaw conference was ending. The three delegates were Lotapaia, Piomingo, the war chief, and Mingotuska, in the garbled spelling of whose name can be detected the Chickasaw "king," Taski Etoka. Taski Etoka, whom the Americans commonly called the "Hare-lip King," was the nephew and successor of Mingo Homa, who had died in 1784, while Lotapaia was apparently acting in the place of James Colbert, who had been killed by a fall from his horse in January, 1784. Between the Chickasaw king and the war chief there existed considerable enmity, reflecting the division of the tribe into Spanish and American factions, but they had been forced into temporary accord by the necessity of seeking from the Americans a trade promised but still unprovided by the Spanish from Mobile. In the treaty, signed January 10, the Chickasaws granted to the United States the same trade monopoly they had given the preceding year to Spain, and with hopes long unrealized ceded to the United States a tract of land five miles in diameter at the lower end of Muscle Shoals for a trading post. Before they could leave, both Chickasaws and Choctaws were robbed thoroughly and impartially by the Cherokees.[21]

The three dubious treaties negotiated at Hopewell were duly reported to Congress, which on April 17, 1786, received them in calm disregard of protests by North Carolina and Georgia. Whatever ambition Congress may have had of increasing its authority or of improving Indian relations was quickly nullified by the conduct of Franklin and Georgia. Because some Cherokees, apparently in naïve reliance on the Hopewell treaty, had killed several

nessee and the Old Southwest, 1783–1800," East Tennessee Historical Society *Publications*, Vol. X, 131, and in a letter by Miró to Gálvez, June 28, 1786, Miss. Prov. Ar., Spanish Dominion, II, 739–40. For Franchimastabe's responsibility for the Choctaw delegation to Hopewell see Serrano y Sanz, *op. cit.*, 36, and Burnett, "Documents Relating to Bourbon County," *loc. cit.*, 337, Long, Davenport, and Christman to Elbert, September 13, 1785. John Pitchlynn, born in 1756, had lived among the Choctaws since 1775.

[21] For the Chickasaw conference and treaty see n. 12 above. McGillivray in his letter of May 1, 1786, to Miró (n. 20 above) says that the Chickasaws were bribed to cede the trading-post site.

trespassers on their land, John Sevier, the president of Franklin, sent an expedition in August, 1786, against the easily accessible Overhills and forced them in the treaty of Coyatee to surrender all their remaining land north of the Little Tennessee.[22] At the very time that the commissioners at Hopewell were ostensibly restoring the Muscle Shoals region to the Indians, Valentine Sevier was leading a group of ninety people down the Tennessee to settle in the Bend. Only a prudent retreat before the onslaught of Dragging Canoe saved them from annihilation at the hands of McGillivray.[23]

On April 2, 1786, the Creek council declared war on Georgia, which had resumed, or continued, the occupation of the territory "ceded" at Augusta and Galphinton. The activities of the war parties, which McGillivray at once unleashed, were apparently unhampered by his counsel to remove the intruders and destroy their property, but to refrain from killing the unresisting. War parties sent against Muscle Shoals had to limit themselves to a survey of the ruins, Dragging Canoe having made other action unnecessary. A third set of Creek warriors joined with the Chickamaugas against the Cumberland settlements in an onslaught so furious that it carried far into Kentucky.[24] Arms and ammunition for these raids were furnished the Creeks from St. Marks and Pensacola. Dragging Canoe received part of his supplies through John McDonald, who after the Revolution had remained among the Chickamaugas as a trader to Charleston and Pensacola. Most of the Chickamauga supplies, however, were brought in by

[22] Ramsey, *op. cit.*, 344–45; Brown, *op. cit.*, 254–55.

[23] Ramsey, *op. cit.*, 377–79; Brown, *op. cit.*, 251; Street, "Houston County," *loc. cit.* These men had accompanied the commissioners of the District of the Tennessee as a guard to Long Island Town, where they had opened a land office and issued land warrants.

[24] It was probably at the hands of one of these raiding parties that John Donelson met his death April 11, 1786. Donelson in the spring of 1781 had moved from French Lick to Daviess Station in Lincoln County, Kentucky. In 1785 he moved his family again to French Lick, while he was at Muscle Shoals in connection with his land speculation. In the fall of that year he went to Virginia and in the spring of 1786 was returning to French Lick through Kentucky with two companions, Tilly and Leach, when he was killed near the Big Barren River. He was buried there (Draper MS Notes XXXII, 309–13; *Calendar of Virginia State Papers*, IV, 120).

French traders from Detroit over the ancient Wabash-Tennessee route. There were about one hundred of these traders resorting to Muscle Shoals, of whom thirty were settled there under a guard of Shawnee and Delaware Indians. The enterprising French traders not only supplied the Chickamaugas, but also visited the Cherokee and Chickasaw towns and went far enough into Creek territory to excite the apprehensions of Panton's factors.[25] It was doubtless with a view of safeguarding these supplies that the Chickamaugas built the new town of Coldwater.

The immediate effect of McGillivray's vigorous attack was an overture for peace from the Cumberland settlements and the appointment by the Georgia legislature of Daniel McMurphy as "their agent to reside in the Creek nation to preserve peace with their Friends the Creek Indians." The arrival of McMurphy (dubbed Yellow Hair by the Creeks) coincided, by design or good fortune, with the absence of McGillivray in New Orleans. His optimistic, or impudent, demands that all traders should have a Georgia license and all travelers a Georgia passport received the support of the still disgruntled Tame King and Fat King, but the other chiefs refused any dealing with him until McGillivray returned. Prior to this event, McMurphy, with commendable prudence, returned to Georgia but, before leaving, wrote a letter to O'Neill at Pensacola, asserting that the Creeks were within the state of Georgia and protesting against the action of Spain in supplying them with arms.[26] The Creek council, called by McGillivray on his return, after listening to the talks of McMurphy, *in absentia*, as relayed through Tame King and Fat King, instruc-

[25] For John McDonald as a trader see P. M. Hamer, "The British in Canada and the Southern Indians," East Tennessee Historical Society *Publications*, Vol. II, 107-34 and A. P. Whitaker, "Spain and the Cherokee Indians, 1783-1795," *North Carolina Historical Review*, Vol. IV, 83-98, 252-69. For the French at Muscle Shoals, see Cherokee Indians, Talks and Treaties, I, 4, Martin to Telfair, October 16, 1786, and I, 128, Davenport to Sevier, July 28, 1786; Papers of the Continental Congress, II, 185, Martin to Thompson, January 5, 1787. Corbitt, "Papers from the Spanish Archives," *loc. cit.*, Vol. XI, 65, Kelley to Panton, January 23, 1787. It was Martin's opinion that the French traders had more supplies at Muscle Shoals than all the Southern Indians could buy in three years.

[26] Although the Spaniards affected to disdain this letter, it caused them considerable worry since it revealed that their aid to the Creeks had not remained secret, as they had tried to keep it.

ted McGillivray (doubtless at his suggestion) to warn the Georgians again to retire east of the Ogeechee.[27]

This warning Georgia answered, apparently before receiving it, with an invitation to the Creeks to meet state commissioners on Shoulderbone Creek on October 15, blandly observing that if the Creeks had any complaints about encroachments, they ought to let the Georgians know what they were. In a tart reply a month later, McGillivray, after reminding the commissioners that the Creeks had spent a considerable portion of their time for the last few years sending unanswered complaints to Georgia, declined any meeting until assured that the 1773 boundary was restored. At the same time he defied Georgia, McGillivray granted the Cumberland people a truce till the following April (1787), being induced thereto by the clamors of Tame King and Fat King, by the need of the Creek people to resume their hunting, and by the information gathered by his reliable intelligence service that the Georgians were negotiating with Franklin for a joint expedition against the Creeks, with whom they were discussing peace.[28]

Undeterred by the attitude of McGillivray, the Georgians continued their diplomatic efforts to promote a conference that might bear fruit commensurate with those won at Augusta and Galphinton. They were so far successful that when the time came for the Shoulderbone meeting, November 3, 1786, the Tame King and the Fat King with their followers put in their appearance and confirmed the two treaties they had previously made. Their reward for this limited complaisance and eminent past exertions on behalf of Georgia was their detention by the Georgians as hostages for the good conduct of the Creeks, one element of the said good conduct, so it was rumored, being the assassination of McGillivray or, as an equivalent, his delivery to the Georgians. The seizure of the two chiefs was perhaps the one act of the Georgians that McGillivray could wholly approve, since it relieved

[27] The activities of McMurphy are described in Caughey, *McGillivray*, 118–24 and 127–28. See also McMurphy's report in Cherokee Indians, Talks and Treaties, I, 129.

[28] The Cumberland envoys to McGillivray were Ewing and Samuel Hogg (Indian Office Records, Retired Classified Files, Ewing to Coffee, December 30, 1815).

him of his two thorns in the flesh and at the same time gave him an opportunity to execrate the Georgian conduct. The net result of the Shoulderbone species of diplomacy was the solidification of the Creeks, for the Tame King "for once in his life time behaved like a Man," frightened the Georgians into releasing him, and came home with his resentment unassuaged by the presents given him. The followers of the unreleased Fat King also now aligned themselves with McGillivray, and even the Seminoles joined in the war. The Georgians, suspecting that their boldness had boomeranged, sent McMurphy and "Young Galphin" to the Creeks, the division of labor between them being that the latter should ask for peace while the former promoted the assassination of McGillivray. McGillivray chased McMurphy out of the country and granted Galphin a truce for the duration of the hunting season.[29]

In the meantime, since the negotiation of the Hopewell treaties seemed to have provoked the Southern states to a no more violent attitude than contempt, the Congress of the United States had apparently felt encouraged to push further the assertion of its authority. On April 3, 1787, just as he was on the point of resuming war after the nominal truce, McGillivray received a letter from Dr. James White stating that White had been appointed United States superintendent of Southern Indians and was on his way to the Creek country to establish peace.[30] Any hope McGillivray

[29] McGillivray's comments on the Shoulderbone proceedings are given in Caughey, *McGillivray*, 139-41. There is a copy of the Shoulderbone treaty in the *Colonial Records of Georgia*, edited by Allen D. Candler, XXIX, 524; the treaty was signed by fifty-nine Creeks, chiefly from Tallassie, Broken Arrow, Cusseta, and Coweta.

[30] Dr. James White was connected with the Blount group of speculators, and it was probably through their influence that he was chosen a delegate to Congress in December, 1785. He had no knowledge of Indian affairs, and at the time he was chosen superintendent had already begun negotiations with Gardoqui, looking, ostensibly, toward the union of the western country with Spain. His career as a conspirator is described in T. P. Abernethy, *Western Lands and the American Revolution*, and in A. P. Whitaker, *Spanish–American Frontier, 1783–1795*. He is often confused with the Colonel James White who founded Knoxville.

The United States Congress on August 7, 1786, had established two Indian districts, one of which included all the tribes south of the Ohio. A superintendent was to have charge of each district, and provision was made for the licensing of traders. On October 6, Dr. James White had been appointed superintendent of

may have had from this mission disappeared when he found that White had arrived in the Creek country convinced that the Augusta and Galphinton cessions had been fairly negotiated, a conviction gained neither from study nor from intuition but from the propaganda to which he had been subjected as he passed through Georgia. This view, however, when expressed to the council aroused such an extreme denunciation from the chiefs that the superintendent returned to Georgia convinced that the Georgia claims were invalid. His mission promoted peace by securing the release of the Creek hostages held by Georgia and a consequent extension of the truce till August.[31]

While McGillivray was fencing with Georgia and the Overhill Cherokees were trying to satisfy Franklin's insatiable appetite for land, the Chickamaugas, disdaining both appeasement and diplomacy, had been bludgeoning away on the Cumberland settlements. In May, 1787, the unilateral delights of this operation were interrupted when the Cumberland people sent an unexpected expedition under James Robertson against Coldwater, which presented the double attraction of accessibility and quiet. Among those killed in the ensuing engagement were several Creek Indians, who, in all probability, were present not merely as innocent bystanders.[32] The truce being thus broken, McGillivray at once unleashed several hundred of his straining warriors against the Cumberlands and sent a small party into the Chickasaw country, where, he had been informed, the Americans were building a fort. The latter, finding some Americans at work, killed a number of them, including Davenport, who had gone out as one of Georgia's commissioners in 1785 to organize Bourbon County and since the failure of that fantastic enterprise had been lingering among the Chickasaws as Georgia's commissary.[33]

---

the southern district and four days later instructed to visit the Southern tribes and report.

[31] White's report on his Creek mission is in *Indian Affairs*, I, 21; McGillivray's comments in Caughey, *McGillivray*, 148–51. According to the report, McGillivray offered to cede the Oconee land provided the United States would set up a buffer state there. In none of his correspondence does McGillivray allude to any such offer.

[32] Clark, *op. cit.*, XX, 730, Robertson to Caswell, July 2, 1787.

Both factions of the Chickasaws had tolerated Davenport because they had hoped through him to secure some modicum of the commerce that both Spain and the United States had promised and neither had supplied. In a joint action springing from a common destitution, Taski Etoka and Franchimastabe in December, 1786, had sent Miró a formal complaint about trade conditions, threatening that if Spain did not provide the supplies promised at Mobile, the two tribes would turn to the Americans.[34] Since no visible commercial improvement followed in the wake of their indignation, they had carried out their threat in March, 1787, by sending a joint delegation to Congress to request the immediate establishment at Muscle Shoals of the trading post for which the Chickasaws at Hopewell had donated the site. From this excursion they secured nothing except the usual presents and the customary extensive collection of promises.[35] Some Americans, apparently on individual initiative unassociated with official encouragement, had established a trading post at Chickasaw Bluffs, but only a thin trickle of goods from it reached the Chickasaws and Choctaws.[36] On March 19, 1787, the Choctaws and Chickasaws, having seen their delegation safely off to the Americans, held a conference with the Spanish commissary, Pedro Yuzón, at Yazoo, where they aired their economic grievances and proposed certain reforms.[37] Having received these proposals, chiefly for cheaper

[33] The killing of Davenport is described in Corbitt, "Papers from the Spanish Archives," loc. cit., Vol. XI, 84, 87, and 88, Ben James to Mather and Strother and to John Joyce, July 23, 1787, McGillivray to Miró, July 25, 1787. From these it is to be gathered that the Creek party was from Coosada and numbered twelve men and a boy. They found Davenport at the home of William Kemp on Wolf Creek, killed both Davenport and Kemp, as well as two of Kemp's boat crew, wounded six other men, and carried off a white boy. After this they plundered the store, carrying off seventy rifles and twelve blankets. There were fourteen Americans present. One Creek was killed.

[34] Serrano y Sanz, op. cit., 31, note 2.

[35] Williams, Lost State, 141; Corbitt, "Papers from the Spanish Archives," loc. cit., Vol. XIV, 101, Fraser to Miró, April 15, 1788; Miss. Prov. Ar., Spanish Dominion, III, 223-55. The delegation was headed by Toboka of the Choctaws and included Cabosa, Mingotaska, John Woods, "Chamby" (Tinebe), and others. They brought back presents to Piomingo, Franchimastabe, and other chiefs.

[36] Corbitt, "Papers from the Spanish Archives," in loc. cit., Vol. XII, 103, O'Neill to Miró, September 8, 1787.

[37] Serrano y Sanz, op. cit., 31-34.

goods and more of them, Miró finally recognized the elementary truth that the Indians could receive supplies only from some one who could furnish them and began negotiations with Panton to supplant Mather and Strother and take over the trade. He sent Juan de Villebeuvre to the Indians to herald the coming dispensation and to counteract American influences. Villebeuvre met the Indians at Yazoo the last of October, heard their excuses for their previous dealing with the Americans, and received, probably with considerable skepticism, their pledges of future good conduct.[38]

When, in the summer of 1787, McGillivray began planning to intensify the war against the Georgians to an even greater degree than had been normal during the truce, he could justly congratulate himself on the smiling state of his fortunes. His warriors had inflicted so much punishment on the Cumberlands that even Governor Caswell had been moved to intercession; in May at Little Tallassie he had presided over a council with visiting delegations of Iroquois, Hurons, and Shawnees and had seen an agreement made to restore their Revolutionary confederation against the Americans; he had outwitted White, killed Davenport, and, with the unwitting aid of Choctaws and Chickasaws, forced the Spaniards to admit Panton into Mobile. The only element of discontent was the pro-Americanism of Piomingo and his followers among the Chickasaws, and he proposed that the Spaniards should bring them into alignment by withholding supplies from them, although the operation might have to be deferred until there were some supplies to withhold.[39]

But McGillivray's consciousness of well-being was considerably diluted when he heard in the fall of 1787 that he was to be deprived of Spanish support, both moral and material. This change of attitude on the part of Miró reflected his fear that McGillivray, by his aggressive tactics, might become involved in a general war with the United States and (what was more deplorable) also in-

<hr>

[38] *Ibid.*, 37–40.

[39] Corbitt, "Papers from the Spanish Archives," in *loc. cit.*, Vol. XI, 82, McGillivray to Miró, June 20, 1787. McGillivray said that the conference had met to restore the union of 1777 and 1779, and that the delegations would return in November to co-ordinate their warfare with that of McGillivray and Dragging Canoe.

volve Spain.[40] His first act was to reduce the quantity of arms (according to McGillivray the quality was not reducible) and to notify him that they were to be used only in defensive warfare. Since defensive warfare was the only kind that McGillivray considered he had been waging, he at once demanded that Miró tell him exactly what his intentions were. Miró then advised him to make terms with the Georgians even if he had to confirm the cessions of Augusta and Galphinton. This unpalatable advice was made even more distasteful by Miró's insistence that in any event the monopoly of Creek trade should be reserved to Spain. From this dilemma of fighting without support or accepting an ignominious peace, McGillivray was extricated by the intervention of the United States Congress, William Augustus Bowles, and the captain general of Cuba.

In a body as deliberative as the United States Congress, the further consideration given to the Creek situation on August 3, 1787, must be considered as practically an immediate reaction to the failure of the White mission four months before. After briefly pondering the issue until October 26, it voted to send a four-man delegation to the South to make new treaties with the Creeks and Cherokees, one commissioner each to be selected by the Carolinas and Georgia to act with the superintendent. White, in order, presumably, to devote full time to conspiracy, closed his brief and discouraging diplomatic career by resigning in January, 1788, and Congress on February 29 appointed Richard Winn of North Carolina as his successor for a term of six months. The instructions given the commissioners to negotiate treaties of peace and friendship, to arrange boundaries, and to eschew land cessions did not carry any implication that they were to consider the treaties of Augusta and Galphinton invalid.

The invitation from the United States to a peace conference not only relieved McGillivray from fear of a general war, but

[40] The Spanish officials were disturbed, too, by McGillivray's growing power (which they thought would render him less dependent on Spain) and by his plans for a confederation of Northern and Southern Indians, which they feared would be dominated by the British in Canada. A very revealing letter in this latter respect is that by Zéspedes (Spanish governor of East Florida) to Valdés, March 24, 1788, in Corbitt, "Papers from the Spanish Archives," *loc. cit.*, Vol. XIV, 86.

also aroused his suspicion that it had originated in Georgia's adversity. Therefore he qualified his acceptance by demanding, as a prerequisite to a conference, the removal of the Georgians from the disputed territory. Nor would he accept as a substitute for a removal, which the agitated commissioners alleged their inability to force, their promise to request Georgia to make no further encroachment. While negotiations were in this interesting stage where neither party was able to advance and neither wished to withdraw, the Creeks received a visitor in the person of William Augustus Bowles.[41]

The arrival of Bowles among the Lower Creeks in June, 1788, was so timely that it is difficult to consider it not prearranged. Whether he came by invitation or on his own initiative, he brought the welcome news that he had landed a supply of arms and ammunition on the east coast of Florida and that McGillivray had only to send a pack train for it. To McGillivray the beneficence of this manna in no way depended either on its origin or on the manner of its transmission, and he blandly accepted Bowles' explanation that it had been sent by an English charitable society in sympathy with Creek distress. With this supply in hand, and a larger one promised for November, he became even more independent in his attitude to Spain and even more adamant toward the commissioners. On August 20, 1788, he sent Miró his "determined resignation" from the Spanish service, being moved thereto by the credence which the Spanish officials were giving to the wild rumors that McGillivray, Bowles, and Panton were conspiring to attack Pensacola, take over the Floridas, and set up an Indian government under British protection. But the sensible Governor checked the gathering storms by writing McGillivray that the captain general had directed him (Miró) "to sattisfie you and your nation," adding slyly that it would doubtless no longer be necessary for McGillivray to resort to extraordinary agencies for supplies. Since Miró, by breaking up Bowles' second expedition, had made it impossible for any immediate supplies to reach

[41] North Carolina did not appoint a commissioner; South Carolina and Georgia appointed Pickens and Matthews. Their letter of March 29, 1788, to McGillivray and his reply of June 4 are in Caughey, *McGillivray*, 174, 180.

the Creeks by this "extraordinary" agency, McGillivray accepted the tendered Spanish olive branch, and agreed, on Panton's urgent advice, to have no further dealings with Bowles.[42] So, his deadlock with other American commissioners already temporarily resolved by their postponement of the conference till the following May, McGillivray, again secure on flanks and rear, could now bestow on the Georgians the attention that they, in his view, deserved.

Since the Chickamaugas were unrecognized as a separate tribe and the Cherokee government was officially at peace, North Carolina could justify its refusal to appoint a peace commissioner on the technical grounds that the state and the Cherokees were not at war.[43] This fortunate state of affairs, however, came to an end in June, 1788, when a force of Franklinites on one of their expeditions foully murdered Old Tassel, who had come out on their own invitation to confer with them. The immediate result of this act was that the inhabitants of Echota and five other towns of the Overhills deserted their towns and moved east of the mountains, hoping to derive from distance a safety that meekness had been unable to bring.[44] The tribal council elected Little Turkey as the successor of Old Tassel and established a new "capital," at Oostanaula in Georgia. Since the majority of the towns now joined in the war, Dragging Canoe seems to have recognized Little Turkey as head chief, thus ending the schism that had existed since 1777. From Oostanaula on June 20 and June 30, the chiefs sent talks to Pickens declaring for peace, but condemning in bitter language

[42] Bowles, like Panton, still awaits a biographer. For his 1788 venture see Caughey, McGillivray, 185-226; Corbitt, "Papers from the Spanish Archives," loc. cit., Vol. XV, 95-101; and Lawrence Kinnaird, "International Rivalry in the Creek Country," Florida Historical Quarterly, Vol. X, 67. Any account of Bowles not based on the Spanish Archives is of little value. D. C. Corbitt and John Tate Lanning's "A Letter of Marque issued by William Augustus Bowles as Director-General of the State of Muscogee," The Journal of Southern History, Vol. XI, 246-61 is an excellent summary of his career.

McGillivray never withdrew his resignation and never again drew a salary from Spain.

[43] Indian Affairs, I, 26, Governor Johnston to the governor of South Carolina, March 19, 1788.

[44] Papers of Continental Congress, III, 425, Talk of the Prince of Notaly, June 5, 1788; ibid., 438, Justices of Abbeville to people on Nolichuchy, French Broad, and Holston, September 9, 1788.

the murder of Old Tassel and the killing of other peaceful Indians by the Franklin people.[45] Martin went among them and remained for a month, trying to quiet them, preventing the wholesale removal they had apparently contemplated, but failing, and perhaps not desiring, to allay their resentment against Sevier and Franklin.

The war which Governor Johnston had been unable to detect became evident to Winn when the Cherokees in August inflicted a stinging defeat on Martin at Lookout Mountain, and on August 29 he appealed to Martin and the Governor to make peace.[46] Since this appeal was fruitless and was followed by another raid by Sevier on the Valley and Middle towns in September, on the twelfth of October he sent a talk to the chiefs themselves, which they answered from Oostanaula November 20, recounting the injustices they had received but avowing their desire for peace.[47] The signatures of Little Turkey, Hanging Maw, and Dragging Canoe attested a Cherokee unity that might be directed either to peace or continued war. In November, the Governor finally acted by issuing a proclamation against warring on the Cherokees, by appointing John Steele as North Carolina commissioner to act with Winn, and by sending Alexander Drumgoole to invite the Cherokees to a peace conference and to go on to the Creek country with a letter to McGillivray soliciting his co-operation.[48] On March 10, Little Turkey, Hanging Maw, and Dragging Canoe accepted the invitation to a peace conference, which they asked to be held at Hopewell; they also agreed to a truce until the conference should be held. But while Drumgoole was at Oostanaula, a delegation of Cherokees was meeting with Winn, Martin, and the three state commissioners on the Keowee, agreeing to a truce and a conference to be held on the French Broad the third Monday in May.[49]

[45] *Ibid.*, III, 429, 435, Talks given at Oostanaula, June 20 and 30, 1788.

[46] *Indian Affairs*, I, 45, Winn to Knox, October 13, 1788.

[47] *Ibid.*, I, 45. Cherokees to Winn, November 20, 1788. On November 1, the chiefs had sent a similar talk to Martin.

[48] For the Drumgoole mission see Clark, *op. cit.*, XXI, 507, 508, 529, and 542. Drumgoole arrived at Oostanaula, January 18, met the Cherokees at Coosawattee, February 6, 1789, and then went on to the Creek country. McGillivray had gone to Pensacola two days before, but Dan McGillivray took the Governor's letter and promised an answer when the chiefs returned from hunting about May 1.

When in May, 1789, McGillivray received from the American commissioners an invitation to meet them in the postponed conference on June 30, he might have refused, with good grace, on the technical ground that their commissions given under the Confederation were not valid in a Georgia that had now joined the "more perfect union." His acceptance, as he carefully explained to Miró, was because the failure of the Spaniards to deliver their promised war supplies left him no alternative to negotiating for peace. The Cherokees had no such legal grounds for avoiding a meeting, for whatever validity the American commissions had possessed for a treaty in 1788 they still possessed in 1789, since North Carolina had not joined the new union, and was therefore, presumably, still a member (with Rhode Island) of the old. The Cherokees, indeed, failed to appear on the French Broad at the appointed time, but they were absent because they had agreed to a conference not on the French Broad but at Hopewell.[50] Steele went to the Cherokee country in June and secured a confirmation of the truce.

The disappointment of the commissioners over Cherokee misfeasance was augmented by the failure of the Creek conference to

[49] *Ibid.*, XXI, 522 and 527, Martin to Johnston, February 2, 1789, and Steele to Johnston, February 19, 1789; *Indian Affairs*, I, 31, Winn to Knox, March 1, 1789.

[50] Draper MSS, Tennessee Papers, 2XX30, Martin to Henry, July 2, 1789. Martin was present on the French Broad as United States agent for the Cherokees and Chickasaws, to which position he had been appointed by Congress on August 20, 1788. In consequence of White's appointment as superintendent, Virginia had closed her Indian agency on January 31, 1787. McGillivray asserted (Caughey, *McGillivray*, 245) that the Cherokees boycotted French Broad on his advice. The Cherokee officials had attended the Lower Creek council in April and asked his protection (Caughey, *McGillivray*, 230). The Cherokees' obstinacy in preferring Hopewell to the French Broad was on account of their fear of Sevier, who in March, 1789, had again raided the Overhill towns. On August 22 a trader named Bellew appeared in New York and presented to President Washington a document purporting to be a memorial adopted at Echota, May 19, by the chiefs of twenty-one Overhill and Valley towns, asking that the intruders on their land be removed and offering to cede to the United States the land in the angle of the French Broad and Holston. Suspecting fraud, Washington sent a reply that the United States could do nothing about the matter while North Carolina remained out of the Union (*Indian Affairs*, I, 56–57). There is no doubt that the memorial was a forgery (Draper MSS, Tennessee Papers, 2XX30, Martin to Henry, July 2, 1789).

materialize. McGillivray, with forebodings too publicly expressed to be altogether sincere, actually set out for the conference, but on passing through the Lower Creeks, he was persuaded by the chiefs to wait until their war parties, then in the field, returned. He was the more easily persuaded since he had just received fresh promises of support from Miró, and had been informed through his intelligence service that the American commissioners had instructions to support the land claims of Georgia. Instead of proceeding, McGillivray requested a further postponement, and to this the commissioners perforce agreeing, a conference was set for Rock Landing on the Oconee, September 15.

It seems likely that the only attractiveness of this meeting to McGillivray lay in the prospects it offered him of regaining his confiscated estate amounting to some $150,000. The hints he had received to this effect were all the more welcome since, after resigning as Spanish commissary, he had no financial resources except such sums as he received from Panton.[51] Taking with him some nine hundred Creeks as a precaution against any Georgian reversion to kidnapping or assassination, McGillivray went to Rock Landing, where he learned that the old commissioners had been replaced by new ones who had not yet arrived—and as a matter of fact did not all arrive until September 30. The three commissioners—Benjamin Lincoln, Cyrus Griffin, and David Humphrys—had been instructed to investigate the treaties of Augusta, Galphinton, and Shoulderbone and to base the terms of their treaty on their conclusions: whether the treaties had been fair or fraudulent, the commissioners were to demand the land in dispute, but in the latter case they were to pay for it. It is charitable to suppose that their action in treating first and investigating later was due to their late arrival. McGillivray was given a draft of a treaty which recognized the validity of the treaty, the suzerainty of the United States over the Creek Nation, and the exclusive right of the United States to Creek trade. The indignant Creek leader summarily rejected the proposed treaty, and, gather-

---

[51] Caughey, *McGillivray*, 245, McGillivray to Panton, August 10, 1789. In this letter McGillivray said that the commissioners had "for some time past been endeavoring to stop my mouth and hands with my family estate . . . ."

ing his empty-handed Indians around him, set out for home without the formality of a farewell.[52]

The satisfaction with which McGillivray regarded his conduct at Rock Landing markedly diminished when Miró warned him that it might well result in war, since the commissioners would be certain to represent his action as an insult to the United States. In such a war McGillivray knew that the United States would have the active assistance of Piomingo's faction of the Chickasaws, whose pro-Americanism had been strengthened by a Creek killing of Piomingo's brother and nephew at the beginning of June.[53] It must have seemed to McGillivray that the first step toward such an alliance was being taken when in December, 1789, the United States sent down the Ohio and up the Tennessee a small military force under Major John Doughty to visit the Chickasaws.[54] The Creeks were vulnerable now on their northern flank because of North Carolina's action in joining the new union (November, 1789) and subsequently ceding (December, 1789) its western lands to the United States. An added source of worry was the sale by Georgia in December, 1789, of vast quantities of land in the present states of Mississippi and Alabama to three land companies. If these companies succeeded in planting their intended colonies at Muscle Shoals and on the Yazoo, the Creeks would then face

[52] There are numbers of discrepancies between McGillivray's account of the conference (Caughey, *McGillivray*, 251–54) and that given by the commissioners (*Indian Affairs*, I, 65–69).The day before he started to the conference McGillivray had heard from Miró that the king of Spain had confirmed the treaty of 1784. This "made me stout in my heart and strong in my mouth" at the meeting (Caughey, *McGillivray*, 254–55, McGillivray to Leslie, October 12, 1789).

[53] Caughey, *McGillivray*, 239, McGillivray to Miró, June 24, 1789; Ayer Collection, No. 722, Piomingo's talk to Martin, September 20, 1789; *Indian Affairs*, I, 77. The Chickasaws had been killed while on their way to the Cherokee conference on the French Broad. In the fall Piomingo went to New York to see the President, stopped off at Long Island to give Martin a talk for Governor Johnston, and on his way home met the commissioners at Richmond, who sent talks by him to Choctaws and Chickasaws.

[54] Colton Storm, ed., "Up the Tennessee in 1790: The Report of Major John Doughty to the Secretary of War," The East Tennessee Historical Society *Publications*, Vol. XVII, 119–32. Doughty's small force was attacked by Creeks and Chickamaugas on the Tennessee near Bear Creek and driven back down the river, finally taking refuge with the Spaniards at New Madrid. He reported to Knox that it would be impossible to maintain a trading post at Muscle Shoals. The expedition was sent as a result of Piomingo's plea for trade.

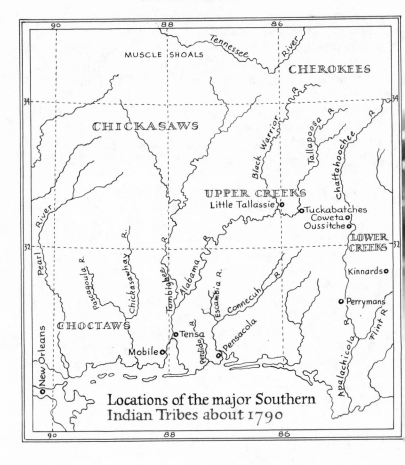

Locations of the major Southern
Indian Tribes about 1790

enemies on three sides, having behind them only the inconstant support of Spain.[55]

To McGillivray, then, the arrival of Colonel Marinus Willett in April, 1790, must have seemed as providential as the appearance of Bowles in 1788. Washington, undeceived by the biased reports of the commissioners and uninfluenced by his associates demanding war, had sent Willett as his personal envoy to invite McGillivray to New York (then the capital) to discuss peace terms. McGillivray's acceptance (after consulting his council) was not due to any reliance on Washington's professed yearning for "justice and humanity," but to his knowledge that the Doughty expedition had failed and that the United States was facing an Indian war in the Northwest. The adversity of the United States was the Creek opportunity.[56] After writing his decision to Panton and Miró so late that he could not receive their protests, he set out overland for New York, accompanied by Willett and twenty-six chiefs.[57] His journey to New York was a triumphal tour, his reception, when he arrived July 21, was that of a visiting emperor, and his stay in the city was one continual ovation. None of this dulled McGillivray's innate caution nor deflected him from his purpose. He refused to make any trade concessions or any acknowledgment of United States suzerainty except over those

[55] C. H. Haskins, "The Yazoo Land Companies," *Papers* of the American Historical Association, Vol. V, 395–437 is the standard treatment of the subject, but was written from insufficient sources and is misleading in numerous respects. See also J. C. Parish, "The Intrigues of Dr. James O'Fallon," *The Mississippi Valley Historical Review*, Vol. XVII, 230–63.

[56] William Willett, in *A Narrative of the Military Actions of Colonel Marinus Willett*, 96–113, describes the visit of Willett to the Creeks. He brought McGillivray a letter from Benjamin Hawkins (then senator from North Carolina) referring to the unfavorable report by the Rock Landing commissioners and urging him to come to New York. Apparently the plan for a New York conference originated with Hawkins. McGillivray in a letter to Panton, May 8 (Caughey, *McGillivray*, 259) outlines Willett's arguments and his own reasons for accepting them.

[57] McGillivray rode horseback the greater part of the journey, the chiefs and warriors were in wagons, and Willett in a sulky. They traveled by way of Stone Mountain, Seneca, Guilford Court House, Richmond, Fredericksburg, Washington, and Philadelphia. Governor Zéspedes of St. Augustine sent Carolus Howard to New York to counsel with McGillivray, which he succeeded in doing despite the vigilance of the Americans. The British officials in Canada sent two agents to New York ostensibly to learn from McGillivray more about Bowles, who was then in Canada appealing to the authorities.

Creeks living within the limits of the United States. He recovered that part of the Galphinton cession lying south of the Altamaha and conceded the remainder of the land in dispute in return for an annuity of $1,500 to be paid by the United States to the Creek Nation; he did this because he knew the Creek title to the land ceded at Augusta had been doubtful, and that it was impossible to dispossess Georgians of land they had already settled.

In addition to the fourteen articles of the treaty, there were six others which the Americans called "secret" and McGillivray called "separate"; they might perhaps, most properly be designated as "contingent" since they depended on the course of future developments for their validity. The first of these provided that the Creeks might have a free post for supplies through the United States in case their present supply system should be dislocated by war, and that after two years the United States might send $6,000 worth of supplies annually if it could arrange to do so. There can be little doubt that McGillivray considered this latter provision as merely a polite way of declining trade relations with the United States, since certainly the latter would never be able to "arrange" any trade without McGillivray's express approval. The free post provision had reference to the threat of war between Spain and Great Britain over the Nootka Sound affair. McGillivray learned of this only when he reached New York and the articles represented his improvisation to meet the apparent danger. Another article provided that McGillivray should have the rank of honorary brigadier general at a salary of $1,200 a year upon taking the required oath.[58] It is evident that this "salary" was, as McGillivray explained to Miró, merely an annuity to McGillivray in compensation for his confiscated estate, which Georgia could not be forced to restore. McGillivray, of course, realized that the payment, in whatever guise, was actually attempted bribery (as was a $100 annuity to the chiefs of Okfuskee, Tuckabatchie, Tallassie, Cusseta, Coweta, and Miccosukee) but his phil-

[58] In a letter to Miró, February 26, 1791 (Caughey, *McGillivray*, 290) McGillivray explicitly said that when he found that the required oath was one of allegiance to the United States he refused to take it. But in the Knox Papers, XXVI, folio 145 (Massachusetts Historical Society) is his signed oath of allegiance witnessed by Justice John Blair of the United States Supreme Court.

osophy permitted him, as in his dealings with Bowles, to accept supplies from any source that was available.[59]

From the standpoint of peace, certain verbal agreements made by McGillivray and Knox at New York were as important as the treaty provisions, whether absolute or contingent. Knox agreed to prevent any settlement by the Yazoo companies and to exert pressure on Georgia to revoke the grants: Washington's proclamation against them followed in August. McGillivray promised to influence Little Turkey to make peace and perhaps promised to prevent his Creek warriors from helping the Northern Indians against the Harmar expedition then under way. The logic of events, if nothing else, was forcing this change of policy on McGillivray for the creation of the Territory South of the River Ohio in May, 1790, cut the connection between Northern and Southern Indians and brought the Cherokees (and also the Chickasaws) into direct contact with federal authority. The first step in asserting this authority took the form of an "Act for Regulating Trade and Intercourse with the Indian Tribes," which was approved by Washington the day after McGillivray arrived in New York. The act, to run for two years, provided that the Indian trade should be limited to traders licensed by the superintendent or other Presidential appointee.[60]

Although McGillivray upon his return from New York revealed to Miró both the open and secret articles of the treaty, he did not completely convince the Spaniards of his candor. When in April, 1791, he was presented with an annuity of $2,000, the gift was perhaps more an evidence of Spanish apprehension than of Spanish confidence. McGillivray, however, accepted it with his usual indifference to the origin of benefits conferred. His financial condition improved still further the following month

[59] The so-called secret articles are given in Hunter Miller, *Treaties and other International Acts of the United States of North America*, I, 344. There is no record that any of the secret articles were ever ratified by the Senate except the trade provision, concerning which the Senate was consulted in advance. The open treaty is given in Kappler, *op. cit.*, II, 25-28. The treaty was signed by McGillivray and twenty-four chiefs on August 7, 1790.

[60] *Annals of Congress*, 1 Cong., 2 sess., II, 2241. This act, repeatedly extended and modified, remained the basic regulation for private traders as long as there were any private traders to be regulated.

when John Heth arrived in Little Tallassie with $2,900 in gold representing the amount due the Creeks for the first year of the treaty.[61] The sense of well-being induced by the monetary accessions was reflected, perhaps, in his genial hospitality to John Pope when he came through the Creek country in June.[62] It was reflected also in his polite manner of evading the repeated invitations to membership in the South Carolina Yazoo Company.[63] The attempt of the Tennessee Company to make a settlement at Muscle Shoals in January, 1791, aroused his wrath, but before he could move against it, the Chickamaugas by prompt action had deftly removed the source of irritation.[64]

In the performance of this public service, the Chickamaugas found themselves acting in unwonted harmony with the United States, for, since the settlement had been denounced by Washington, Governor Blount (of the Territory South of the River Ohio) had notified the Indians to deal with it as they saw fit. One is tempted to believe that the restraint shown by the Chickamaugas in merely driving off the settlers instead of killing them was due less to any amelioration of Indian character than to a possible sympathy for any group defying the United States. For the Chickamaugas had been consistent in disregarding the truce to which they had consented, and had continued their raids with unabated enthusiasm. But when Governor Blount invited the Cherokees to meet him in Knoxville in July, 1791, for the long-delayed treaty of peace, the chiefs of the Lower Towns attended and took the leading part in the negotiations. The Chickamaugas were probably too well-conditioned to American diplomacy to feel any

[61] The account of the United States with the Creeks from August 7, 1790, to August 7, 1791, is given in *Indian Affairs*, I, 127. The total payment to the Creeks was $3,700, comprising $1,500 annuity, $1,200 for McGillivray's salary, $600 for the six chiefs, and $400 for two interpreters. Of this amount $600 had been advanced to McGillivray in New York and $200 to Cornell for interpreting.

[62] Pope's observations on the Creeks were incorporated in his well-known *Tour through the Southern States and Western Territories of North America*, 46–52.

[63] For the invitation given McGillivray to join the company see the letter of Alexander Moultrie to McGillivray, February 19, 1790, in *Mississippi Valley Historical Review*, Vol. XVI, 391–92. McGillivray's rejection of this and other overtures is indicated in Caughey, *McGillivray*, 280–81.

[64] Brown, *op. cit.*, 318–19; Ramsay, *op. cit.*, 560.

surprise when Blount introduced his peace program by demanding, in complete violation of his instructions, a cession of the Muscle Shoals region. Their automatic rejection of this demand was delivered with such emphasis that the Governor found it necessary to shift his ambitions and ask for the land between the Holston and French Broad. Since this Overhill territory was, in reality, already lost, and would serve for a battleground quite as well ceded as unceded, the Indians finally agreed to sell after protesting the price and declaring their intention of sending a delegation to the President to ask for more. They also conceded free use of the Tennessee and gave permission for a road through Cherokee territory from eastern Tennessee to the Cumberland settlements.[65]

On the same day that some of the Chickamauga chiefs were making peace on the Holston, others were meeting on the Miami with Northern Indians planning war. Their agreement to make peace was taken probably on the advice of McGillivray, whom Knox had consulted on the matter at New York; their participation in the Miami war council was a result of a close accord with the Shawnees existing since 1777. In confirmation of this friendship a group of Chickamaugas had gone north at the close of the Revolution to live on the Scioto, while a number of Shawnee families had moved south to live at Running Water.[66] Using the liaison services of these groups, Dragging Canoe had maintained contact with the British Indian officials at Detroit, while the British Indian agent, Alexander McKee, had a representative among the Chickamaugas in the person of George Welbank, through

[65] *Indian Affairs*, I, 203–206. Blount's instructions for this treaty have been lost; it seems probable that he had been instructed to secure the land on the Holston, which the forged memorial of 1789 had represented the Cherokees as willing to cede. In December, 1791, a delegation of four Cherokees (led by Bloody Fellow) with two interpreters went to Philadelphia to solicit an increase in the annuity fixed by the treaty at $1,000. They arrived December 28, and as a result of conferences with Knox secured an increase to $1,500. The Cherokees argued that they had never received any payment for the land taken at Hopewell.

[66] Carter, *op. cit.*, II, 193; Royce, "The Cherokee Nation," *loc. cit.*, 165; *Indian Affairs*, I, 264; Papers of Continental Congress, II, 531. There were about seventy of the Chickamaugas settled in Ohio on Paint Creek, from which location they made continual raids against northern Kentucky. The Shawnees at Running Water numbered about one hundred.

whom he sent letters and supplies to Dragging Canoe.[67] As a result of these influences a considerable number of Chickamaugas participated in the defeat of St. Clair and were so inflamed by their success that they abandoned whatever pretense they had previously made of observing the Holston agreement.[68]

The restlessness of the Southern Indians engendered by the war in the Northwest furnished the setting, and perhaps the occasion, for the reappearance of Bowles among the Creeks. Although it is impossible to speak with precision of his aims and purposes, it is certain that he desired to prevent the execution of the New York treaty. His evident collusion with Welbank indicates a prearranged co-operation with the Northern Indians and with the British agents in Canada. His designs required the overthrow of McGillivray and, probably, the elimination of Panton, Leslie and Company, which, although it saw eye to eye with Bowles on the treaty, would certainly oppose any attempt against McGillivray. If Bowles could have secured the support of Panton, it is not likely that he would have been deterred by any consideration for the firm of Miller and Bonamy (Nassau), which had outfitted him.

Late in September, 1791, Bowles, anchoring his ship (in which he had come from New Providence) at the mouth of the Ochlocknee, went on overland to Oussitchie (Osochi) on the Flint, where his father-in-law, Perryman, was chief. Here, by distributing presents and promises, he gained the support of the villagers, who listened with apparent approval to his denunciation of the treaty and presently proclaimed him "General and Director of the Affairs of the Nation." The turmoil caused by his few but noisy followers forced McGillivray to postpone the running of the treaty line and to send Heth away with his mission uncompleted. Unable on account of Indian custom to seize Bowles while protected by his father-in-law, McGillivray put a price on his head

[67] The best account of Welbank's activities is Hamer's "The British in Canada," *loc. cit.*, 117ff.

[68] Piomingo led a small force of Chickasaws to assist St. Clair. Affronted by St. Clair's apparent neglect, the Chickasaws left the day before the defeat, alleging that they had news of an invasion of the Chickasaw country by the Creeks (W. H. Smith, ed., *St. Clair Papers*, II, 250, 254, 256, 302; *Indian Affairs*, I, 266–91; A. W. Putnam, *History of Middle Tennessee*, 363).

and, confident that Bowles' support would not survive the exhaustion of his supplies, set off unperturbed on a prearranged visit to New Orleans. As a matter of fact, the supplies of the "General and Director" soon came to an end, and his seizure of Panton's store near St. Marks, whether in hostility or as an emergency measure, only postponed the day of reckoning. On February 26 the director, at the end of his resources, accepting an invitation from the Spanish governor, boarded a Spanish ship for New Orleans. The new Spanish governor, the Baron de Carondelet, opposing the New York treaty, was apparently hoping to use Bowles to supplant McGillivray, whom Carondelet distrusted and whose authority he was seeking to destroy.[69]

The withdrawal, or abduction, of Bowles did not end or even ease the tensions among the Southern Indians. Throughout the year 1792 they were continually pulled and hauled by sundry outside agencies into antagonistic courses. One of these external pressure groups was the Northwest Indians, who, elated by their victory over St. Clair, were urging a general alliance of Southern Indians for the purpose of completing a work so auspiciously begun. The most avid missionaries in this movement were the mingled Shawnee, Creek, and Chickamauga warriors who had drifted back to Running Water after the campaign ended. Welbank, now living among the Lower Creeks as the political heir of Bowles, advocated the alliance, and Dragging Canoe devoted to it the final energies of his failing life. Since there could be no alliance unapproved by McGillivray, Dragging Canoe went to Little Tallassie to see his old ally, and McGillivray, whether in evasion or in assistance, advised him to visit the Chickasaws. It would be difficult to say whether the rivalry of Piomingo and Taski Etoka was the result of their different attitudes toward Spain and the United States or whether their different attitudes reflected their rivalry. At any rate, the tribe was so evenly divided

[69] In addition to the references on Bowles given in n. 42 above see Lawrence Kinnaird, "The Significance of William Augustus Bowles' Seizure of Panton's Apalachee Store in 1793," *Florida Historical Quarterly*, Vol. IX, 156-92; Corbitt, ed., "Papers Relating to the Georgia-Florida Frontier," *loc. cit.*, Vol. XXII, 186-89; Caughey, *McGillivray*, 305-306, 307-309. An account of Bowles' "capture" is in Miss. Prov. Ar., Spanish Dominion, III, 765ff.

that the only common action it could take was the negative one of preserving the *status quo*. Apparently, however, Dragging Canoe converted Taski Etoka to his view, with the result that from this time on the latter became the leading advocate of Indian confederation in the South. Shortly after his return from the Chickasaws, Dragging Canoe died at Lookout Mountain Town, March 1, 1792, as a result, it is said, of a too vigorous celebration of certain successful Chickamauga depredations near Nashville.[70] As his successor, the Chickamaugas elected John Watts, the nephew of Old Tassel.

Directly opposed to the policies of Dragging Canoe and Taski Etoka were the efforts of the Americans to enlist the Southern Indians in a projected campaign against the Northern tribes. Their insistence that they were doing this, not because they needed help, but because otherwise the restless Indians would enlist with their Northern brethren, reveals a commendable knowledge of Indian psychology and an impossible plan for dealing with it. In January, 1792, President Washington took the first step (as yet unauthorized by law) in this course by appointing temporary agents to reside among the Indians, thus resuming the practice that had lapsed with the ending of Martin's agency. Leonard Shaw became agent to the Cherokees, James Seagrove to the Creeks, and (in March) James Robertson to the Chickasaws and Choctaws.[71] Each of these was instructed to recruit the Indians of his agency for service in Wayne's army: six hundred Indians were to be secured, and they were to be armed and supplied by the United States, to be led by General Pickens, and to rendezvous at Fort Washington (Cincinnati) in June. As a supplement to the evangelical campaign by the agents, Blout was authorized to hold a

---

[70] The date of Dragging Canoe's death is given by Brown, *op. cit.*, 329, without citation of authority. A letter from Welbank to McKee January 16, 1793 (Hamer, "British in Canada," *loc. cit.*), refers to Dragging Canoe as having recently died.

[71] The appointment of agents was suggested by the Cherokee delegation in Philadelphia asking for an increase in annuity. Shaw accompanied the delegation back to the Cherokee country, bringing with him talks for the Chickasaws and Choctaws, which were forwarded to them by Blount when he invited them to the Nashville conference. Robertson's appointment was a compensation for damages received from Chickamaugas and Creeks.

conference with the Chickasaws and Choctaws at Nashville in July.[72]

The mutually antagonistic plans of the Northern Indians and the United States were checkmated by the activities of Carondelet, who opposed all Indian collaborations with the United States and distrusted an Indian confederation dominated, in all probability, by the British. With the immediate purpose of undoing the treaty of New York, he sent a trusted agent, Pedro Olivier, in February, 1792, to live among the Creeks as commissary, while he dallied with the idea of supporting Bowles against McGillivray. But it soon became evident that Olivier could do nothing to lessen the authority of McGillivray over the Creeks or to prevent him from carrying out the treaty as he seemed determined to do. Nor was Carondelet able to supplant McGillivray with Bowles unless he were prepared also to discard Panton, whose loyalty to McGillivray was beyond question. The one course open to Carondelet was to continue Miró's policy of supporting McGillivray while attempting by Panton's influence to lure him away from his present course. Accordingly, in the spring of 1792, Carondelet sent Panton to Little Tallassie. Panton arrived April 30 just as McGillivray was preparing to set out for Rock Landing to help mark the treaty line fixed by the Treaty of New York. What passed between the two men is not known, but whatever it was, it caused McGillivray to abandon his trip to Rock Landing and to go instead to New Orleans to see Carondelet.[73]

After his conversation with McGillivray, Panton went on to the Chickamaugas. He arrived while the chiefs were away conferring with Blount at Coyatee, receiving the annuity due under the treaty of Holston, and blandly denying any knowledge of the forty murders and two hundred cases of horse stealing which had

[72] The government's desire to enlist the Southern Indians is evident in its instructions to Shaw and Seagrove at the time of their appointment and in the correspondence of Knox with Blount, Seagrove, and McGillivray, during February, March, and April (*Indian Affairs*, I, 253–66, and in I. O. R., Old Records Division, Adjutant General Division, War Department (MSS).

[73] McGillivray's letter to White, May 6, 1792 (Caughey, *McGillivray*, 321) makes it clear that it was Panton's influence which induced him to abandon his trip to Oconee and to go to New Orleans instead. Panton's unexpected visit would have missed McGillivray had the latter not been detained by high waters.

occurred on the territorial frontier since the treaty.[74] Staying at the home of John McDonald, the former commissary, Panton summoned Watts from the conference, delivered to him O'Neill's invitation to come to Pensacola for a free supply of ammunition, and added that if he needed anything more, he could get it from Panton at cost. To these fair prospects Watts promptly surrendered and set out at once with Panton, several Chickamaugas, and the largest pack train the tribe was able to improvise. Arriving at Little Tallassie about the first of June, Watts and Panton had a conference with McGillivray, after which McGillivray set out for New Orleans while Panton, Watts, and the others went on to Pensacola.[75]

What McGillivray did at New Orleans he did not do because he was forced by Carondelet, but because he had been persuaded by Panton, whom Seagrove, in one of his infrequent moments of insight, had declared to have more influence with McGillivray than any man living. In the resulting brief treaty of July 6, 1792, the Spaniards guaranteed all the lands "belonging to and actually possessed by the Creek nation" in 1784 and promised to furnish the Creeks ample and sufficient supplies not only to defend their country but also to regain their "encroached lands." In return, McGillivray guaranteed the territory of Spain in Louisiana and West Florida. In addition to these obligations the treaty *recommended* that the Creeks give (at a time unspecified) to all white people living within the Creek limits of 1773 a demand that they withdraw in two months; there was no commitment by McGillivray to remove them by force. The treaty was to be in effect only until His Most Gracious Majesty's pleasure was known, and McGillivray probably had no difficulty in foreseeing what the reaction of His Majesty would be to a treaty which bound Spain rigidly but left the Creeks free. In return, apparently, for his complaisance in signing a treaty so favorable to himself, McGillivray received an increase of his pension to $3,500 a year.[76]

[74] Blount's report of the Coyatee conference is in *Indian Affairs*, I, 267–69.

[75] Details of Panton's visit with the Chickamaugas are given in the statements of James Leonard and Richard Finnelson, *ibid.*, 191–95, 288–89. It is evident from McGillivray's letters to White (n. 73 above) that Leonard was mistaken in saying that McGillivray accompanied Panton to the Chickamaugas.

[76] The text of this treaty is given in Caughey, *McGillivray*, 329–30.

Hardly had McGillivray returned home when he received a letter from Carondelet asking him to influence the Chickasaws and Choctaws against attending a conference with the Americans in Nashville. As a matter of fact, the Creeks, even before Carondelet wrote, had already exerted their "influence," perhaps at the suggestion of Taski Etoka, who had visited the Creek country while McGillivray was absent. In the Choctaw conference called on June 23 to hear the American talks, certain Creek warriors appeared, and by pretending drunkenness broke up the meeting. They then finished their work by driving the Americans out of the country and issuing to the conniving Choctaws a warning against going to Nashville.[77] As a result of their efforts only 110 Choctaws attended the conference, which, as McGillivray tolerantly commented, was a small number considering the ingrained Indian yearning for the food and presents always distributed at these meetings. The Chickasaw delegation was much larger, comprising the entire Piomingo faction of the tribe with an addition of the usual number attracted by entertainment. Taski Etoka boycotted the meeting, but some of his followers were present as spies: Tinebi (Chananby), his nephew and heir apparent, and Ugula Yacabe (Wolf's Friend), second warrior of the nation, a rival of Piomingo's devoted to Spanish interests, and others. The Piomingo faction had its ardor for the Americans considerably cooled by the time it reached Nashville, for at a council on Duck Creek, Captain George convinced them that the Americans were trying to involve them in the northwestern war in order to kill off all the Indians and take their land. Happily, Blount's announcement that Wayne's campaign had been postponed left the Chickasaws free to proclaim their martial ardor without the inconvenience of displaying it. Ugula Yacabe protested so vigorously against any Muscle Shoals trading post that Blount promised to abandon the plan. It is uncertain whether the precision with which Piomingo outlined the Chickasaw boundaries was meant as a hint to the Americans or to the Cherokees.[78]

[77] *Ibid.*, 332-33, McGillivray to Carondelet, July 22, 1792; *Indian Affairs*, I, 278.

[78] *Indian Affairs*, I, 284-88. During the conference Piomingo referred to Chenanbe (Tinebe) as king of the Chickasaws. As a matter of fact Taski Etoka

The twenty-three Cherokees in attendance at the Nashville conference were there primarily as spies for their nation, always uneasy at any conjunction of its unpredictable neighbors. Upon their return they stirred the nation by reporting that James Robertson was threatening to destroy the Five Towns in retaliation for the continued outrages emanating from that source. While the Five Towns were making preparations to deal with this coming invasion, John Watts arrived opportunely at his home at Willstown (near Fort Payne, Alabama) and summoned the chiefs of the nation to that place in September to hear his report.

When the chiefs gathered at Willstown, they found that Watts had brought back a letter from O'Neill pledging Spanish support for the Cherokees in defending their homes; as an earnest of which support the Spaniards had given Watts ammunition requiring seven pack horses to carry and accoutrement for two hundred horsemen. Not all of Watts' three months' trip had been spent at Pensacola; on his return he spent some time among the Creeks, a large delegation of whom had accompanied him home. It was Watts' suggestion that since they had plentiful supplies, they might well now begin their defensive warfare, to which the promise of Spanish support was limited, by an anticipatory attack on the Holston country. To this measure the upper Cherokees, being most exposed to a Holston reprisal, raised the objection that the failure of their corn crop had left them destitute of food. The result of the deliberations at Willstown was that the Lower Cherokees declared for war, in which it was understood the Upper Cherokees would have no official participation.

In a meeting at Lookout Mountain Town a few days later, the Lower Cherokees after planning their campaign against the Holston country, became so drunk in the subsequent celebration that they were unable to go on the campaign they had planned. This was perhaps just as well, for Blount, warned by Agent Shaw, Interpreter Carey, and others, had mobilized the militia.[79] Learning

was still king, but McGillivray describes him as wandering in exile among the Choctaws (Caughey, *McGillivray*, 346–49, McGillivray to Panton, November 28, 1792).

[79] The Cherokees ascribed their war preparations to Robertson's threat (*Indian Affairs*, I, 280) and there is no good reason for thinking they were dis-

this, Watts put Blount off his guard by conciliatory letters, secretly changed his plans to an attack on the Cumberlands, and on September 30, 1792, made a sudden (and unsuccessful) attack on Buchanan's Station, near Nashville. The war thus begun continued with flourishing fortunes until February 6, 1793, when Watts and Blount arranged a three-weeks' truce until the meeting of the Cherokee council.

In October, 1792, in order to assure themselves of continued Spanish support, the Lower Cherokees had sent to New Orleans a six-man delegation including Bloody Fellow and Bold Hunter. After the Cherokees arrived in New Orleans (in December), Taski Etoka and Franchimastabe appeared, the former bringing proposals from the Shawnees for a general confederation and the latter accompanied by several hundred half-famished fellow-citizens. The relations of Spain with the Choctaws and Chickasaws had been peaceful since Panton had taken over the trade monopoly. There had been stirrings of discontent among the apprehensive Choctaws when Spain established a fort in the triangular cession of 1777, but the matter had been amicably settled by a formal treaty May 14, 1790, by which the Choctaws and Chickasaws agreed that the Spanish rightfully had title to the land in question as heirs of the British.[80] At the New Orleans conference, Taski Etoka, who was making himself the spiritual heir of Dragging Canoe, suggested to Carondelet that Spain make a defensive alliance with the Southern Indians, and Bloody Fellow asked that the Spaniards build forts on the Tombigbee and at Muscle Shoals so as to insure their line of communication with the Cherokees.[81] It was suggested by the gratified but cautious Carondelet that the Indians should lay these proposals before their tribal councils and return to New Orleans in the spring of 1793 for final action

sembling. The proceedings at Willstown were reported to Blount by the traders Finnelson and Deraque and by James Carey (*ibid.* I, 289-91, 328). At this meeting Shaw, because it became known he was warning Blount, was threatened with death by the Creek delegation and was sent under guard of friendly Upper Cherokees to Seneca.

[80] *American State Papers, Foreign Relations*, I, 280.

[81] A full account of this meeting is to be found in Miss. Prov. Ar., Spanish Dominion, IV, 611ff. See also Caughey, *McGillivray*, 343-44, Carondelet to McGillivray, November 11, 1792.

on them. Since the Piomingo faction had not been represented at the New Orleans meeting, Bloody Fellow and two of his companions went home through the Chickasaw country with the purpose of persuading them to unite with the other Southern Indians. Before the Chickasaw council on February 13, 1793, the Cherokee ambassadors presented their arguments reinforced by talks sent to Piomingo and Ugula Yacabe by Carondelet and by McGillivray to the nation. But Piomingo was not to be placated; the Chickasaw council, dominated by him, not only rejected the plan for a confederation but even declared war on the Creeks.[82]

It is unlikely that McGillivray had expected his advice (sent at the solicitation of Carondelet) to be accepted by the Chickasaws or was sorry to have it rejected. He had little faith now in a general alliance, however great his zeal had been five years before. He wanted only to preserve the *status quo* as long as possible; having made two incompatible treaties, he could preserve his integrity only by failing to execute either. After his treaty with Carondelet, he never began war against the Americans, nor did he ever give them notice to withdraw within their limits of 1773. The treaty placed him under no obligation to do either, and he resisted Carondelet's timid urgings by pleading the lack of arms. He gave up his "salary," much to the consternation of Knox; he refused all Seagrove's importunities for marking the boundary, asserting that the Creek council had rejected the proposed bounds (which was quite true) and that the ill will resulting from mutual depredations made it unsafe for any surveying party to take the field (which was also quite true).[83] This course left the Georgians in possession of the ceded land quite as effectively as if the boun-

[82] *Indian Affairs*, I, 441.

[83] McGillivray himself never had a meeting with Seagrove, who, for fear of assassination, refrained from visiting the Creek country. In May, 1792, while waiting for Panton to return from the Chickamaugas, McGillivray sent some of the Creek chiefs to meet Seagrove at Rock Landing and in November permitted some of the Lower Creeks to visit him for the sake of receiving supplies, which the United States was donating because of Creek famine conditions caused by a prolonged drouth (Downes, "Creek-American Relations," *loc. cit.*, 350–73; *Indian Affairs*, I, 314, Seagrove to McGillivray, October 8, 1792). The United States contributed some $10,000 worth of supplies for famine relief. These the Creeks received with gratitude but without commitments about ending their raids or running the line.

dary had been marked. But McGillivray knew he could not remain indefinitely resting on his oars, and so, as he confided to Panton, he was "approaching to a despondency." In addition to his mental worries, his health seems to have been shattered by the fatigues, and perhaps the dissipations, incident to the New York trip. The "cursed gout" kept him chained to his fireside with his legs paralyzed from the knees down. Thus sore beset in mind and body he continued to rule the Creeks, satisfy Carondelet, and placate the United States until finally in December, 1792, he summoned his weary flesh and spirit for a visit to Panton in Pensacola. There, at eleven o'clock on the night of February 17, in the house of his friend and his father's friend, he died.

"Poor fellow," said the sorrowing Panton, "he has left us at an untoward time."[84]

[84] Caughey, *McGillivray*, 354, Panton to Carondelet, February 20, 1793.

V

A Time of Indecision

1793-1798

I<small>T IS NOT LIKELY</small> that McGillivray himself would have classified as "untoward" that Creek–Chickasaw war which he had done nothing to avoid and much to provoke. But to Spain and the United States, to Panton, Leslie and Company, and to the Northern Indians the war was both an embarrassment and a threat. The United States deplored it because of the probability that the naïve Chickasaws might expect some tangible evidence of the friendship that the United States had been so profusely professing as a substitute for material assistance, and so involve the nation in a southern war at the very time it needed all its energies for the northern one. Spain disliked it because it was manifestly impossible to complete an Indian confederation while two of the prospective allies were earnestly trying to destroy each other. Moreover, the United States might use the war as a pretext for extending its power in the South at Spanish expense. Panton viewed the war as a nuisance interrupting his Indian trade, while the Northern Indians feared that the Creeks would become so engrossed in the delights of killing their neighbors that they would neglect the greater but more remote opportunities in the Northwest.

By way of implementing their earlier proposals made through Dragging Canoe and Taski Etoka, the Northwestern Indians in the fall of 1792 had sent south an accredited delegation of nine Shawnees and a white man to secure formal pledges of aid from the Southern tribes. These had spent the winter among the Five Towns, probably with their brethren at Running Water, where they doubtless enjoyed the seasonal activities of hunting and raiding the Cumberlands.[1] Early in January they had gone on to the Lower Creeks accompanied by a number of Cherokee chiefs and warriors.[2] Although they came earlier than was expected and in the absence of McGillivray, the chiefs received them with all the formalities prescribed by intertribal etiquette, built a new "square" for them near Broken Arrow, and appointed times for their talks, February 18 at Coweta for the Lower Creeks and March 7 at Tuckabatchee for the Upper.[3] The scarcity of food in the Creek larder, not yet recovered from the faminine of 1792, rendered the entertainment of the ambassadors an embarrassing problem until Welbank, although his own supply line from the Bahamas had been cut by the Spaniards, managed by some commercial legerdemain to secure stores from Pensacola. These, with a modicum of arms and ammunition, he distributed among the diplomats through the agency of Little Prince, chief of Broken Arrow.[4]

It is evident that while the "broken days" (the Indians on calling a meeting sent to those summoned as many little sticks as there were days before the conference and the recipients broke a stick each day) were running, the Shawnees were interspersing among their feasting and hunting activities a considerable bit of private missionary work. Word of this activity caused Agent Seagrove such acute mental distress that he boldly resolved to interfere, provided it could be done by proxy. Continuing his preference for performing the duties of his agency by correspondence

[1] Hamer, "The British in Canada," *loc. cit.* The "white" man may have been a Canadian or one of the Cherokees from the Scioto band.

[2] John Watts said (*Indian Affairs*, I, 447) that the Shawnees were accompanied to the Creeks by Glass, Turkey, Dick Justice, Hovalta, Charley, Water Hunter, Breath, Drunkard, Doublehead, Person Stricker, Spider, Chuluch, and an interpreter.

[3] McGillivray, writing to Carondelet, January 15, 1793, said the Shawnees were expected in the spring (Caughey, *McGillivray*, 351-53). Their reception by the Creeks is described by Thomas Carey to Blount, March 20, 1793 (*Indian Affairs*, I, 435-36).

[4] Hamer, "British in Canada," *loc. cit.* Welbank when the Shawnees arrived, was at the mouth of the Ochlocknee building storehouses for the supplies expected from Nassau.

rather than by personal exposure, he wrote from Georgia to his agents among the Creeks, directing them to kill or capture the Shawnees, adding, by way of incentive, that he would pay a pack load of goods for a captive, half a pack for a scalp.[5] The lieutenants of Seagrove, fearing the effect on the Creeks of introducing such advanced ideas into their untutored conceptions of diplomatic usage, refrained from carrying out their instructions, with the result that in due season the Shawnee orators delivered their talks to the Lower Creek council in the name of the thirty-three tribes they claimed to represent. They urged the Creeks to make common cause with them against the Americans; the British had promised supplies; the Creeks should attack Georgia and the Cumberlands as a diversion; and they should send direct aid to the Northwest.[6] In answer to these pleas, the Lower Creek meeting took no official action, but most of the towns decided for war.[7] With the Upper Creeks, the Shawnees seem to have had no such success, their talk being accepted by only two of the towns. Mad Dog, chief of Tuckabatchee and leading chief of the tribe since McGillivray's death, was presumably trying to continue McGillivray's policy of keeping the war against the Americans unofficial and, as far as possible, inactive. Moreover, since his brother and nephew had been killed by Piomingo's party, the Chickasaw war as a war of revenge took precedence over an American war that was merely a war for principle.

As the Tuckabatchee meeting was ending, a small body of Lower Creeks raided the store of Robert Seagrove (brother of

[5] At the conference with the Creeks in November, 1792, Seagrove had arranged with a number of Indians and half-bloods to keep him informed about Creek events. Among these were James Holmes, Timothy Barnard, Jack Kinnaird, the Cornells, Little Prince of Broken Arrow, and the White Lieutenant of Okfuskee. Seagrove's correspondence with these about the Shawnees is given in *Indian Affairs*, I, 375ff.

[6] Welbank, who was present at the Lower Creek meeting, distrusted the Shawnee statement about British aid and asked the chiefs to defer action until he could go to Sandusky to verify it. It is evident from Hamer, "British in Canada," *loc. cit.*, that no responsible British official had made any such promise.

[7] Cusseta, a traditional "white" (peace) town was openly for peace with the Americans. The chief hostile towns were Coweta, Broken Arrow, Ossitchie, and Euchee. The two hostile towns among the Upper Creeks were Coolome and Tallassie, where the Tame King, Opothle Mico, was still incensed over his imprisonment at Shoulderbone.

the agent) on the St. Marys, killed six men, and carried off a considerable quantity of merchandise for home consumption. The possibly sagging morale of the Shawnees was apparently so restored by this action that they remained another month in the congenial atmosphere before departing for the Cherokees. Although the hospitality of the Creeks had possibly felt the strain of a three-months' visit, it is difficult to believe, as the Americans fondly reported, that they accelerated the departure of their guests by putting a price on their heads.

Back among the Lower Cherokees, the Shawnees found that housing facilities had been increased by the building of a new square for them at Running Water. Agent Shaw, having become antagonistic to Blount (presumably at the instigation of Shaw's Cherokee wife), had departed for Philadelphia with the ostensible purpose of regaining their lost land for the Cherokees, pledging the Cherokees to a seventy-five-day truce while he was absent.[8] This truce the Cherokees were faithfully observing—except toward Georgia, the Carolinas, Virginia, Kentucky, and the Territory South of the River Ohio. With a desire to negotiate some measure of reconciliation between theory and practice, Secretary of War Knox had urged Blount to send Watts, Little Turkey, and other chiefs to Philadelphia to visit President Washington, reasoning that the Cherokees would feel constrained to keep the peace as long as their chiefs were in American hands. At the time of the Shawnees' return, Watts (with the same reasoning) was busy evading this invitation, being reluctant to interrupt the local indulgence in the simple pleasures of murder and arson.

In a general meeting of both Upper and Lower Cherokees at Willstown on May 13, the Shawnees gave their formal talks, after which the chiefs debated what they should do. It is probable that the opposition to war shown by Little Turkey was sincere and was due, in part at least, to a message sent him by Mad Dog. After the meeting, Little Turkey wrote to Alexander McKee that the nation had declared for war, and to Blount that the nation was

---

[8] *Indian Affairs*, I, 437, Carey to Blount, March 19, 1793. In February, 1793, Blount had appointed John McKee as deputy agent and was employing him on tribal business (*Ibid.*, I, 435).

for peace.[9] These mutually contradictory statements were both true since the Cherokee Nation had completely mastered the art of keeping the nation officially out of a war in which its every constituent part was participating. As a matter of fact, the Lower Cherokees had for many weeks been streaming to the Northwest without in any way diminishing their more local depredations. Immediately after the meeting, the Shawnees, accompanied by Welbank, set out for the Maumee Rapids, where the Northwestern Indians were waiting to receive their report before holding a conference with the Americans.[10]

In the meantime the Creek-Chickasaw war had continued with increasing verbal intensity, but, thanks to the peace efforts of the Spaniards, without any great hostile contact between the belligerents. The Chickasaws, too weak to take the field, had fortified themselves in their towns after the fashion formerly taught them by the English, and, while awaiting the attack which the Creeks were too wary to deliver, had made the expected appeal to the United States for help. James Robertson, their agent, was limited to the sending of food, but enlarged the definition of the term to include such guns and ammunition as he could collect. Wayne sent them a greater supply by water to Chickasaw Bluffs, including in the cargo a quantity of paint and whiskey.[11] It was the official attitude of the United States that these supplies were not furnished for war purposes, but solely to encourage the Chickasaws in the normal pursuits of peace. The Creeks, however, hearing about the transaction and apparently distrusting the Chickasaw capacity for discrimination, protested vigorously to

[9] *Ibid.*, I, 357, Little Turkey *et al.* to Blount, May 23, 1793; Hamer, "British in Canada," *loc. cit.*, Little Turkey to McKee, May 20, 1793. Little Turkey was undecided whether to declare for war or peace and wrote to Panton for advice, saying that he had formerly relied on McGillivray for counsel (Corbitt, "Papers Relating to the Georgia-Florida Frontier," *loc. cit.*, Vol XXIII, 388).

[10] Welbank remained in the north until the fall of 1793, when he returned to the Cherokees. There in March, 1794, he was robbed, and suspecting (erroneously) that the robber was a Creek, he set out for the Creek country. He was killed (by mistake) at Eufaula. McDonald secured his papers and sent them to Alexander McKee.

[11] *Indian Affairs*, I, 429–30, Knox to Blount, May 14, 1793. Wayne's supply consisted of 500 guns, 2,000 lbs. of powder, 4,000 flints, one Armorer with tools, 4,000 lbs. of lead, 1,500 bu. of corn, 50 lbs. of vermilion, 100 bu. of salt, and 100 gal. of whiskey.

the president.[12] As a substitute for supplies of which he was destitute, Seagrove gave the Creeks encouragement to prosecute a war which he hoped might distract their hostile attentions from the Georgians.

Under such conditions the Spaniards, unencouraged and unassisted, strove persistently, if not altruistically, for peace. Since Piomingo was invulnerable to argument, they employed the less subtle method of withholding supplies from his partisans and of undermining his authority among his people. In both respects they had a powerful weapon in Panton, Leslie and Company. American supplies, open or clandestine, were insufficient to enable Piomingo to prosecute the war, and he could secure more neither from Panton at Mobile nor from Turnbull at Los Nogales.[13] The resulting discomfort among Piomingo's followers made them vulnerable to the representations of his rivals. The chief of these was Ugula Yacabe (Wolf's Friend), a war chief second in authority and influence only to Piomingo himself, a devoted follower of Taski Etoka, and a friend and confidant of Villebeuvre, the Spanish commissary among the Choctaws and Chickasaws. His efforts were powerfully seconded by the Colberts, who had been associated with Panton in the English regime.[14] They gained such an ascendance that, in June, Ugula Yacabe, presumably with the approval of the tribal council, sent peace talks to the Creeks.[15]

Among the Creeks, the Spaniards had to contend only against the feeble seductions of Seagrove and the determination of Mad Dog. Upon McGillivray's death the Spaniards rejected, apparently with wisdom, Panton's advice to name McGillivray's brother-in-law (Milfort) regent of the tribe until McGillivray's son should

[12] *Ibid.*, I, 408, Mad Dog *et al.* to President Washington, July 2, 1793.

[13] In 1792 the Spaniards, over the opposition of McGillivray and Panton, had authorized Turnbull to build a store on the Yazoo. He had been an American trader from Nashville, was influential among the Indians, and was undoubtedly of considerable help in checkmating Piomingo.

[14] The work of Ugula Yacabe and the Colberts in opposing Piomingo is described in detail in Miss. Prov. Ar., Spanish Dominion, V, 131ff. One of the Colberts also bore the title of Piomingo (Mountain Leader) and the two Piomingos are often confused, as in F. W. Hodge, *Handbook of American Indians North of Mexico*, B. A. E. *Bulletin No. 30.*

[15] Miss. Prov. Ar., Spanish Dominion, V, 51.

come of age, but relied on Olivier and such chiefs as they could influence to hold the tribe steady in its alliance with Spain. But the mantle of McGillivray fell neither on Milfort nor on Olivier but on Mad Dog, who, whether by formal election or by tacit consent, assumed the duties of head chief. Mad Dog had been in McGillivray's confidence and inherited the dead leader's animosity toward the Chickasaws as well as his lack of faith in a general Indian confederation. These factors and his own personal resentment against Piomingo made him the chief obstacle in the way of Spanish peace efforts. But Carondelet persevered. In May he sent Olivier to the Chickasaws to second the peace efforts of Ugula Yacabe; at his direction Milfort (so he said) recalled a Creek army of twelve hundred which had started for the Chickasaw country, and Panton went up into the Creek country from Pensacola with the threat of cutting off supplies.[16] Yet when the overtures of Ugula Yacabe came to the Creek council on June 4, 1793, they were rejected, and the "war" went on for another month before the Spaniards were able to effect an uneasy peace.[17]

The Creek council of June 4, which rejected the Chickasaw peace overtures, also considered the question of Creek representation in the conference of the four nations proposed for perfecting the Indian confederation discussed the preceding year. Mad Dog opposed a conference as unrealistic, asking Olivier, in hope or derision, if Piomingo would be present. The opposition of the Cornells probably indicated only that they were in the pay of Seagrove. Some of the chiefs, objecting to going so far, suggested that the meeting be held on the Tombigbee, where the Creeks would not be so exposed to a corrupt Choctaw environment. In any case, the council decided that the Creeks could attend no conference at all until after they had celebrated their feast of the ripe corn.[18]

[16] Caughey, *McGillivray*, 357–59, Milfort to Carondelet, May 26, 1793; *Indian Affairs*, I, 387–88, Seagrove to Knox, May 24, 1793.

[17] *Indian Affairs*, I, 395–96, Weatherford to Seagrove, June 11, 1793; *ibid.*, I, 465, Robertson to Smith, July 20, 1793. August 17, 1793, Robertson wrote Smith (acting governor of the Territory) that the Creeks had lately sent delegates to the Chickasaws with an invitation to come to Tuckabatchee and confirm the peace (*ibid.*, I, 466–67).

[18] *Ibid.*, I, 395–96, Weatherford to Seagrove, June 11, 1793; Miss. Prov. Ar., Spanish Dominion, V, 44, Olivier to Carondelet, June 4, 1793.

The Choctaws also developed scruples about sitting in conference with Creeks and Cherokees, who might be expected, judging from past performances, to steal all the horses and other property of the Choctaws while the conference was in progress.[19] These indications of an incomplete spiritual accord between Creeks and Choctaws caused Carondelet to consider the holding of two conferences, one at Los Nogales for the Choctaws and Chickasaws, and another at Mobile for Creeks and Cherokees. But evidently reasoning that segregation was an insecure foundation for concerted action, he finally called on all four tribes to meet together at Los Nogales in October.[20]

A preliminary step toward the contemplated confederation had been taken on May 10, 1793, when the *pequeña partida* (eastern division) of the Choctaws ceded to Spain the land on the Tombigbee (where the French had formerly erected Fort Tombecbe), whereon Spain should build a storehouse and a fort for the common security.[21] In the general meeting of the four tribes held at Los Nogales October 28, 1793, neither Bloody Fellow nor Taski Etoka, the two architects of confederation, was present. The Chickasaw delegation, led by Ugula Yacabe, apparently included no chief of the Piomingo faction. The Cherokees, openly avowing the superior attraction of their war against the Americans, had commissioned the Creeks to represent them. The four chiefs representing the Creeks had been named by Olivier, and none of them was of the highest rank; it is uncertain whether this was an evidence of lack of enthusiasm or of reluctance to risk the lives of their head chiefs among their prospective allies. Franchimastabe led the large Choctaw delegation, which included the head chiefs of the three divisions. By the terms of the treaty here made, the Cherokees joined the other three nations under the protection of Spain, and the four formed an alliance, offensive and defensive, among themselves and with Spain, which

[19] Miss. Prov. Ar., Spanish Dominion, V, 64–65, Carondelet to Gayoso, August 19, 1793. In saying this, Franchimastabe was apparently making an oblique reference to Choctaw misfortunes at Hopewell.

[20] *Ibid.*, V, 55.

[21] The text of this treaty made at Boutucca is given in Serrano y Sanz, *op. cit.*, 90.

power was to mediate with the United States the question of Indian boundaries.[22]

In the sequel, if not in the design, this power of mediation was the most significant article of the treaty. Spain had supported the Indians against the United States primarily as a means of increasing their dependence on Spain: now Indian hostilities were no longer necessary to insure a dependence already confirmed by formal treaty. Consequently, Spain made prompt use of her power of mediation to end the Creek and Cherokee attacks, which, if continued, might have involved both Indians and Spaniards in a full-scale war with the United States. The first effects were seen among the Creeks, whom Panton and Olivier encouraged in inviting a visit from Agent Seagrove.

The expectation of President Washington that Seagrove would be a resident agent had remained unrealized because of Seagrove's fear (perhaps not unjustified) of assassination if he entered the Creek country. After McGillivray's death Seagrove on three separate occasions fixed a date for visiting his charges, and each time felt forced to postpone it because of hostile encounters between Creeks and Georgians.[23] Unable to condone such a solicitude for continued existence in a mere agent, the War Department gradually became restive and, after a series of ineffective hints, gave him positive orders to enter the Creek country.[24]

Delaying only long enough to solicit and receive from the Creeks a bodyguard of 130 friendly chiefs and warriors, Seagrove on November 5 set out from Fort Fidius on the Altamaha and in due season came to the peace town, Cusseta. Warmly welcomed here, he went on to Tuckabatchee, where Mad Dog had called a meeting of the National Council. Here he was met and welcomed by Olivier and delivered his talk to the nation. He remained in the Creek country until April 25, 1794, living with Olivier at Little

[22] *Ibid.*, 91–92.

[23] *Indian Affairs*, I, 378, 393, 411, Seagrove to Knox, April 19, July 6, and October 9. The first of these episodes was the plundering of the Seagrove store at Traders' Hill; the second was the murder of David Cornell, June 20, while on an embassy to Seagrove; and the third was the calling out of the Georgia militia by Governor Telfair in September for an invasion of the Creek country.

[24] *Ibid.*, I, 366.

Tallassie and always under close guard, ostensibly to prevent malcontents from hampering his labors by assassination. One may suspect that the tales of homicidal intent were concocted by the Creeks in order to justify their watchfulness; and that, under the pretense of guarding him as an ambassador, they were in reality detaining him as a hostage. In his long sojourn, his polite hosts made elaborate agreements with him for an exchange of prisoners, a surrender of criminals, and even a restoration of stolen horses. On the question of trade and of marking the boundary, the Creeks evaded any commitments, having been advised by Panton and Olivier to be at peace with the Americans but to yield neither trade nor territory. When Seagrove finally departed in April, 1794, after several real or pretended attempts on his life, he left behind him Timothy Barnard as his deputy among the Upper Creeks and James Jordan among the Lower. Upon his return the Georgia militia, always dependable, negatived all his work for peace by attacking the Indian delegation which accompanied him.[25]

The attainment of peace between Cherokees and Americans was more arduous because of their accumulated bitterness and their mutual inability to control their irresponsible people. The first of these irresponsible acts after the Willstown meeting came in June, 1793, when some of the territorial militia under Captain John Beard, in direct violation of instructions from Governor Blount, attacked a friendly group of chiefs gathered at Coyatee for the purpose of arranging their long-deferred trip to Philadelphia. In this act of unrelieved villainy, Hanging Maw, war chief of the Upper Cherokees, was gravely wounded; but John Watts, war chief of the Lower Cherokees, led his vengeful warriors in a series of retaliatory raids so damaging that in October, 1794, Brigadier General John Sevier himself felt constrained (in violation of instructions) to invade the accessible territory of the Lower Cherokees in Georgia, where he burned several towns, including

[25] *Ibid.*, I, 485, 487. Seagrove was escorted home by Mad Dog, the Hallowing King of Coweta, and forty assorted chiefs and warriors. Seagrove took six of the chiefs with him to Augusta to visit the Governor, while the others hunted on the frontier. It was the hunters that the Georgians attacked.

Oostanaula.[26] It was in November after, although not in consequence of, this visitation that a delegation of Cherokee chiefs, including Little Turkey, John Watts, and Bloody Fellow, went to Los Nogales, where in an intertribal conference they formally signed the confederation treaty of the month before.[27] It seems likely from the personnel of the delegation that it went to solicit from the Spaniards aid, not in making war, but in making peace. Certainly, it was peace that Carondelet enjoined on them. On their return they brought a commission as commissary to John McDonald, whom the Spaniards hoped to use in controlling trade and promoting peace in the same way that they were using Olivier among the Creeks.[28]

In the execution of his twofold duties, McDonald was confronted with many difficulties. The supplies, which by the treaty of 1793 the Cherokees were to receive through Pensacola, were by April, 1794, beginning to grow scanty as a result of depredations on Spanish shipping by French privateers subsequent to the British-Spanish alliance of May, 1793. But the same alliance that brought this embarrassment to Spain also extricated her from it when in July, 1794, the British sent in supply ships to Pensacola.[29]

The first faint promise of peace appeared in June, 1794, when as a result of deceit, caprice, ambition, war weariness, or Spanish counsel, a Lower Cherokee delegation led by Doublehead, accepting a renewed invitation from Blount, visited Philadelphia. In a series of amicable conferences with Knox, they promised peace and received, in deferred (and probably uncontemplated) pay-

[26] The details of these alternating depredations are to be found in Brown, *op. cit.*, 384–405.

[27] *Indian Affairs*, I, 475, McKee to Blount, December 5, 1793.

[28] McDonald was appointed on the advice of Panton, who wrote Carondelet that the Americans had offered McDonald $1,000 a year to act as their commissary (Corbitt, "Papers Relating to the Georgia-Florida Frontier," *loc. cit.*, Vol. XXIII, 78–79, Panton to Carondelet September 7, 1792; *ibid.*, Vol. XXIII, 383, *idem* to *idem*, October 15, 1793). Blount wrote Knox in May, 1794, that he had just received a letter from McDonald, written a year earlier, asking to be employed by the Americans (*Indian Affairs*, I, 531). McDonald wrote Alexander McKee, April 10, 1794, that he had received his appointment from the Spaniards but had not accepted it (Hamer, "British in Canada," *loc. cit.*). He did accept it and continued to draw his salary until 1798.

[29] *Indian Affairs*, I, 487, deposition of William Jones.

ment for the land ceded at Hopewell, an increase in the Cherokee annuity from $1,500 to $5,000. The advance collection of this money engendered in the delegation such a strong, although temporary, enthusiasm for the possibilities of peace that they returned in late October with the intention of not again going to war.[30] While Doublehead was absent, two events occurred that may have inclined the Cherokee heart to an acceptance of the peace (with increased pay) which he had negotiated. One of these was the news of Wayne's victory at Fallen Timbers and the subsequent collapse of Indian resistance in the Northwest.[31] The other was the destruction of Nickajack and Running Water by a combined force of Territorial and Kentucky volunteers in September.[32] On November 7, 1794, practically all the chiefs of the Upper and Lower Cherokees met Governor Blount at Tellico Blockhouse in a conference confirming the peace.[33] The absence of Doublehead from this conference was probably to avoid embarrassing inquiries about the nondistribution of the $5,000 he had brought back with him.

To the United States in 1793 and 1794, the Creeks and Cherokees had given peace but nothing more. Both tribes remained bound to Spain not merely by formal alliance but by the stronger

[30] The Doublehead mission is described in Brown, *op. cit.*, 399–400, 438–39.

[31] Several hundred Cherokees and Creeks went north to fight against Wayne, while several companies of Chickasaws and a few Choctaws joined him. Piomingo led a company of sixty as far as Nashville, where he left them, and with Colbert and other chiefs went to Philadelphia. On July 11 he was received by the President. Mucklisha, one of the chiefs, was given a captain's commission, and the tribe promised an annuity of $3,000 (Haywood, *op. cit.*, 424ff.; H. B. Cushman, *History of the Choctaw, Chickasaw and Natchez Indians*, 424ff.). He also secured from Washington a written guarantee of Chickasaw boundaries as Piomingo described them. As the Chickasaws and Choctaws were returning home after the battle of Fallen Timbers, they were assaulted by some white people in Cincinnati, September 8 and 9, and some of the Indians were badly hurt with clubs and stones. Secretary Sargent ordered out the militia to guard the Indian camp, and a Cincinnati grand jury indicted two of the assailants, one of whom escaped and the other tried and acquitted (C. E. Carter, *Territorial Papers of the United States*, III, 421, 422–23, 423–24, 426–27).

[32] *Indian Affairs*, I, 632–35, Reports of Ore, Robertson, and Blount; Miss. Prov. Ar., Spanish Dominion, V, 431, McDonald to Carondelet, September 20, 1794.

[33] *American Historical Magazine*, Vol. IV, 82–94 (correspondence of James Robertson); *Indian Affairs*, I, 536–38.

ties of trade. The Creeks, under the careful tutoring of McGillivray, had never admitted American trade, while the exclusive trading rights granted to the United States by the Cherokees, Chickasaws, and Choctaws had stimulated that nation only to a profusion of promises and preparations. Until 1794 the United States had been content to copy the British Indian organization without any subsequent effort to make it function; it made provision for licensed traders but neglected to grant them any licenses. The modicum of trade brought in illegitimately and clandestinely by unlicensed traders only served to impress on the Indians their practically entire dependence on Panton, Leslie and Company for the supplies necessary to maintain that high standard of living and fighting which they had adopted from their white neighbors. Panton, indeed, by 1794 had eliminated all competition except a few unlicensed traders among the Cherokees and Chickasaws, and Turnbull among the Choctaws; the latter he was preparing to drive out by establishing a store at the mouth of the Yazoo.[34] He was confident he could overcome any private competition, but was dismayed on learning from Washington's message to Congress in December, 1793, that the United States was contemplating an establishment of government stores for the Indian trade. In the last two years the Panton interests had survived the depredations of Bowles, the death of McGillivray, the capture of ships by French privateers, the completion of Turnbull, and the devastation of Spanish red tape. Panton reflected, sadly and erroneously, that he could not meet this last blow of government competition. He wrote to Carondelet on May 2, 1794, proposing that Spain either buy out the firm for $400,000 or make it a loan of that sum for ten years without interest.[35]

The evident reluctance of Congress to accept Washington's repeated suggestions for establishing government stores was due more to its dislike of the socialistic flavor of the proposition than to any knowledge Congress had that such a measure had once

[34] Corbitt, "Papers Relating to the Georgia-Florida Frontier," *loc. cit.*, Vol. XXIII, 382, Panton to Carondelet, August 18, 1793.

[35] *Ibid.*, Vol. XXIV, 150–53. Governor Folch recommended the loan to the home government, but no action was taken, probably because of the Treaty of San Lorenzo.

been tried by South Carolina and had dismally failed. By the act of March 3, 1795, Congress strained its philosophy to the extent of appropriating $50,000 for the purchase of trade goods to be sold in that year to Indians within the limits of the United States. The avowed purpose of this act was to secure control of the Indians by controlling their trade; and since it was the Southern Indians who were the most restive, Washington decided to expend the entire appropriation in the South. Accordingly, a beginning was made with the Creeks and Cherokees, who were at once the most dangerous and the most accessible, by establishing "factories" (stores) at Tellico Blockhouse and at Colerain. But the quantity of trade goods had been so depleted by the demands of the Greenville treaty and the Cherokee annuities that it was not until the fall of 1795, when new supplies came from England, that merchandise could be sent to either factory.[36]

The placid assumption by the United States that the Tellico factory would serve the Chickasaws as well as the Cherokees ignored not only such realities as distance and tribal animosities, but also the aggressive steps being taken by Carondelet and Panton to extend their control over Chickasaw affairs. Taski Etoka had died in 1794 and had been succeeded by his brother Tinebe, who was closely allied to Ugula Yacabe and was even more pro-Spanish than his predecessor had been.[37] From him and other chiefs of the anti-Piomingo faction, the Spaniards secured a grant of land at Chickasaw Bluffs, where in May, 1795, they erected Fort San Fernando de las Barrancas. This measure, inspired by the threat of the new Yazoo companies, extended Spanish trade as well as Spanish influence because Panton, apparently recovering from his earlier dejection, now established a store at the Bluffs and thus increased his monopoly of Chickasaw trade.[38]

The building of Fort San Fernando was the final effort of

[36] *Indian Affairs*, I, 583-84. Tellico Blockhouse was in present Tennessee on the Tellico tributary of the French Broad. Colerain was in Georgia on the St. Marys River about thirty miles up the river.

[37] Miss. Prov. Ar., Spanish Dominion, V, 473, Gayoso to Carondelet, October, 1794.

[38] Samuel C. Williams, *Beginnings of West Tennessee in the Land of the Chickasaws*, 53-55. Panton's store here was under the direction of John Forbes, with Kenneth Ferguson as clerk.

Spain's American officials in their apparently successful struggle to dominate the territory disputed with the United States and, as a step toward that domination, to control the Indians resident therein. It is one of the ironies of history that the Treaty of San Lorenzo (Pinckney's Treaty), which made all their efforts vain, came at a time when these efforts seemed most likely to succeed. The mass of Southern Indians had perhaps never understood what was involved in the dispute of Spain and the United States over territory which both conceded to belong to the Indians themselves. But all Southern Indians realized that the Treaty of San Lorenzo ended their alliance with Spain and that for the future they could depend on Spain neither for support against encroachment nor for mediation in their quarrels with the United States. To the Choctaws and Chickasaws, this Spanish support was of only theoretical importance, since neither had white neighbors near nor any boundary in dispute. But to the Cherokees it meant acquiescence in the American interpretation of the Hopewell line; and to the Creeks, the execution of the long-evaded provisions of the Treaty of New York.

The handwriting on the wall became visible to the Creeks in the spring of 1796, when messengers arrived from Agent Seagrove summoning them to Colerain for a treaty with United States commissioners Benjamin Hawkins, Andrew Pickens, and George Clymer. Had the Creeks known that the United States had been prodded into this treaty by the Georgians and that Georgia commissioners were to be present, it is unlikely that their desire to placate the United States or their long-suppressed yearning for free rations would have led them to accept.[39] When on their arrival at Colerain they found the Georgia agents there accompanied by a considerable number of Georgia militia, they no doubt applauded their own perspicacity in storing meat supplies along the route to facilitate their return. But the United

[39] The Georgia legislature had passed an act for settling the lands south of the Altamaha and had asked the United States to secure the lands by treaty. Washington, after consulting the Senate, named the commissioners and invited Georgia to have agents in attendance to guard the interests of the state. The Georgia agents were James Hendrick, James Jackson, and James Sims. They brought with them on their ship a quantity of goods with which to pay for the land they hoped to secure.

States commissioners, by placing a federal guard around the Creek camp, prevented the militia from exerting its customary diplomatic influence and so enwrapped the Georgia agents in the coils of protocol that they felt constrained to withdraw to their ship. Under such conditions the Creeks were emboldened to give an emphatic and derisive rejection to the inept demands of the Georgians for a land cession. To the commissioners they expressed their willingness to carry out the terms of the Treaty of New York, objecting only to the commissioners' contention that the boundary line followed the Apalachee fork of the Oconee. Before the inflexible attitude of the commissioners, they finally conceded the point, and on July 29, 1796, having protracted their oratory and eaten American food for twelve days, they signed the treaty.⁴⁰

Supplies for the Creeks during the negotiations had been furnished from the government factory at Colerain, which had finally opened for business in January, 1796, after a considerable delay in the erection of a storehouse and the gathering of goods. The commissioners explained to the assembled Indians the arrangements that the government had made for their welfare provided they paid higher prices for what they got, paid for it in cash, and came for it themselves. This "felicity," the commissioners explained, the Creeks could expect to be permanent, since Congress by an act of April 18, 1796, had appropriated $150,000 as a revolving capital for the Indian trade and had authorized the President to establish factories on the Indian frontier wherever he found it desirable.⁴¹ In response to a suggestion from the commissioners, the Creeks ceded a tract of land, five miles square, on the Indian side of the Oconee, to which the factory should be removed from

⁴⁰ A detailed account of the negotiations at Colerain and the text of the treaty is given in *Indian Affairs*, I, 586–618. The Georgia agents protested against the treatment they received, Georgia protested against the treaty, and Washington declared it "unsuccessful." There were about four hundred Creeks in attendance at Colerain.

⁴¹ Edward Price, the factor at Colerain, did not arrive at his post until January 6, 1796, and found on arrival that the factory goods had been much damaged in the sea transit to Colerain (Department of the Interior, Indian Office Records [hereafter cited as I. O. R.], Retired Classified Files, Price to Frances, January 11, 1796).

Colerain. This amiable conduct on the part of the Creeks was caused neither by their elation over the $6,000 they received for the tract nor by any enthusiasm for a cash-and-carry system of commerce but to the condition of their trade, which was at times precarious. The imminence of war between Great Britain and Spain made it difficult for Panton to keep his traders supplied, and trade with the Americans had made only a modest beginning. Seagrove began granting trading licenses in 1796, but both the licensed traders and the many unlicensed ones had difficulty getting supplies. The factory was forbidden to sell to traders.[42]

The comparatively small attendance of the Upper Creeks at Colerain had been due in part to the counter attraction of a new war with the Chickasaws. This war had begun in January, 1795, when a party of Chickasaws on a visit to Nashville presented to Robertson five Creek scalps, which they had lifted from their respective possessors on Duck River. Anticipating Creek disapproval of their action, the Chickasaws asked Robertson for aid, which Robertson gave with some manifest uneasiness over the correctness of his attitude. In addition to supplying other munitions of war, Robertson encouraged the recruiting of men in the Cumberland settlements to such effect that when a Creek invading column reached the Chickasaw towns, there were some fifty Americans present to aid in the successful defense. Meanwhile, the Spaniards, as in the former war, worked actively for peace; Gayoso, at Los Nogales, in the latter part of May sent an agent to the Chickasaw king, who readily agreed to the ending of a war which he had not begun and in which he had not participated. A resulting peace overture from the Chickasaws in June was accepted by the Creeks in July without materially affecting the

---

[42] By Panton's contract he had the option of remaining in business or of closing it in case of a war between Spain and Great Britain. At Spanish request he had continued in business after the Treaty of San Lorenzo, and was now given permission to remain. Seagrove began granting licenses in February, 1796, and granted eight during the year; Price granted nineteen in the next two years (I. O. R., Retired Classified Files, Register of Licenses, February 27, 1797). The factory goods were removed from Colerain to the new post at Fort Wilkinson in the spring of 1797 (I. O. R., Indian Trade Letter Book, Fort Colerain and Hawkins, 1795–1812). Price, who was evidently not of a conciliatory disposition, was continually involved in quarrels with the army officers at Fort Wilkinson until his death in February, 1799.

course of hostilities, since in neither the proposals nor the acceptance did the factions at war take any part. The Chickasaws, too weak to take the field even with American assistance, kept within their fortified towns, from which in September they beat off another Creek attack led by Mad Dog. Meanwhile, William Colbert applied to Blount for aid and, being refused, went on to Philadelphia, where the new Secretary of State and War, Timothy Pickering, gave him scant sympathy. Pickering, in fact, had already written Blount and Robertson a scathing reprimand of their conduct, blaming the Chickasaws for provoking the war and peremptorily ordering Blount to mediate. Blount called the Creeks to meet him at Tellico on October 10, and in November sent the trader J. D. Chisholm to them. Mad Dog agreed to peace and sent proposals to the Chickasaws by Chisholm, as a result of which a truce was arranged pending a meeting of the two parties with Blount at Knoxville. After these amenities had been observed the war went on as before.[43]

In December, 1796, the Creeks were surprised by a visit from Benjamin Hawkins in his new capacity as "principal temporary agent" of Southern Indians, to which position he had been appointed on December 1, 1796, thereby taking on the duties, without the title, of superintendent.[44] The Creeks welcomed him so warmly that he remained among them for three months, getting

[43] Haywood, *The Civil and Political History of the State of Tennessee,* 447–63; Benjamin Hawkins, *Letters of Benjamin Hawkins, 1796–1806,* Collections of the Georgia Historical Society, IX, 448, 449, 451, Thomas to Seagrove, November 11, 1795, December 5, 1795, and February 19, 1796; F. J. Turner, "Documents on the Blount Conspiracy, 1795–97," *American Historical Review,* Vol. X, 574–606, statement of J. D. Chisholm to Rufus King; P. M. Hamer, ed., "Letters of William Blount," East Tennessee Historical Society *Publications,* Vol. IV, 122–33; Ayers Collection No. 292, Foster to Haynes, October 25, 1795, and No. 926, Pickering to Henley, July 22 and August 26, 1795; Cherokee Indians, Talks and Treaties, pt. II, 442, Franche to Mathews, July 28, 1795; *ibid.,* pt. II, 458, Cornell to Seagrove, November 28, 1795.

[44] The office of superintendent lapsed June 1, 1796, when the Territory South of the River Ohio, the governor of which was *ex officio* superintendent, became the state of Tennessee. Foreseeing this, the Secretary of State on May 9, 1796, had advised the President of his right to appoint a new superintendent (Carter, *op. cit.,* IV, 42). Washington, however, named Hawkins as "principal temporary agent." Seagrove was relieved of his agency at this time and set up a store at Colerain to supply traders (on credit) with the goods they could not obtain from the factory.

acquainted with his charges, discouraging the war against the Chickasaws, and inquiring into the state of their trade, which he noted (without any indication of disapproval) was almost completely monopolized by Panton.[45] The visit with the Creeks was, however, merely a prelude to Hawkins' immediate business, the running and marking of the Cherokee and Creek boundaries as specified in the act of May 19, 1796. Accordingly, late in March he set out from the Creek country for Tellico, where on April 1 he was to meet Andrew Pickens and James Winchester, who had been named to assist him. In his subsequent efforts in the Cherokee country, he was aided by the Cherokees and opposed by the white squatters, neither of whom seems to have learned from experience that the sequel to encroachment was not removal but cession.[46]

Cherokee disgruntlement, minor in comparison with their active antagonism of former years, was revealed to Hawkins in a conference at Tuskegee on April 25. Here, without success and probably without expectations, the Cherokees protested the American interpretation of the Hopewell line and the decadent condition of the merchandise sold them at the factory. The factory goods, hauled in wagons from Philadelphia through the long valley of Virginia, as a rule reached Tellico Blockhouse appreciably diminished in quantity and deteriorated in quality. Notwithstanding their dissatisfaction with the goods and the high prices, the Cherokees had been compelled to resort to the factory for much of their supplies, since the private traders, licensed and unlicensed, were unable to bring in adequate supplies and Panton,

[45] Hawkins' good will toward Panton is shown by a letter he wrote him from Coweta, February 2, 1797, tendering his help if Panton's business should become affected by the war between Great Britain and Spain (*Letters of Benjamin Hawkins*, 69). Panton in reply said he had no hope of competing with the factory system, but was continuing his trade out of consideration for the Indians (McClung Collection, Panton to Hawkins, February 28, 1797).

The account of Hawkins' activities during 1797 is taken from his *Letters* unless other reference is cited.

[46] For the juggling of language in the Hopewell treaty and a description of the Cherokee line, see Royce, *The Cherokee Nation*, 153–55. Royce, *Indian Land Cessions*, pt. II, plate CCXL, shows the line as run at this time, and its later construction. Hawkins was able to run the Holston treaty line only fifty miles, being unable to penetrate the mountains. It was later finished by Pickens as shown in Royce, *Indian Land Cessions*, plate CLXI.

Leslie and Company had withdrawn from the Cherokee trade.[47] In October, 1796, Panton had sent his junior partner, John Forbes, from Mobile to Knoxville to liquidate the firm's Cherokee business and to arrange for collecting the debts due—which amounted to about $3,000; apparently his efforts received the co-operation of the factory officials.[48]

At the Tuskegee conference the Cherokees protested against the activities of Zachariah Cox, expressed their apprehension over the Creek-Chickasaw war, and voiced their bewilderment over the "Blount conspiracy." The moribund project of establishing a settlement at Muscle Shoals had been revived as a result of a second sale by Georgia of her western lands in January, 1795, to four land companies, one of which was the Tennessee Company, headed by the unsavory Cox.[49] As a result of the Cherokee protests, reinforced by Choctaw and Chickasaw expostulations, Hawkins gave Cox such a decided warning that it undoubtedly contributed to his abandonment of the project, thus preserving the Muscle Shoals region as a bone of contention among Creeks, Cherokees, and Chickasaws for another quarter-century. As a method of settling the Creek-Chickasaw war, which was still rumbling along, Hawkins, after persuading the Creek council to adopt resolutions for peace, arranged to have a conference of the four tribes in Cherokee territory in August under the supervision of Silas Dinsmoor, Shaw's successor as Cherokee agent. The Chickasaws had appealed to Hawkins for aid, which Hawkins

[47] The Cherokee factory had not been able to open for trade until January, 1796, since which time it had done a considerable business. The operations of this factory are recorded in I. O. R., Cherokee Factory, 1795-1812. There were licensed traders among the Cherokees in 1795; unlicensed traders had been in evidence at all times and continued to be. Governor Sevier of Tennessee strongly opposed the factory and did what he could to hamper it (Donald L. McMurry, "The Indian Policy of the Federal Government and the Economic Development of the Southwest, 1789-1801," *Tennessee Historical Magazine*, Vol. I, 36).

[48] Corbitt, "Papers Relating to the Georgia-Florida Frontier," *loc. cit.*, XXIV, 266-67, Forbes to Carondelet July 22, 1796. While in Knoxville, Forbes also conferred with John McKee, who had the title of "Agent Resident at Tellico Blockhouse."

[49] Haskins, "Yazoo Land Companies," *loc. cit.;* S. G. McLendon, *History of the Public Domain of Georgia*, chaps. III, VIII, and XI; I. J. Cox, ed., "Documents relating to Zachariah Cox," *Quarterly Publication* of the Historical and Philosophical Society of Ohio, Vol. VIII, 31-114.

refused. On June 14, 1797, he dismissed James Robertson as Chickasaw and Choctaw agent for the given reason that Robertson was unable to reside among the Indians. In the following August he placed them under the Choctaw agent, Samuel Mitchell, whom he appointed at that time. With the Treaty of San Lorenzo the Choctaws, because of their position, assumed more importance in the eyes of the American government and the Chickasaws relatively less. The Chickasaws had other reasons for worry for, although Panton had not removed his store from Chickasaw Bluffs when the Spaniards abandoned their fort there in the spring of 1777, it was scantily stocked and the Chickasaws were still forced to get most of their supplies from Mobile. The $3,000 in annuity goods which Piomingo had gleaned from the United States on the occasion of his visit to Philadelphia in 1794, however gratifying as a mark of friendship, so increased in value in the course of the long journey to Nashville that there was little to be distributed. Private traders, lacking in altruism, charged even higher prices than did either the American government or Panton, Leslie and Company.[50]

The tentacles of Blount's conspiracy were reaching out in the spring of 1797 to ensnare not only the Cherokees but all the Southern Indians. When Chisholm, Blount's emissary to the Creeks and Chickasaws in 1795, returned to the Cherokee country after the failure of his ostensible mission, he bore a petition signed by a number of British traders among the Indians asking that they be made citizens of the United States. If the petition was not granted, the traders had plans for arousing the Indians to an attack on the Spanish Floridas, and, after their conquest, for setting up a new government there under British protection. In the fall of 1796, Chisholm presented the petition at Philadelphia, to which place he, as interpreter, had accompanied a group of sight-seeing Indians, including John Watts and James Carey of the Cherokees, Malcolm McGee and George Colbert of the Chickasaws, and John Pitchlynn of the Choctaws. After a cold reception by the government, Chisholm had approached the British ambassador without receiving any encouragement and, after a conference

[50] Ayer Collection, No. 926, Pickering to Henley, May 11, 1795.

with Blount (then a senator from Tennessee), had sailed to England to solicit British aid. His plans, originated by himself, Blount, or the traders, called for a simultaneous attack on New Orleans by the Choctaws and on Pensacola by the Creeks and Cherokees. In his absence Blount attempted through Carey certain overtures to the Cherokee chiefs. But Carey proved unable to keep the matter secret, with the result that on July 8, 1797, he was haled before a justice and acrimoniously questioned by Hawkins, Byers (the factory manager), Dinsmoor, and Henley (agent of the War Department). With his revelations the fantastic project evaporated. It is impossible to say how many chiefs had been solicited or how deeply they were involved.[51]

The failure of Hawkins to visit the Chickasaws in 1797 indicated, possibly, his disapproval of their current conduct; his abstention from Choctaw affairs was no doubt due to a prudent desire to avoid conflict with the Spaniards, who in the summer of 1797 had not yet retired from their posts in the Choctaw country. In October, thoroughly tired by his physical and spiritual exertions among the demanding Cherokees, he went once more to Cusseta, where he intended to reside in order to give his personal attention to the Creeks. The only matter of moment that seemed to require his intervention was the Creek-Chickasaw war, which was lumbering on despite all the efforts to stop it. On October 27 he met the Lower Towns chiefs at Coweta, where Tussekiah Mico reported on his peace mission to the Chickasaw king. The peace arranged by the intertribal conference in August had lasted only until the Upper Creek towns had an opportunity to attack, and it was unlikely that the Chickasaws would fail to retaliate. The Lower Creek council sent Mucklassee Mico to the Chickasaws in an effort to forestall further hostilities by confirming the peace. The Chickasaw war was an Upper Creek matter and so could be viewed by the Lower Towns with considerable detachment. But when Hawkins began to hint at a cession of Creek lands east of

[51] Turner, "Documents on the Blount Conspiracy," *loc. cit.*; *American State Papers, Foreign Relations*, II, 20–27, 66, 78; *Annals of Congress*, 5 Cong., 2 sess., 2383; Kate White, "John Chisholm, a Soldier of Fortune," East Tennessee Historical Society *Publications*, Vol. I, 60; Isabel Thompson, "The Blount Conspiracy," *ibid.*, II, 3–21.

the Ocmulgee, all the Creek objectivity abruptly disappeared, and their refusal was so blunt that the principal temporary agent abandoned the subject. After employing his leisure time in completing the organization of his department, Hawkins on December 6 set out for Fort Wilkinson, whence he went on in January to run the New York treaty line.[52]

The ability of the Cherokees to withstand pressure proved less than that of the Creeks. As a result of a memorial from the infant and self-assertive state of Tennessee, President Adams appointed commissioners to secure from the Cherokees such a land cession as would restore their lands to the trespassers dispossessed by the Holston treaty, and would amplify the then attenuated figure of white holding in the state. In justified anticipation of opposition, the commissioners were given several alternative demands they might present, the last being to get whatever they could. This last proved to be the only practicable procedure. The Cherokees, indeed, when they reluctantly met the commissioners at Tellico Blockhouse in June, refused to make any cession at all. But at an adjourned meeting in September, they relented to the extent of ceding a tract west of the Clinch and two others east of the Tennessee. The official records do not reveal the methods by which this change of heart was brought about.[53]

[52] During his spring visit to the Creeks Hawkins had appointed Timothy Barnard, James Burgess, and Alex Cornell as deputy agents among the Creeks, and Richard Thomas as clerk to the chiefs. In the fall he appointed Sackford Maclin as assistant agent.

[53] *Indian Affairs*, I, 631, 638–41; Royce, *The Cherokee Nation*, 174–81. Adams first appointed Fisher Ames, Bushrod Washington, and Alfred Moore as commissioners. Neither Ames nor Washington accepted, and in March, 1798, George Walton and John Steele declined and Thomas Butler was appointed. Governor Sevier named Robertson, Lachlan McIntosh, and James Stuart to attend and look after the interests of Tennessee. Stuart resigned and was replaced by James White. Robertson did not attend.

V I

Bowles

1798-1803

To any reflecting mind the delay of the Spaniards in delivering their fortified posts north of 31 degrees might well appear to be owing to their fear of a British (or American) attack down the Mississippi rather than to a national talent for procrastination or to a local reluctance to abandon territory with such great effort won. Nor is it necessary, or even possible, to consider the Indian opposition to the running of the dividing line a result of Spanish encouragement or Spanish perfidy. The basis of this opposition was not regret for the withdrawal of the Spaniards nor grief over the prospective loss of territorial unity. It arose from an unreasoning fear that, in some way they did not understand, the running of the line would be a prelude to the loss of their lands and of their independence. It was inevitable that this fear should be chiefly a fear of the United States, where the government had thrice since 1795 solicited land cessions, where the land speculators continually threatened, and where the frontiersmen unceasingly encroached. In July, 1798, a council of Chickasaws and Creeks meeting at Tuckabatchee to confirm peace had made recommendations that henceforth no Indian land be alienated unless the head chiefs of all four nations were present and consenting.[1] The experience of the Cherokees at Tellico the following September showed that intertribal agreements were as impotent as tribal determination to prevent spolia-

[1] *Letters of Benjamin Hawkins,* 490. This meeting was presided over by Mad Dog.

tion. Among the Chickasaws and Cherokees, because of distance or despair, opposition to the line found no expression; among the Choctaws it was so feeble as to be crushed by correspondence.[2] Only among the Creeks did it result in open hostility.

It can hardly be doubted that the dividing line served the Creeks in great measure merely as an occasion for a display of an already well-developed anti-Americanism: what the Americans favored, certain Creeks felt bound to oppose. The leader of the anti-American faction was the Tame King of Tallassie, in whose attitude was reflected a still unassuaged and carefully nurtured resentment over the Shoulderbone incident of ten years before and also a violent and sincere antipathy to the civilizing program Hawkins was attempting to put into effect among the Creeks.

When Hawkins had come among the Creeks in 1797, his conventional English sensibilities were outraged by the Creek working combination of political anarchy and economic communism. With the typical American inability to tolerate nonconformity, he had set to work at once to refashion the Creeks in the American image by promoting a stronger governing authority and by encouraging the hitherto undeveloped idea of private property. He had strengthened the authority of the town chief, systematized the sessions and procedure of the national council, and converted the head chief into a "Speaker" of the council. By his popularity among the Creek women he had induced some of them to take up spinning and weaving. He had succeeded in having some of the land fenced, had introduced the plow into an extremely primitive agriculture, and had encouraged the raising of cattle and hogs. He wished to have the tribal lands placed under town ownership, although he opposed individual ownership because, Creek nature being what it was, it would make the land too easily alienated. All these things the principal temporary agent considered good, because not only would it recreate the Creeks in the American pattern, but would also, by instilling order, promoting peace, and increasing agriculture, enable the Creeks to maintain themselves on a more restricted domain and thus to have surplus acres for cession to a benign and fostering American government.

[2] Andrew Ellicott, *The Journal of Andrew Ellicott*, 98.

His political reforms appealed to the chiefs, his economic reforms to the women, in whim by Creek custom rested the ownership of all products of home and field. The rank and file of the Creek men had no liking for the political new order and were deeply opposed to the economic reforms, which, in addition to violating Creek custom, would tend to excite in the women an even greater degree of insubordination than they ordinarily displayed. To the agent's exhortations to raise cattle and hogs, the Creek masculine mind responded more cheerfully, since both, as species of game, were under control of the men and had the added attractiveness of not requiring any great output of manual exertion. But on the other aspects of the reforms, the Creeks were divided between the old communist-conservatives and the new capitalist-progressives. The rift between the two was destined to increase until it brought the nation to the very verge of destruction.

The commissioners for running the line encountered no Indian opposition as long as they operated in the domain of the poverty-stricken and apathetic Choctaws, but when they reached the Tombigbee, where the Creek territorial claims began, the pressure of accumulated warnings caused Ellicott, the American commissioner, to send for Hawkins. In the ensuing conference, to which the Creek chiefs came, near the confluence of the Escambia and Conecuh rivers, the Creeks hesitantly agreed to furnish the commissioners the escort of two chiefs and twenty warriors that they had promised at Colerain. However, the escort would guard them only to the Chattahoochee; beyond that river was the country of the Seminoles, with whom the commissioners would have to deal as best they could.[3] The significance of this act was impaired by the absence of the Tame King and his followers, who had boycotted the conference and gone, with or without an invitation, to Pensacola to confer with Governor Folch.

When Hawkins, unexpectedly appearing, surprised the assembly, the unembarrassed Governor, with consummate courtesy, perhaps not untainted by guile, consigned the Indians, as resi-

[3] *Ibid.*, 206; Corbitt, "Papers Relating to the Georgia-Florida Frontier," *loc. cit.*, Vol. XXV, 162, Panton to Gayoso, May 12, 1799.

dents of the United States, to him to be dealt with and, incidentally, entertained. Hawkins addressed them with his customary vigor, but apparently not with his customary suavity, upbraiding them for their hostile attitude, and declaring that the United States was determined to run the line even if it cost the lives of a thousand men. Unimpressed by these statistics, the Tame King, after receiving the few gifts Hawkins had been able to improvise, departed to prepare impediments for the surveyors, but held his warriors in check for twenty days while he sent Methogley, the second chief of Miccosukee, with a protest to Seagrove, in whom the disgruntled Creeks had come to have great confidence since his dismissal by the United States.

Methogley, claiming to be the spokesman not only for the Seminoles, but also for all four nations, told Seagrove of the alleged misconduct of Hawkins among the Creeks, of his threatening speech at Pensacola, and of a warning given him (Methogley) by a Spaniard at St. Marks that the Spaniards and the Americans had agreed to divide the Indian land between them as a preliminary to enslaving the Indians. His closing assertion that the Indians he represented were determined to prevent the running of the line, even if in so doing they had to fight both Spain and the United States, was probably made merely to create an impression of Indian impartiality, since Spain's zeal for running the line had never visibly risen above the level of resignation. In his reply, Seagrove refrained from comment on the indictment against Hawkins (of which he undoubtedly approved), reminded Methogley of the Creek promise at Colerain to protect the surveyors, and ridiculed their fear of the loss of land and liberty.[4]

The Creeks and Seminoles who dogged the surveyors from the Escambia to the Chattahoochee limited their hostility to stealing, but at the Chattahoochee they were assembled in such large numbers as to leave no doubt that here they meant to halt the line. When Ellicott, who had gone by sea and up the Apalachicola, joined the surveyors on the Chattahoochee, he was met by Timo-

[4] Methogley's talk, June 14, 1799, and Seagroves' reply the following day are given in No. 927 of the Ayer Collection; Methogley said that Hawkins had summoned him, Thomas Perryman, and Kinhijah, the first chief of Miccosukee, to escort the surveyors, but that they had not gone.

thy Barnard, whom Hawkins had sent down to parley with the malcontents. In the ensuing conference the Indians took such little pains to conceal the hypocrisy with which they protested their peaceful intentions that Ellicott became alarmed and on the advice of James Burgess, a then friendly half-blood, again sent for Hawkins. The principal temporary agent, either from excessive optimism or inadequate knowledge, judged that the line-running could continue without trouble, and the Creek escort declared itself willing to go on. But when Ellicott dropped down to the mouth of the Flint, the Indians began to advance on his camp, stealing his horses, sabotaging his boat, and firing sporadically at the surveyors. Judging from these manifestations of disapproval that further progress was impossible, Ellicott abandoned the survey, dismissed his escort, and started on his patched-up boat down the Apalachicola to go by sea to the St. Marys, at the headwaters of which the line was to terminate. At the mouth of the Apalachicola on St. George's Island, he found William Augustus Bowles, who had been shipwrecked there as he was coming into Florida on his final intervention in the affairs of the Southern Indians.[5]

Bowles had come to Florida with the intention of setting up an Indian state which would aid the British by harassing the Spaniards and would be assisted by the British with such supplies as would enable it to maintain itself. Bowles was, however, primarily a Creek patriot to whom a war with Spain was merely the necessary price he must pay for British support in establishing his Indian state. Consequently, his first concern after leaving the island of his shipwreck was to call the Creeks and Seminoles to a conference at Wekiwa, where he had established his headquarters on the Apalachicola, and, with their consent and approval to proclaim the state of Muscogee with himself as its director general. He thus on October 26, 1799, reassumed the title which his partisans had given him on October 22, 1791.[6] To his supporting Indians he announced that there would be no more Indian lands

<hr>

[5] Panton, Leslie and Company MSS, Greenslade Papers, Ferguson's Declaration, June 16, 1800.

[6] Ayer Collection, No. 100, Bowles to ——, October 31, 1799.

ceded and no dividing line run: the latter he would prevent by writing personal letters to the King and President. The favor he gained by this announcement was increased by his promise to bring in British goods by Christmas.[7]

The Director General and his supreme council did not specify the boundaries of the state of Muscogee, but no one conversant with the previous activities of Bowles can believe that he meant to exclude either the Upper or Lower Creeks. His decree of October 31, 1799, ordering out of Muscogee by November 8 all commissioned agents of Spain and the United States indicates that he meant to include them, and his later statement that only his innate generosity prevented him from having Hawkins assassinated carries the same suggestion.[8] For the time being he limited his activities to Florida, since it was only for operations in Spanish territory that he could expect British support. But the decree of October 25, 1799, opening to trade the ports of Apalachicola and Ochlocknee, certainly affected Creeks as well as Seminoles, as did that of November 26 offering land to white settlers in Florida east of the Apalachicola.

Among the Creeks, the Tame King promptly declared himself an adherent of Bowles, judging correctly that from his past record and present program he would be a powerful ally in solidifying Indian sentiment against Hawkins and the United States. Many of the Lower Creeks who in 1791 had supported Bowles, even against McGillivray, now welcomed him back. Against this increasing tide of discontent, the sorely tried agent acted promptly, although perhaps neither wisely nor too well. In a meeting of the Creek national council at Tuckabatchee in November, 1799, he denounced Bowles and demanded that the council go on record as opposing him. This the complaisant council did the next day in a formal address by Mad Dog, asserting that Bowles had never been a Creek chief and that the Creeks would have killed him in 1792 if he had not left the country. Mad Dog condemned the selling of tribal land by Bowles to white settlers and rejected his

[7] Georgia Department of Archives and History, Creek Indian Letters, pt. II, 584, Report of Emoutla Haujo, from Coweta Tallahassee, December 16, 1799.
[8] Ibid., pt. II, 590, Bowles to Jackson, June 6, 1800; Corbitt and Lanning, "A Letter of Marque and Reprisal," loc. cit.

promise of trade, saying that the Creeks wanted trade only from Panton.[9]

On the advice of Hawkins the council somewhat pointedly implemented its anti-Bowles declaration by organizing the Upper Creek towns into nine military groups, each under the direction of a warrior in sympathy with Hawkins and the council.[10] The Lower Creek towns were so strongly in favor of Bowles that the council made no effort to organize or control sentiment among them. Hawkins also insisted that the Tame King should be publicly whipped by the Creek authorities as a punishment for his action on the Flint in coercing the surveyors to abandon the line after the nation had consented to have it run. The council, submissive as it was, was much opposed to an action so unprecedented in Creek history and so in violation of Creek custom. It was only on Hawkins' angry insistence that they finally agreed to it, and then only on his assumption of all responsibility for the results. Mad Dog himself led the seventy-two warriors who seized the old king and three of his associates, bound, and publicly flogged them.[11] The humiliation, however pleasant to Hawkins, only increased the recalcitrance of the Tame King and added to the number of his adherents. It is evident, too, that some of the chiefs, including Mad Dog, in shame for their action in mishandling a Creek (a thing McGillivray himself never presumed to do), began to compare their present subservience with their former status when they stood with McGillivray.

The Creek followers of the Tame King, although they had no cause for hostility toward Spain, continued their support of Bowles when on April 5, 1800, he declared a state of war existing between Spain and Muscogee, being induced thereto apparently not by his commitments to Great Britain, but by the action of Spain in capturing and burning his headquarters at Wekiwa (February 3). Unwilling to limit his military activities to proclama-

[9] *Florida Historical Quarterly*, Vol. XI, 33–36, Talk by Efau Haujo at Tuckabatchee, November 25, 1799. Efau Haujo (Mad Dog) mentioned that Bowles had illegally secured a cession of land from the Seminole Potato King.

[10] Hawkins, *The Creek Country*, 49.

[11] *Letters of Benjamin Hawkins*, 417–19, Hawkins to the Secretary of War, May 8, 1802.

tions, Bowles on April 9 invested the Spanish fort at St. Marks with a force of Seminoles and Creeks and on May 19 forced, or at least received, its surrender. In his accompanying seizure of Panton's store up the Wakulla, he acted, perhaps more from economic than from military necessity, for although Panton was not a belligerent, Bowles' line of supply from the Bahamas was too precarious to be dependable. From this time on, the Spanish officials in Florida bombarded the Creek council with exhortations to restrain the warring Indians, while Panton began to threaten the suspension of trade unless reparation were made for his pecuniary losses.[12]

Governor Folch put a price of $4,500 on Bowles' head, but as Hawkins, in pride or chagrin, observed, no Indian attempted to win the reward. Whether Bowles' immunity to assassination was due to the primitive state of the Indian culture, his own popularity, or the alertness of his sixty-man bodyguard it is impossible to say. After the capture of Wekiwa, he had removed his headquarters to Miccosukee, and here he continued to reside after the Spaniards recaptured St. Marks (June 23, 1800), sending his talks to the Creek towns by Perryman and Kinhijay. So exasperated was Hawkins by these tactics that in October, 1800, he goaded the chiefs of Cusseta and Coweta to send a talk (written by Hawkins) to Mad Dog demanding that he lead a Creek force to Miccosukee and take Bowles by force from the Seminoles. This demand Mad Dog refused, knowing that all the Lower Creek towns below Uchee had gone over to Bowles, and that the Upper Creek warriors would refuse to follow him into a sanguinary civil war.[13]

It may be uncertain whether Bowles considered the Cherokees a part of his state of Muscogee, but undoubtedly his program was known to them, and, with the example of Creek success in

[12] Spanish Transcripts, Library of Congress, Legajos 2372, p. 90, Burgess to Bowles, July 3, 1801; *ibid.*, p. 100, Spanish Governor at New Orleans to Creeks, December 1, 1801; I. O. R., Retired Classified Files, Hawkins to Dearborn, July 18, 1801.

In the conference at Willstown twelve nations were represented either by delegations or official messages—all of which were friendly to the United States (I. O. R., Retired Classified Files, Meigs to Dearborn, October 4, 1801).

[13] *Florida Historical Quarterly*, Vol. XI, 36-39, Daniel McGillivray to Panton, October 13, 1800.

halting the line, may have heartened them when in September, 1801, they were again asked for a land cession. The imperfect unity of the tribe, wrought by the murder of Old Tassel and the subsequent death of Dragging Canoe, was breaking on the issue of civilization versus the ancient ways, with the Upper Cherokees submissively, and even cheerfully, accepting the American program, while the Lower Cherokees rejected it all except the raising of livestock. Since the ideological differences among the Cherokees coincided with geographical divisions, they were even more virulent than among the Creeks. In 1801 the Lower Cherokees were making tentative moves toward the formal division of the tribe into two parts on the line of the Chilhowie Mountains, and some of them were advocating the removal of the Lower towns west of the Mississippi, where they would be beyond the bounds of the United States and out of reach of its dreaded civilization.[14]

However divided otherwise, the Cherokees had a community of dissatisfactions. In addition to their common feeling of shame over the land cession of 1798, they all entertained a common antipathy to their agents and a common antagonism to the factory at Tellico. Dinsmoor, who was well liked by even the most sullen of the Cherokees, had been dismissed in March, 1799, by President Adams, who was out of sympathy with the program of civilizing the Indians and gravely doubted if it could be done. Dinsmoor's successor, Major Lewis, confined his activities among the Cherokees so exclusively to the women and his energies at Tellico so continually to the bottle that no Cherokees mourned when he was replaced in March, 1801, by Return Jonathan Meigs.[15] The Cherokees were inclined to be distrustful of Meigs because of his age and because he had other duties in addition to those of his agency. The Cherokee complaint against the factory was that it sold inferior goods at exorbitant prices. The replacement of Byers by J. W. Hooker, as factor, in March, 1801, however much of an improvement politically, did not remedy matters, for Hooker felt obliged to raise prices even above the 33 1/3 per cent advance

[14] *Letters of Benjamin Hawkins,* 361–63, 384–86, Hawkins to Dearborn, August 10 and September 6, 1801.
[15] I. O. R., War Department Letter Book A, 29, 37.

practiced by his predecessor. The high prices, resulting from the long haulage of goods from Philadelphia, enabled the South Carolina traders to undersell the factory. By 1801 the factory had debts to the amount of $6,515 owing to it, and it was Meigs' opinion that it could never operate except at a loss.[16]

On June 4, 1801, President Jefferson appointed General Wilkinson, W. R. Davie, and Benjamin Hawkins commissioners to hold treaties with the four Southern tribes, beginning with the Cherokees, from whom they were instructed to secure a land cession and permission for roads through their territory to Georgia and Natchez.[17] The Cherokee chief, Glass, coming to Washington with a Cherokee delegation about a week later, heard of this project and laid down such an intense verbal barrage against it that the astonished President assured him it would not be pressed. The Secretary of War Dearborn at once wrote to the commissioners that in view of Glass's tirade they should "treat the subject [of land cessions] with great tenderness."[18]

With a skepticism born of experience, Glass, upon his return, summoned a Cherokee council at Oostanaula in order to forewarn his people of possible tribulations in store. To this council, deliberating both Glass's report and the commissioners' summons to a conference, the Lower Cherokee chiefs, by accident or design, failed to receive an invitation, whereupon suspecting that the Upper Cherokees were secretly planning again to betray the nation as they had allegedly done in 1798, they secured an invitation from Hawkins to attend the treaty making. As a matter of fact, the Oostanaula council, driven by indignation to an unwanted display of independence, resolved not to attend the conference and wrote the commissioners a letter so bellicose that it frightened the authors themselves. Upon reflection, they substituted one which accepted a conference but insisted that it be held at Oosta-

---

[16] *Indian Affairs*, I, 654; I. O. R., Retired Classified Files, Meigs to Dearborn, December 25, 1801. By the end of 1800, Tellico had received $55,066 worth of merchandise and had sold it all but $10,171 worth. It had taken in from the Indians $47,000 worth of fur and peltry. The debt of $6,575 was probably due mostly from the military and agency personnel.

[17] Davie subsequently resigned and Andrew Pickens was named in his place.

[18] *Indian Affairs*, I, 650, Dearborn to commissioners, July 3, 1801.

naula instead of at Southwest Point, as the commissioners had proposed. After much altercation, the commissioners fixed the conference by ultimatum, at Southwest Point, but apparently in winning this contest of wills they exhausted their resolution and quietly acquiesced when Doublehead, speaking for the nation, refused, with pointed references to speculators in high places, both land and roads. Little Turkey, fearing the aftermath of this tribal non-co-operation, did not attend the conference but remained at Oostanaula, from which place he summoned the delegates of the four tribes to meet on September 20 (the beginning of the Cherokee fall festival) at Willstown in order to concert measures for preserving their land.[19]

The Chickasaws were more united and even more resolute than the Cherokees against a land cession. The schism that had so long paralyzed them was now ended, and the tribe was living placidly under the nominal rule of Tinebe (who the Americans called Chinnimbi or Chamby). The civilization program, which had so divided the Creeks and Cherokees, had not yet reached the Chickasaws, nor were there among them any discernible symptoms of unrest that could be traced to the influence of Bowles. The prevalent movement away from their fortified villages resulted rather from the ending of the Creek war than, as Hawkins thought, from a desire for farming. Their dislike for their new agent, Samuel Mitchell, who had moved up to them from the Choctaws early in 1801, led them rather to a disregard of his advice than to opposition to his measures. Co-operation with the United States was now a tribal policy endorsed by the king, Ugula Yacabe, the three Colberts, and the other leading chiefs, but it stopped short of a land cession. Instead, they demanded that the commissioners, when they arrived at Chickasaw Bluffs, October 15, confirm the boundaries guaranteed them by Washington in 1794. These boundaries the commissioners, having already abandoned any idea they may have had of a land cession, were quite

[19] The details of this abortive conference are given in the *Letters of Benjamin Hawkins*, 359-86. For an account of Glass's conference with the Secretary of War, see I. O. R., War Department Letter Book A, 72-83.

willing to confirm since the Chickasaw lands thus defined extended so far to the east as to cover the route of the proposed Nashville-Natchez road and thus rendered it unnecessary to go through Cherokee territory at all. The request for the road was granted after only the minimum delay required by tribal etiquette, but the request for houses of entertainment along the road was warily refused. The signatures of seventeen chiefs, including the king and two Colberts, attested both the friendliness and the unity of the tribe. Their complaisance in signing the treaty was rewarded by a gift of merchandise valued at $2,695, in addition to two hundred gallons of whiskey and one thousand pounds of tobacco.[20]

Although the hunting season had begun and the Six Towns absented themselves, the Choctaw conference which began at Fort Adams, December 12, 1801, was largely attended by the Choctaws in the expectation of securing for the duration of the meeting a respite from the famine now continually besetting them. The Choctaws had a new agent in the person of John McKee, who had replaced Samuel Mitchell in 1799.[21] But no agent could do much toward alleviating the Choctaw distress which stemmed from the imminent exhaustion of their inadequate hunting grounds. Unable to secure peltry sufficient to exchange for needed, or at least customary, supplies, the tribe was existing precariously on goods furnished on credit by Panton, who was beginning to display more interest in collecting old debts than in contracting new. Such central government as the tribe had possessed had virtually disappeared, and each of the three divisions was going its own independent way. Hungry and submissive, the Choctaws readily agreed to the commissioners' request for the Natchez road through their territory and a delimitation of their Natchez cession to the British, to which, of course, first the Spaniards and now the Americans had fallen heir. After six days of

[20] *Indian Affairs*, I, 652, Commissioners to Dearborn, October 27, 1801; Kappler, *op. cit.*, II, 55–56.

[21] Rowland, *Mississippi Territorial Archives*, 289. Mitchell had incurred the animosity of Winthrop Sargent, governor of Mississippi Territory, who had stigmatized him "as either a knave or fool—and I believe the latter."

conferring at United States' expense, they received a parting gift of merchandise to the value of $2,038 and a supply of tobacco; to Hawkins' astonishment they refused a gift of whiskey.[22]

For the Creek conference the commissioners had been instructed not only to ask for a land cession but also to insist on getting it. The reason for the insistence was Jefferson's desire to placate Georgia into a cession of her western lands as the only practicable method of delivering a state-rights President from the embarrassment of administering the Mississippi Territory erected within the Georgia limits by his Federalist predecessor. The lands demanded of the Creeks were these: a tract between the Apalachee and the Tugalo, a tract between the Oconee and Ocmulgee, and the lands between the Altamaha and the St. Marys. In order to legitimatize the position of some sixty families who had settled on the first of these contrary to law, the United States had contemplated its purchase from the Cherokees the preceding year, but had abandoned the plan in the face of Glass's tirade. Apparently considering the Cherokee refusal to sell as an evidence of Creek ownership, the United States now solicited it from the Creeks. The land south of the Altamaha—the Tallassie country—was the land allegedly ceded to Georgia at Galphinton but left in Creek hands by the treaties of New York and Colerain.

After the Choctaw meeting the commissioners went overland to the Creek country, where Hawkins found that in his absence Creek affairs had gone from bad to much worse. In May, 1802, Bowles had summoned the Tame King of Tallassie and Little Prince of Broken Arrow to join him in an attack on St. Marks, assuring them that he had two thousand troops and was expecting more from Providence. Excited by these fair prospects, the two set out for Florida with several hundred followers.[23] Attendance at the conference, therefore, which began at Fort Wilkinson on the Oconee, May 24, was limited practically to the Upper Creeks. Not only did most of the Lower towns boycott the conference in order to follow Bowles, but from Florida the "legal and constitu-

[22] *Letters of Benjamin Hawkins*, 410–12, commissioners to Dearborn, December 18, 1801; *Indian Affairs*, I, 659–63; Kappler, *op. cit.*, II, 56–57.

[23] Spanish Transcripts, Legajos 2372, pp. 178, 183, Dureauzeaux to Folch, May 2 and May 8, 1802.

tional head of Muscogee" on June 4 sent the commissioners a protest against the treaty making, denouncing it as illegal and fraudulent and declaring they would be bound by no treaty except one made at a place previously selected by the Creeks and agreed to by the four nations.[24]

Before this protest was received or even written, Wilkinson had opened the conference in language which perhaps reflected his irritation over the theft of his baggage among the Creeks. By this time the Georgia Compact had been signed, but the commissioners apparently said nothing about it, perhaps judging that the feeble prospects for Creek co-operation would not be strengthened by any publication of the pledge by the United States to extinguish all Indian land titles in Georgia. The commissioners made no demand for a cession of the Apalachee-Tugalo tract, the Creeks having forestalled it by the novel device of disclaiming ownership and having implemented their disclaimer by a boundary agreement with a Cherokee delegation on the treaty grounds. The other two tracts the commissioners asked to buy, so that the Creeks might have sufficient means to pay their debts and provide for the aged and infirm after the manner of the Americans. Unimpressed by this opportunity to balance their budget and at the same time to initiate a social welfare program, the Creeks refused both demands. The Tallassie country, they said, belonged to the Lower Creeks and could not be sold without the consent which they were not present to give. The readiness with which the Creeks gave this answer suggests that the Florida exodus of the Lower Creeks, while publicly denounced, was not wholly unapproved and had, perhaps, not been entirely unencouraged. They refused the land between the Oconee and Ocmulgee on the sentimental grounds that it was their ancestral home and for the material reason that it was their best hunting ground. After this interchange the Creek chiefs were eager to return home, where, as they slyly informed Hawkins, their assistance was needed in the agricultural operations he had sponsored. The commissioners, on the other hand, sought to procrastinate on the grounds that they were expecting Georgia delegates to put in their appearance.

[24] *Ibid.*, Legajos 2372, p. 415.

The stalemate continued until June 12, when Hawkins addressed the Indians, detailing their outrages against Georgia, denouncing the Lower Creeks for their support of Bowles, and reminding them of the blessings brought to them by the United States. The agent's zeal had apparently not been diminished by the news he had just received that he had been demoted from virtual superintendent of all Southern Indians to merely agent of the Creeks.[25] Following this speech, the Creeks held a council, as a result of which they announced they would make a cession. In their official report the commissioners referred to this change of heart as a miracle, thereby relieving themselves of any necessity to explain how it was brought about. The "miracle," however, did not extend so far as to bring a cession of all the land requested, but only a narrow strip of the Tallassie land along the old border and less than one-half of the territory between the Oconee and Ocmulgee. For these two tracts the Creeks received a perpetual annuity of $300 for the tribe as a whole, a ten-year annuity of $1,000 for the governing chiefs, $10,000 worth of merchandise to be distributed, and $15,000 with which to pay their factory debts and the Georgian claims for damages done them since the treaty of Colerain.[26]

At the close of the negotiations Mad Dog dictated to Hawkins a talk to be sent to the Seminoles demanding, in the name of thirty-two Creek towns, some Cherokee and Chickasaw, that they abandon Bowles and their war against Spain. This demand he proposed to send down by James Burgess, but on the insistence of a chief who distrusted Burgess, he named the chiefs of Tuskegee

[25] Although the Congressional act creating Mississippi Territory in 1798 had specified that the territorial governor should be *ex-officio* superintendent of Southern Indians, Hawkins had continued to exercise the authority of superintendent. The first governor, Sargent, had protested voluminously against this anomaly but without success. But Jefferson listened to the protests of Claiborne, and on February 23, 1802, Dearborn ordered him to exercise the authority to which his position entitled him. Henceforth the Choctaw and Chickasaw agents reported to Claiborne, the Cherokee and Creek agents directly to the Secretary of War (Rowland, *Mississippi Territorial Archives*, 13, 21, 32, 47, 108, 155, 289, 293; I. O. R., War Department Letter Book A, 166–68).

[26] The official report of the commissioners is given in *Indian Affairs*, I, 668–81. The text of the treaty is in Kappler, *op. cit.*, II, 58–59. For a map of the land ceded see Royce, *Indian Land Cessions*, pt. II, plate CXXII.

and Autossee to accompany him.[27] With this letter Mad Dog closed his career as leader of the Creeks, announcing to them that in the future Creek councils would be held at Acheaubofau, where the Foosehatchee Micco lived. According to Creek forms this was an abdication in favor of the Foosehatchee Micco, commonly called Opoie Micco. Mad Dog gave age as his reason for abdicating, but it can hardly be doubted that he was forced out by Hawkins, of whose program he was becoming increasingly doubtful and whose demands at Fort Wilkinson he had opposed. Mad Dog had been co-operative, but, wearing the mantle of McGillivray, he had not quickly enough learned how to serve.

[27] Burgess living on the lower Flint had been a go-between for the Creeks and Bowles (Spanish Transcripts, Legajos 2372, pp. 82–90.

VII

Debts, Bribes and Cessions

1803-1811

AMONG THE Southern Indians prior to 1803, only the Creeks and Cherokees had experienced the loss of territory, the one to the covetousness of Georgia and the other to Tennessee. From neither could the Indians expect any future surcease of pressure, since Georgia now had the Compact as a lever for its demands, and in Tennessee the insatiable speculators were still intent on engrossing the land, possession of which, technically gained under the North Carolina confiscation of 1783, had been denied, or at least postponed, by the Hopewell treaty. Moreover, in 1802 the Choctaws and Chickasaws became for the first time subject to pressure when news of the retrocession of Louisiana caused Jefferson to believe that the left bank of the Mississippi must be cleared of Indian title preparatory to its defensive settlement against the strong and inconstant French beyond.[1] In addition to these unpleasing prospects, the Creeks, Chickasaws, and Choctaws were beginning to be importuned by Panton, Leslie and Company for tribal land cessions in payment for the individual trading debts eluding collection. Subjected to pressure from all these directions, the harassed tribes found it impossible long to preserve their domains undiminished.

It was apparently Jefferson's belief that, although sheer obstinacy might cause the Indians to refuse land cessions to a benevolent government, their primitive honesty would incline them to

[1] James D. Richardson, *A Compilation of the Messages and Papers of the Presidents, 1789–1907*, I, 352, Jefferson to Congress, January 18, 1803. North of the Ohio pressure was brought to bear on the Sac and Fox tribe for the same reason.

pay their debts. He would encourage the Indians first to accumulate these useful debts at the government stores and then to liquidate them by land cessions.[2] This plan promised quicker returns than could be obtained under the Federalist program which deferred the denuding of the Indian until he became civilized. Already on April 30, 1802, Congress, after scrutinizing the records of the existing factories, had given them a year's lease of life, presumably in recognition of their diplomatic importance since they were apparently without any mercantile functions.[3] But for the two new factories which Jefferson decided to establish for the Choctaws and Chickasaws, trade would be merely a by-product of the debt promotion. The inevitable site for the Chickasaw post was Chickasaw Bluffs; the location of the Choctaw factory at St. Stephens was dictated neither by nearness to the Choctaws nor by accessibility from United States trading centers, but by the hope that so placed it might block the trade of Panton, Leslie and Company from Mobile.[4]

[2] Williams, *Beginnings of West Tennessee*, 63. Jefferson said that the way the government could obtain Chickasaw lands was "to establish among the Chickasaws a factory for furnishing them all the necessaries and comforts they may wish (spirituous liquors excepted) encouraging them and especially their leading men to run in debt for these beyond their individual means of paying; and whenever in that situation they will always cede land to rid themselves of debt." See also I. O. R., Retired Classified Files, Riley to Meigs, November 29, 1806: "Mr. Hockker [Hooker] told . . . that when he was at the Norard that in conversation with Mr. Jefferson he asked him if he could get the Cherokee to run in debt to the amount of ten or twelve thousand dollars in the public store. Mr. Hockker told him for answer fifty thousand. Well, says he, that is the way I intend to git there countrey for to git them to run in debt to the publick store and they will have to give there lands for payment. Mr. Hockker's answer was if that is your Deturmeanation you must git sum other pursun to keep the store."

[3] The act of 1796 authorizing the factories had expired, and the factories had been running for several years without legal authority.

[4] On July 3, 1802, Jefferson appointed Joseph Chambers as factor for the Choctaws and, five days later, Thomas Peterkin for the Chickasaws (I. O. R., Letter Book A., 242, 246). James Wilkinson and Governor Claiborne were asked to recommend a site for the Choctaw factory, and they concurred in naming St. Stephens (Official Letter Books of W. C. C. Claiborne, Mississippi Department of Archives and History, 151, 153; *Indian Affairs*, I, 682-83). Ten thousand dollars worth of goods were sent to the Choctaw factory even before its site was determined. The goods were brought up the Mississippi and stored at Fort Adams until Chambers was ready to receive them (I. O. R., Letter Book A, 547). The Chickasaw factory was opened in the fall of 1802, but that at St. Stephens was apparently delayed till early in 1803.

James Edward Oglethorpe, founder of the Georgia colony
From a pen and ink sketch
by S. Ireland, 1785

Thomas Jefferson
From the portrait by Mather Brown, 1786

*Charles Francis Adams Collection
and Frick Art Reference Library*

But, as a matter of fact, it was Panton, Leslie and Company which enabled Jefferson to secure his cession without recourse either to the slow process of civilization or to the more rapid method of debt. For Panton, Leslie and Company already had the debts; all that was necessary was for the Indians to make their cessions to the United States and pay their debts with the money received.[5] This felicitous arrangement seems to have first suggested itself to Secretary Dearborn when in May, 1802, he was informed by John McKee, the able and departing agent for the Choctaws, that Panton, Leslie and Company were seeking from the Choctaws a land cession, to which the United States had given approval through him (McKee) in 1797.[6] After mastering his horror over this evidence of unpatriotic collusion between his Federalist predecessor and an alien merchant, Dearborn suggested that, although the improved moral standards incident to a Republican regime forbade the countenancing of an Indian cession to the firm, the sound principle of debt collecting might be preserved by its payment with funds secured by a cession to the United States. As a measure of accommodation to the Choctaws, he was willing to accept a cession between the Tombigbee and the Alabama; when he heard of the retrocession of Louisiana, he desired, instead, a cession on the Mississippi littoral. General Wilkinson, then among the Choctaws on the business of running the lines between them and the United States, was instructed to work with Dinsmoor, the new agent, in securing Choctaw approval; James Robertson was sent to the Chickasaws in December, 1802, as a sorely needed reinforcement for Agent Mitchell. Both tribes were

[5] I. O. R., Retired Classified Files, statement of William Simpson, August 20, 1803. According to this statement the Indian debt to Panton, Leslie and Company amounted to $172,139, of which $112,512 was Creek, $46,091 Choctaw, $11,-178 Chickasaw, and $2,358 Cherokee.

[6] Dunbar Rowland, ed., *The Mississippi Territorial Archives, 1798–1803,* 484–85, Dearborn to Claiborne, June 11, 1802. McKee, as a special agent of the War Department, had visited Panton at Mobile in 1797. His offer to Panton had been made probably to secure Panton's influence over the Indians for the peaceful running of the boundary line with Spain. Following the receipt of this assurance from McKee, Panton had solicited and received permission from Governor Gayoso to accept Indian cessions in the United States. The Creek troubles prevented any immediate progress, and Panton died at sea March 26, 1801. John Forbes succeeded him as head of the firm, which retained its old name until 1804, when it became John Forbes and Company.

under pressure from Forbes, who saw in the new arrangement the only practicable method of bringing about a reassociation with funds lost for many years.[7]

Meanwhile, Hawkins, still trying for the Ocmulgee lands, requested Forbes to come and exert over the reluctant Creeks such influence as a creditor might naturally be supposed to have over a debtor. Forbes arrived among the Creeks when they were at Acheaubofau holding a conference with the four nations to consider a common policy on land cessions. To this conference boldly came William Augustus Bowles, apparently aware that Hawkins and Forbes were planning to seize him, but trusting in the devotion of his Miccosukee, the support of the Cherokees, whom he had summoned by special invitation, the aid of his Creek partisans, and probably the Creek custom that no act of violence be done in a peace town. All these things failed him: Forbes alienated the Seminoles by stipulating the elimination of Bowles as a prerequisite to accepting a land cession which, in the hope of getting trade restored, they were offering in payment of their debts and reparation for their robberies; the Cherokees (with whom Bowles lodged) apparently became convinced that he was an impostor when he was unable to show English credentials; his Creek supporters had boycotted the meeting as they did all meetings which discussed land sales; and Opoie Micco was so goaded by Hawkins that he finally ordered the seizure in a town dedicated to peace. The chiefs, embarrassed by the possession of their captive taken without premeditation, received and accepted from their thrifty agent the cynical advice to turn him over to Spain for the offered reward.[8]

[7] Silas Dinsmoor had been appointed Choctaw agent on March 12, 1802, but did not reach his post until August, traveling over the Natchez Trace and delaying among the Chickasaws to help settle a dispute between that tribe and certain Delawares living with them. Dinsmoor established his agency in the valley of the Chickasawhay near the present Quitman, Mississippi. In 1807 it was removed to the Pearl River Valley a few miles above Jackson. His trip south is described in a letter to Meigs, July 31, 1802. (I. O. R., Retired Classified Files). Robertson wrote to Meigs, December 18, 1802, that Forbes had tried to persuade the Chickasaws to sell their Mississippi front, but that the Chickasaws would sell only east of the Tennessee and north of the Duck (ibid.).

[8] Mrs. J. W. Greenslade, transcriber, "A Journal of John Forbes," *Florida Historical Society Quarterly*, Vol. IX, 279–89; I. O. R., Retired Classified Files,

Having thus consigned their would-be director general to a living death, the council proceeded to adopt a resolution that land sales in the future would be valid only if made by the entire nation. Forbes advised the Creeks to pay their Panton, Leslie and Company debts by selling the Ocmulgee land to the United States rather than by ceding Florida land to himself, but finally agreed (with the Seminoles) to take a cession on the Ochlocknee. The Chickasaws complained of the improper conduct of their agent, Samuel Mitchell and the Choctaws complained that their boundaries were being incorrectly run and marked.[9] The Cherokees complained that Meigs was threatening to take by force the road from Tellico to Athens (Georgia), which they had refused, and interpreted Hawkins' reassurances as advice not to grant.

The demand of the United States for the "Georgia Road" was based on the unwarranted assumption that it, by providing a shorter haulage for supplies to the government factory, would breathe new life into that moribund institution. Uninfluenced by such a prospect, the Cherokee council on April 20, 1803, had delivered a refusal so unanimous as to discourage any man less persistent than Meigs, who merely reported to Dearborn that their action reflected not hostility but apprehension. As a measure presumably of instilling in the tribe a more trusting spirit, Dearborn instructed Meigs to bribe Vann and other influential chiefs. Meigs apparently gave his attention to this diplomatic detail while the other chiefs were absent at Acheaubofau, only to find all his clandestine missionary work rendered vain by the report of the returning Cherokees that Hawkins had approved their refusal. When, in answer to his protest, Hawkins sent a written disavowal of any such approval, the Cherokees, rendered helpless by bribery and fearful of too greatly offending, gave way, and in October ceded the right of way. The Cherokees came to this decision on the occasion of receiving their annuities, which they observed were falling

Bowles to Cherokee chiefs, March 18, 1803. The Cherokee chiefs gave Bowles' invitation to Meigs, who sent a copy of it to Hawkins.

9 Wilkinson, after the signing of the Creek treaty of 1802, had gone to the Choctaws, with whom on October 17 he had made a convention for the marking of their line between the Chickasawhay and the Tombigbee. The Choctaws appointed Mingo Pooscoos and Latala Homa to represent them on the survey, which was finished August 31, 1803.

largely into the hands of Vann and his friends. After the concession, Meigs recommended the worthy Vann as a proper person to be employed in opening the road.[10]

While Forbes was among the Creeks urging the sale of their Ocmulgee lands, assisting in the undoing of Bowles, and tentatively agreeing with the Seminoles on a land cession in Florida, his agent, William Simpson, had conferred with Dinsmoor, Wilkinson, and the Choctaws in the Choctaw country. In September, Forbes came to take part in the discussions. A tribal cession was made difficult by disunity; none of the three divisions showed enthusiasm over relieving the others by a sale of its own territory. The willingness of the southeastern district to pay its debts by a cession of land between the Tombigbee and Alabama was perhaps induced by the knowledge that this territory was claimed by the Creeks.[11] The refusal of the United States to buy did not emanate from any reluctance to accept a clouded title, but from a desire for land on the Mississippi. As a preliminary to securing this, Wilkinson, with unwonted distrust of his own art of persuasion, in the fall of 1802 sent Homastubbee, the chief of the northern district, in which the desired lands lay, to Washington with a delegation of his chiefs to see the President.[12]

Pressure upon the Choctaws lightened with the Louisiana Purchase, but Cherokees and Creeks found no rest from the demands of a land-hungry country. In the spring of 1804, Meigs and Daniel Smith, as United States commissioners, invited the Cherokees to confer with them on the subject of ceding the Wafford tract in Georgia and their Kentucky and Tennessee lands north of line from the Duck to the Hiwassee. As a measure for promoting this additional subtraction from the Cherokees' dwindling domain, the commissioners were authorized to bribe Vann again: two or three hundred dollars was the amount estimated necessary to secure from him a second betrayal of his countrymen.[13] Suspecting, and

10 I. O. R., Retired Classified Files, minutes of the Cherokee council, April 20, 1803; Meigs to Dearborn, May 4, 1803; Dearborn to Meigs, May 30, 1803; Meigs to Hawkins, August 2, 1803; Hawkins to Meigs, September 30, 1803; Meigs to Dearborn, October 20 and October 25, 1803.

11 For the Creek protest against this Choctaw sale, see I. O. R., Retired Classified Files, Wilkinson to Dearborn, October 1, 1803.

12 Carter, *op. cit.*, V, 212.

perhaps knowing, that their chiefs were being bribed, the Cherokees countered by delegating all tribal business to Cheistoya, Broom, and Taluntuskee.[14] Whether the authority of Little Turkey had been terminated by his death or resignation it is impossible to say; the triumvirate was apparently a device for bridging the interval till his successor might be chosen. As an apparent result of the Cherokee defense measure, the commissioners in the treaty of Tellico, October 13 and 14, were able to secure only the small Wafford tract in Georgia; the Cherokees not only refused the larger cession, but on the day following the treaty entered a protest against the contemplated sale by the Chickasaws of land claimed by the Cherokees.[15]

We may legitimately suspect that the enterprise of getting the Ocmulgee lands from the Creeks had languished not only because of Wilkinson's preoccupation with the Choctaws, but also because of the virulence of Creek opposition and Hawkins' disapproval of Forbes' Seminole grant.[16] Opposition to land cessions was but one item in a chronic anti-Americanism which condemned the entire progressive movement and demanded a return to the primitive life of communism and isolation. The heart and soul of the movement was the aged and unrepentant Tame King, whose avowed purpose was to deliver the Creeks from evil by chasing Hawkins back to his ancestral home. From Opoie Micco, nominal chief of a nation hopelessly divided, Hawkins and Meriwether, who had been sent by Dearborn to assist him, had secured a promise to lead a Creek delegation to Washington; but the trip continued to be postponed, ostensibly because of deaths and sickness

[13] I. O. R. War Department Letter Book B, Dearborn to Meigs, April 23, 1804.

[14] I. O. R., Retired Classified Files, Cheistoya to Meigs, August 28, 1804.

[15] *Ibid.*, October 15, 1804. For the Wafford tract the Cherokees received $5,000 and an annuity of $1,000. This treaty remained unratified and apparently forgotten until 1824. At that date the War Department could find no copy of the treaty except the duplicate which the Cherokees possessed.

[16] The grant to Forbes of the land between the Apalachicola and Wakulla rivers, made May 25, 1804, at Cheeskatalofa, was in compensation for the two seizures of Panton's store on the Wakulla by Bowles in 1792 and 1800. The deed was signed by twenty-two chiefs of the Seminoles and Lower Creeks. The grant cancelled $47,000 of the Creek debt, being damages of $27,000 at 6 per cent interest. The grant contained about 1,500,000 acres of land (*American State Papers, Public Lands*, IV, 81–87; *Indian Affairs*, I, 750–51, Forbes to Dearborn, September 5, 1806).

in the delegation, actually, perhaps, because of internal dissensions. Finally, in November, 1804, Hawkins met Opoie Micco and some of the opposing chiefs at his agency on the Flint and, overruling the chief's desire for a further postponement because of the small Creek representation, pressed for a decision. The bedeviled speaker braved the turbulence of the opposition so far as to offer a cession of the land for enough to pay their debts and give each town an annuity of $500; the Forbes purchase, he hinted, had already materially decreased the debt, and, since the United States was selling land for two dollars an acre, it could afford to pay the price asked. At the introduction of this mercenary note into the proceedings, Hawkins apparently became so agitated as to forget his instructions and offered the Creeks $200,000 in United States stock at 6 per cent interest for the land desired. This Opoie Micco continued to refuse until the conference began to experience the throes of dissolution, when, with an unexplained change of heart, he accepted, subject to formal ratification at Tuckabatchee.[17]

The agitation for a Choctaw cession, which Dearborn had apparently permitted to languish after the Louisiana Purchase, had been continued by creditor Forbes with so much vigor that in August, 1804, the United States received a petition secured by Forbes from the northern district of the tribe asking the United States to buy the land between the Big Black and the Yazoo so that the district could pay its debts. Unable to neglect any opportunity of securing land, even if unneeded and undesired, Dearborn appointed James Robertson and Dinsmoor commissioners to treat with both Choctaws and Chickasaws. They were to secure, if possible, all the Choctaw Mississippi front, and all the Chickasaw front north of a line from the Duck to the Mississippi, as well as their land northeast of the Tennessee. The past friendliness of the two tribes would be rewarded by allowing them a price of two cents an acre for their lands on the Mississippi, which was double the price usually paid for Indian land. For the other Chickasaw lands such a high price was unjustified even by sentiment, since the lands in question were claimed by the Cherokees. Ethics

[17] *Indian Affairs*, I, 691–92. Hawkins to Dearborn, November 3, 1804.

forbade the United States to buy from any one the property of another except at a reasonable price.

For the Choctaw conference to be held at St. Stephens in June, Dinsmoor went to New Orleans and brought in a stock of provisions such as no Indian and few commissioners had ever seen before.[18] Whether by his extraordinary outlay Dinsmoor hoped to strengthen the diplomatic powers of the commissioners or to soften the hearts of the Indians, his labor was done in vain, for to the chagrin of the well-fed commissioners, the chiefs of the northern district refused to make any cession at any price. Either the chiefs had experienced a change of heart for which there is no explanation in the scanty remaining records, or else the petition of the preceding year had been fraudulently obtained. It is not to be supposed that the commissioners relied exclusively upon entertainment to alter the determination of the strangely resolute chiefs, but made liberal use of those allied arts of bribery and intimidation, which had become basic ingredients of American Indian diplomacy. Finally, perhaps when the larder began to show signs of complete exhaustion, they adjourned the futile conference till November and set out for the Chickasaws.

---

[18] No account of this abortive conference is given in *Indian Affairs*. The conduct of the commissioners called forth a reprimand from Dearborn: "Mr. Chambers' bill for necessaries, conveniences, and luxuries for the commissioners very far exceeds what had been contemplated. . . . Among the extraordinary articles for an Indian treaty in the woods for two commissioners may be noticed the amount of $200 for raisins, anchovies, cinnamon, nutmegs, pickles, etc., and other articles in like proportion" (I. O. R., Letter Book B, 100–101, Dearborn to Robertson, August 2, 1805).

"The document which has been presented to my view and which has occasioned more surprise than any other is Mr. Chambers' bill for articles furnished Commissioners, particularly such as appear to have been intended for their own use. Those articles, generally, so far exceed what I could have contemplated as to produce impressions not very favorable to the prudence or discretion of those who directed the arrangements. . . . The quantity and expense of articles of the highest luxury, such as could not have been intended for Indians, exceed all reasonable bounds. The amount of the most delicate spices, anchovies, raisins, almonds, hyson tea, coffee, mustard, preserves, English cheese, segars, brandy, wine, etc., etc., etc., could not have been either necessary or useful. Many of the articles ought never to have appeared on a bill of expenses for an Indian treaty, especially in the wilderness. . . . Such accounts of expenses at an Indian treaty have, I presume, never before been exhibited to our Government, and it is to be wished we may never have a second exhibition of the kind" (*ibid.*, 101–102, Dearborn to Dinsmoor, August 28, 1805).

Although the commissioners disregarded their instructions to hold the Chickasaw conference in the "principal town" in favor of a meeting at the Bluffs, where the factory provided greater facilities of food and drink, it may be assumed that they did not neglect Dearborn's injunction to inform Colbert and other reluctant chiefs "early in the negotiations" that they could expect special consideration "for their friendly dispositions." The conference, which opened July 17, attracted, in addition to Colbert and other chiefs, former Agent John McKee, a representative of John Forbes, and a throng of traders bent on vending their liquid wares. No amount of "consideration," however, could induce the chiefs to cede any land except that northeast of the Tennessee. Of the $20,000 that they were to receive for this disputed territory, the Chickasaws were to pay Forbes $12,000 in liquidation of their debts. On the necessity of paying these private debts through a tribal land cession, Colbert and Simpson, by an interchange of letters (read at the conference on Colbert's insistence), had agreed, but the Chickasaws questioned unavailingly their obligation to assume the debts of the white traders among them and protested successfully the payment of interest, the justification for which was beyond their understanding. With a caution inherited perhaps from his Scotch father, Colbert insisted that the $20,000 should be paid in specie in the Chickasaw country. He would not give Simpson an order on the United States for the amount due, but did give him a written promise to pay as soon as the money arrived. Future debts, Colbert grimly commented, would have to be paid by the individuals contracting them. The treaty, signed July 23, 1805, stipulated that, in addition to the $20,000 for the land, the United States should pay chiefs Colbert and Ockoy $1,000 each for services (unspecified) and give King Tinebe an annuity of $100 as a "testimony to his personal worth and friendly disposition."[19]

[19] The seventy-page journal of the Chickasaw commission is in I. O. R., Retired Classified Files, July 6–25, 1805. Detailed as it is, it should be supplemented by Heloise H. Cruzat, transcriber, "Journal of an Indian Talk," *Florida Historical Society Quarterly*, Vol. VIII, 131–42. The treaty is in Kappler, *op. cit.*, II, 79–80. For a map of the cession see Royce, *Indian Land Cessions*, plates CLXI and CLXIII.

After the failure of the Choctaw conference in June, Dearborn had upbraided the northern chiefs for their "unmanly and dishonest behavior," declaring his intention to charge them with the entire cost of the conference, including, presumably, the extensive bill of fare for the commissioners themselves. On their return to the Choctaws in November, the commissioners were instructed to negotiate with the southeastern chiefs for a cession of the Tombigbee lands, which the United States had formerly refused to buy. But no such cession was made, whether because the commissioners broke their instructions and refused to buy or because the Choctaws, perhaps as a result of Creek protests, refused to sell. Only the strenuous efforts of Forbes, seeing the payment of his Choctaw debts a second time eluding him, finally induced the Choctaws to grant and the commissioners to accept a cession of land along the Florida border between the Mississippi and the Tombigbee. Of the $50,500 to be given for this territory, $48,000 was to go directly to Forbes for the debt. The tribe received an annuity of $3,000, and three of the chiefs were to receive $500 each, plus an annuity of $150. Samuel Mitchell, their former agent, was one of the witnesses to this treaty, into which the Choctaws, in humor or humanity, had a provision inserted for the support of his two illegitimate Choctaw children.[20]

While Robertson and Dinsmoor were regaling themselves and practicing among the Choctaws and Chickasaws those arts of diplomacy deemed most suitable for Indian comprehension, Hawkins and Meriwether, their former treaty rejected by the Senate, continued to beset the distracted Creeks for a cession of the Ocmulgee lands. A council called by Opoie Micco at Tuckabatchee on June 26 to hear them on "the subject of their mission" seems to have attracted a full attendance except from the Creeks themselves. In addition to Hawkins and Meriwether, there were

[20] Kappler, *op. cit.*, II, 87–89; *Indian Affairs*, I, 750–51, Forbes to Dearborn September 5, 1806; James D. Richardson, ed., *Message and Papers of the Presidents, 1789–1817*, I, 434–35. Jefferson was so disappointed in the treaty that he did not submit it to the Senate until January 15, 1808, when American relations with Spain were of such a nature as to give value to a tract on the Florida line. For Forbes' further difficulties in collecting this debt, see R. S. Cotterill, "A Chapter of Panton, Leslie and Company," *Journal of Southern History*, Vol. X, 275–92.

present certain commissioners from Georgia, urging, to the dismay of the Creeks and the exasperation of Hawkins, the fulfillment of the twice-outlawed "treaties" of Galphinton and Shoulderbone. Thirty-seven Cherokee chiefs attended for the double purpose of consulting Opoie Micco on the then prospective sale by the Chickasaws of land allegedly Cherokee, and of enjoying a vacation from the demands of Meigs and Smith for another land cession. A delegation was there from the "western nations" seeking to enlist the Creeks in an allied war against the Osages, who at that time seem to have been disporting themselves with even more than their customary unneighborliness. Delegations from the Chickasaws and Choctaws were expected, although it is not evident that they ever arrived. On the other hand, the meeting was boycotted by the Fat King and his adherents fanatically opposed to the civilizing program, of which land cessions seemed to be a fundamental feature.

The meeting listened, doubtless with sympathy, to the representatives of the "western nations," who claimed with a probable lack of precision that their talk had already been taken by fourteen nations, including the Choctaws, Chickasaws, Cherokees, Delawares, and Shawnees. Although war against the Osages was always popular and generally in progress among the Southern Indians, the Tuckabatchee meeting seems to have taken no official action, owing doubtless to the efforts of Hawkins, who, with the other agents, had been instructed to prevent an attack on a tribe now, since the Louisiana Purchase, under the protection of the United States. The Cherokee delineation of Chickasaw iniquity caused the Creeks to become greatly agitated but apparently produced no additional activity. The chief worry of Opoie Micco was the defiant and disdainful absence of the opposition, without whose presence no legal cession could be made. Having in vain sent an express to the Fat King to ascertain his reasons for so conducting himself, Opoie Micco proposed, since the opposition would not come to the council, to take the council to the opposition and to hold a meeting at Ossitchee. Hawkins vetoed this proposal, remembering certain insults and indignities tendered the commissioners at that place the preceding year and likely to be repeated and multiplied at a second opportunity. His counsel that Opoie Micco take his warriors and compel the opposition to come to Tuckabatchee was rejected by Opoie Micco for the less logical and less impossible project of holding an exclusively Indian meeting with the opposition at Cusseta.

As a preliminary to this meeting, called for July 23, Hawkins repeated to the chiefs, at Opoie Micco's request, the talk he had made at the Tuckabatchee conference to the effect that they should act without regard to the opposition and should make the land cession in return for the help of the United States in promoting civilization among them. The Cusseta meeting, as was to be expected, settled nothing. The opposition attended (since Hawkins was not there), stormily opposed a cession of any kind, and at one time in a caucus among themselves drafted a letter to Hawkins threatening to run him out of the Creek country or confine him among the Upper Creeks. Opoie Micco had enough remaining influence to prevent this composition from being sent. He called another Creek meeting for Tuckabatchee in ten days, at which time the attending chiefs authorized the sending of a delegation to Washington to confer with President Jefferson.[21]

The Cherokees went home from Tuckabatchee perhaps exulting that they were too late for the conference which they had promised to hold with Meigs and Smith at Watkin's Ferry on the Hiwassee on July 2. They did not, however, escape the subject, for the commissioners continued to batter at them throughout the summer and into the fall of 1805. The triumvirate appointed the preceding year had resigned their powers to the national council, which chose Black Fox (Inali) as chief of the nation succeeding Little Turkey. This measure apparently made no contribution to healing the schisms or composing the factions rending the nation. Taluntuskee and Doublehead were so at odds with the national council that they fell an easy prey to Meigs' by no means subtle exercises in bribery. Vann was a chronic traitor, whose services Meigs could command any time he needed subterranean assistance.

[21] *Letters of Benjamin Hawkins*, 431–446; I. O. R., Retired Classified Files, Hawkins to Meigs, June 12, 1805.

With the help of these worthies, Meigs and Smith finally gathered the elusive Cherokees together and inveigled them into two treaties at Tellico on October 25 and 27. By these treaties the hapless Cherokees ceded all their remaining land north of the Duck and a line thence to the Hiwassee and, in addition, the right of way for two roads, one from Stone's River to the Georgia Road and the other from Tellico through Muscle Shoals to the Tombigbee. Provisions in the treaty for certain reservations designed for Doublehead and Taluntuskee reveal the ethical machinery of the negotiations; other chiefs doubtless received their rewards in ways less susceptible to investigation by their betrayed countrymen. For their concessions at these times the Cherokees received (in addition to the bribes) a payment of $15,600 and an annuity of $3,000. They also had the comfort of knowing that some of the money was for land claimed by the Chickasaws and already sold by them.[22]

The Creek delegation which journeyed to Washington in the fall of 1805 had been carefully screened to include only chiefs thoroughly committed to "co-operation" with the United States. William McIntosh, just beginning his parasitic career, headed the delegation and was its spokesman in interviews with the President on November 2 and 3. Jefferson requested not only a re-cession of the Ocmulgee lands (at a lower price) but also the road through Creek territory from the Ocmulgee to Fort Stoddart, which Hawkins had assured the Creeks they could defer. McIntosh in reply asserted that the United States, with the Tennessee River navigation and the Natchez Trace, did not need the road it was asking, which, if it were granted, would only cause trouble between Creeks and travelers. He did not refuse a re-cession of the Ocmulgee land but insisted on the original price, saying that the Creeks had previously sold their land too cheaply but had learned from half-bloods and white men what it was really worth. The result of this verbal fencing was that on November 15 the Creeks signed a treaty granting the road and re-ceding their land east of

---

[22] *Indian Affairs*, I, 677; Royce, *The Cherokee Nation*, 190–93; Kappler, *op. cit.*, II, 82–83; Royce, *Indian Land Cessions*, plate CLXI.

the Ocmulgee in return for an annuity of $12,000 for eight years, to be followed by one of $11,000 for the next ten.[23]

Although the Cherokees had advanced considerably in civilization since the United States had begun its instruction in 1792, they were still too primitive to appreciate the technique of bribery and corruption as practiced by Meigs and Smith. Popular opinion was forming to ostracize the offenders, and the national council was deliberating their death. Under such uncongenial conditions, the United States, still unsated, thought it best to conduct its further negotiations in Washington, where the chiefs would be unhampered by vulgar disapproval of their conduct. Doublehead, Vann, and Taluntuskee led the delegation which accompanied the faithful Meigs to the seat of government, and there on January 7, 1806, ceded to the United States their land between the Duck and the Tennessee.[24] The ease with which this cession was obtained is not to be explained wholly by the reservations made for certain chiefs nor by the $100 annuity given to Black Fox. The land ceded had all been claimed by the Chickasaws and sold by them in part to the United States the preceding year. It was territory that the Cherokees had perhaps never owned, had probably never occupied, and would, since the Chickasaw cession, certainly never possess. The Cherokees were, therefore, perhaps justified in considering the $10,000 they received as in the nature of a gratuity.

The epidemic of land cessions which for several years had been devastating the Southern Indians ended with the Cherokee pact of 1806, and seven years passed before a Southern tribe suffered a recurrence of the plague. Indian respite during this period was the result not of Indian resistance, but of the forbearance of the United States, distracted by a vain struggle for neutrality, an assertion of doubtful claims to a portion of West Florida, and the

23 Kappler, *op. cit.*, II, 85–86; I. O. R., Letter Book B, 154–60, conversation of McIntosh with the President. The treaty was signed by Oche Haujo, McIntosh, and four others. Hawkins and Timothy Barnard were among the witnesses.

24 *Indian Affairs*, I, 704; Kappler, *op. cit.*, II, 90–91; Royce, *Indian Land Cessions*, plate CLXI. The treaty was signed by Doublehead, Vann, Taluntuskee, Chulioa, Sour Mush, Turtle at Home, Broom, John Jolly, and six others. Benjamin Hawkins was one of the witnesses.

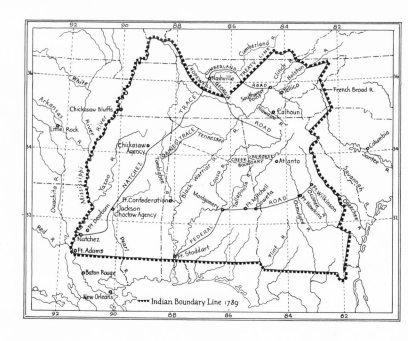

Indian Boundary Line 1789

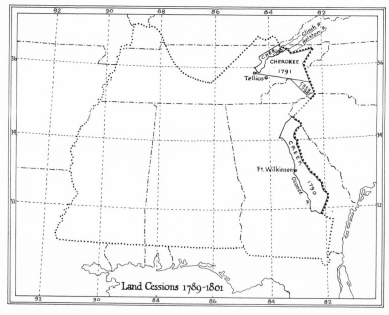

Land Cessions 1789-1801

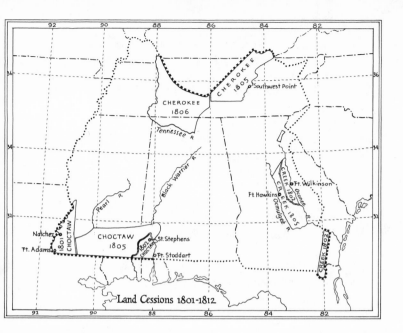

Land Cessions 1801-1812

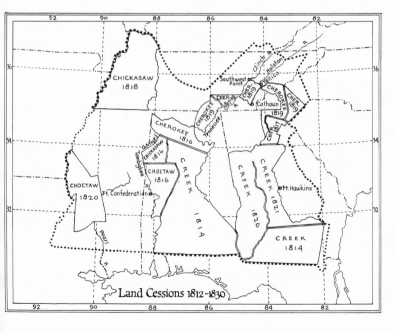

Land Cessions 1812-1830

prosecution of an alleged conspiracy on the part of Aaron Burr.

The passing of the plague left behind it many dissatisfactions and discontents. After the cession of 1805, Hawkins returned to his task of promoting civilization and discord among the Creeks, but his illness in 1806 gave his charges the pleasure of a postponement in the opening of the road they had so reluctantly granted in their last treaty.[25] It was probably with equal satisfaction that in May, 1806, they refused a demand by Forbes that they pay, out of the proceeds of their Ocmulgee lands sale, the remainder of their debt to him; from their treaty of cession they had, with Hawkins' approval and probably at his suggestion, omitted any stipulation for such a payment, and they now contended that the debt had been cancelled by the Seminole cession.[26]

Among the Choctaws, Dinsmoor was absent from his agency the greater part of 1806, presumably recuperating from his diplomatic and gastronomical efforts of the preceding year. Without unmerited disparagement of the agent, it might be said that Choctaw affairs ran as smoothly without as with him, but exaggerated rumors of Spanish overtures caused the War Department in September, 1806, to order him back to his agency.

There was considerable discontent among the Choctaws with the treaty of 1805, but apparently it found its only active expression in a refusal (in all probability temporary) by certain disgruntled chiefs to accept presents proffered by the United States.[27] There is no evidence that the Choctaws experienced any distress because the treaty failed to be ratified and Forbes' debt consequently left unpaid.

[25] This road, commonly called the Federal Road, was a horse path and was to be used by the United States only for the mail service. Consequently it was the Post Office Department that was most interested in seeing it opened. In April, 1806, the postmaster general instructed Hawkins to open the road from Athens, Georgia, through Coweta and Tuckabatchee to Fort Stoddart on the Tombigbee. The road was to be from four to six feet wide and was to have trees felled across the streams. Hawkins, being ill, entrusted the opening of the Athens-Coweta section to Meriwether and stationed at Tuckabatchee a postrider who promised to make twenty-five miles a day through Creek territory. In February, 1807, the postmaster general appointed Dennison Darling as postmaster at Coweta and postrider from Athens to Fort Stoddart. The correspondence on this subject is given in Carter, *op. cit.*, V, 395–515.

[26] *Indian Affairs*, I, 750–51, Forbes to Dearborn, September 5, 1806.

[27] Carter, *op. cit.*, 434, Toulmin to Lattimore, December 6, 1805.

The Chickasaws in May, 1806, received a new agent in the person of Thomas Wright, Silas Mitchell having departed after his discharge without leaving behind him any of those pledges of affection such as had signalized his residence among the Choctaws.[28] The Chickasaws were feeling outraged by the Cherokee presumption in ceding territory already ceded by the Chickasaws and apprehensive over their cession of land the Chickasaws still retained. With Dearborn's assurance that purchase of the Cherokee claim did not constitute a denial of Chickasaw ownership, Colbert seemed temporarily appeased.[29]

Among the Cherokees the most evident aftermath of the January treaty was an increasing condemnation of the chiefs who had negotiated it. In the summer of 1807 came the killing of Doublehead, who had formerly faithfully defended and lately faithlessly betrayed the interests of his countrymen. Since the offender had recently supplemented treason with murder, it is uncertain whether his death resulted from private vengeance or public decree.[30] The death of Doublehead was an embarrassment to Meigs, whom he had promised (doubtless for a consideration) to aid in running the east line of the recent cession in such a way as to enclose considerably more land than had been ceded. Deprived of Doublehead's service, Meigs was compelled to have recourse to the more open and less promising method of applying to the national council, which evasively withheld its consent. Undismayed by this lack of co-operation, Meigs collected a coterie of chiefs open to inducements—Black Fox, Glass, Turtle at Home, Richard Brown, and Sowolotah—with whose connivance and aid he and James Robertson on September 7 ran the more ample line. The open "convention" which recorded this performance awarded the Cherokee tribe $2,000 for the land taken; a secret provision gave $1,000 and two rifles to the chiefs "transacting the business." Meigs, as successful in prophecy as in diplomacy, com-

28 I. O. R., War Department Letter Book B, 224, Dearborn to Wright May 27, 1806.

29 *Ibid.*, War Department Letter Book B, 171–74, Dearborn to Colbert, and Colbert to Dearborn, February 21, 1806. Colbert was evidently in Washington at this time.

30 Brown, *op. cit.*, 451–53.

mented that the co-operating chiefs would have their hands full explaining to the Cherokees and, consequently well deserved this "silent" consideration.[31] In contrast to this transaction, the treaty of December 2, ceding to the United States a small tract on Chickamauga Creek for iron works, appears a reputable affair, and the opposition of Vann indicates that it was in the tribal interest.[32]

The experiment in corruption performed by Meigs had involved mainly, or at least most successfully, the chiefs of the Lower Cherokees, who at one time had shown the most unrelenting hostility to the United States. These, however, owed their selection for this honor neither to their present habitation nor former belligerency, but to their control of the tribal government. Their position not only exposed them to the seductions of bribery but also permitted them to distribute among themselves and their friends the annuities sent to the tribe as a whole. The resentment of the Upper Cherokees against this monopoly of annuities (and perhaps against the monopoly of bribes) reached such a height early in 1808 that they sent a delegation to Washington to explain their grievances. To Jefferson, the delegation, after recounting the manifold derelictions of the Lower Cherokees (tactfully omitting the subject of bribery), proposed that the two districts dissolve the political bonds which had hitherto connected them and that the Upper Cherokees become citizens of the United States. Jefferson's approval was burdened with the impossible condition that the two districts agree on a dividing line; the opposition to a division, he suggested, might, if a minority, express its disapproval by removing west of the Mississippi, where it would receive new territory in exchange for that abandoned.[33]

For Jefferson, the idea of a Cherokee division had little interest and that of United States citizenship for the Cherokees no interest at all, since neither afforded any prospects of land ces-

[31] *Indian Affairs*, I, 754, Meigs to Dearborn, September 28, 1807.

[32] Elias Earle of South Carolina early in 1807 proposed to the United States that he would erect and manage the iron works if the Cherokees would cede the land. Meigs paid, or promised, $5,000 for the land. Because of objections from Tennessee, the Senate postponed action on the treaty until 1810 and then rejected it (Royce, *The Cherokee Nation*, 199–201; *Indian Affairs*, I, 722, 753).

[33] I. O. R., War Department Letter Book B, 376, Jefferson to the Upper Cherokee delegation, May 4, 1808, and Dearborn to Meigs, May 5, 1808.

sions, and the former, as Meigs warned him, effectually denied it. What he desired was Cherokee removal, since thereby the coveted Indian territory could be secured more readily and completely than by the tried methods of civilization, coercion, and corruption, although these might, and in fact did, continue to be useful as accessories.[34] Following the Washington conference, while the Upper Cherokees, in accordance with Jefferson's advice, attempted to reach an agreement with the Lower Cherokees on a tribal division, Meigs, in accordance with his instructions, investigated and promoted the sentiment for tribal removal. Black Fox, Taluntuskee, Glass, John Jolly, and other chiefs who had shown themselves amenable to persuasion on former occasions, now, doubtless for the same reasons, became advocates of removal. At an illegal and clandestine council, held in concert with Meigs in Tennessee, Black Fox named a delegation to visit Washington and sign an agreement for removal. But the resolute resistance of Major Ridge, the killer (or executioner) of Doublehead, not only thwarted the plan but brought about the deposition of Black Fox and the appointment of a delegation representative of both districts.[35]

To the Upper Cherokee delegates asking for a division of the tribe on the line of the Hiwassee Mountains, Jefferson replied that the United States would recognize such an arrangement only if the Lower Cherokees agreed. The Lower Cherokees he advised to send exploring parties to the country of the White and Arkansas rivers.[36] Apparently the first of the Lower Cherokees to follow this advice was Taluntuskee, whose readiness to emigrate was perhaps not wholly uninfluenced by the fate of his brother-in-law, Doublehead. In the spring of 1809 he led an exploring party to Arkansas, as a result of which he reported to Meigs in July that he had 1,130 Cherokees ready to remove.[37] Some of the

[34] The classical treatment of the preliminaries to removal is Annie Heloise Abel's *The History of Events Resulting in Indian Consolidation West of the Mississippi*, The American Historical Association *Annual Report* (1906).

[35] Thomas L. McKenney and James Hall, *A History of the Indian Tribes of North America*, II, 90-91.

[36] I. O. R., War Department Letter Book B, 414-17, Jefferson to Cherokee Deputies, January 1, 1809.

[37] *Ibid.*, Retired Classified Files, Meigs to Cherokee council at Willstown, November 2, 1809.

sycophant chiefs doubtless considered it advisable to emigrate first and explore later.

At the time that there seemed to be no escape from the dilemma of division or removal, both equally repugnant to the rank and file of the Cherokees, the bickering chiefs, perhaps compelled by popular opinion, composed their differences and restored a measure of unity to the disintegrating tribe. In September the national council appointed a committee of thirteen, to which it entrusted the management of the nation; no chief who had taken a prominent part in the recent orgy of land cessions, in the advocacy of division, or in the agitation for removal attained membership on this committee.[38] The renewed unity of the tribe revealed itself in rejecting overtures for a cession of its Kentucky land,[39] in the adoption of an act of amnesty accompanied by a prohibition of clan vegeance,[40] in a formal dissociation of the tribe from the policy of removal,[41] and in the refusal of a request from the United States for a right of way from east Tennessee to the Coosa.

At the same time that the Cherokees were being asked to grant a right of way from eastern Tennessee to Turkeytown on the Coosa, the Creeks were solicited to grant its continuance through their territory to Fort Stoddart. The desire of the United States for such a road arose from dissatisfaction with affairs in West Florida, where the Spaniards continued to deny the territorial claims of the United States and to hamper with tolls the sending of supplies past Mobile to the factory at St. Stephens. The road from Georgia to Fort Stoddart, granted by the Creeks in 1805, began to be used in the spring of 1807, but the jealous Creeks restricted its use to the mails as had been stipulated in the treaty. In 1808, Hawkins had been instructed to get Creek consent for

[38] *Ibid.*, Retired Classified Files, Cherokee chiefs to Meigs, September 27, 1809. In this letter only eleven of the thirteen members of the committee are named: John McIntosh, The Ridge, Richard Brown, Turtle at Home, Charles Hicks, John Walker, George Waters, Thomas Pettite, Doghead, George Lowry, and Tur-cock.

[39] *Ibid.*, War Department Letter Book C, 2, Secretary of War to Meigs, July 15, 1809. In 1808 the tribe had rejected similar overtures for some of their remaining Tennessee land (Royce, *The Cherokee Nation*, 201–202).

[40] Mooney, *Myths of the Cherokee*, 86–87; *Indian Affairs*, II, 283.

[41] I. O. R., Retired Classified Files, Cherokee Managers to Meigs, April 11, 1810.

horse mails down the Coosa route; and in 1810, Meigs asked the same of the Cherokees as far as their territory extended. Both tribes refused.[42] The refusal was owing not only to a justified suspicion of ulterior motives on the part of the United States but also to conflicting claims to the Upper Coosa country, which was beginning to trouble Creek-Cherokee relations.

In April, 1809, James McIntosh had taken a boat load of merchandise down the Conasauga and Coosa destined for the white settlements on the Tombigbee. At Turkeytown, a Cherokee town on Creek territory, he had been stopped by the Creek chief, Tustenugge, who notified Hawkins. Investigation revealed certain irregularities such as a forged passport from Hawkins and a forged letter from the President to the Cherokee chiefs. Tustenuggee's confiscation of the cargo inspired a protest from McIntosh to Meigs, and from Meigs to Hawkins, but Hawkins refused to release the cargo.[43] Not anticipating, or perhaps disregarding, the attitude of the two tribes the Secretary of War William Eustis in June, 1810, instructed the commanding officer at Fort Stoddart to send Captain Gaines to explore the country along the Black Warrior–Coosa divide to the Hiwassee and back by way of the Hightower (Etowah) and Coosa while Captain Wilkinson went up the Federal Road and the Coosa to join him on the Hiwassee.[44] In the fall of 1810, after these explorations were made, the Creeks protested to Washington, and in January, 1811, they had the dubious satisfaction of an assurance from Madison that the surveyors were only locating a possible roadway and had no designs on their land.[45] When the Creek council again refused consent, Hawkins was instructed by the irritated Secretary of War to inform them that the United States was determined to have the road with or without Creek consent.[46] In December,

---

[42] *Ibid.*, War Department Letter Book B, 408, Dearborn to Hawkins December 12, 1808; *ibid.*, Retired Classified Files, Meigs to Cherokee council, April 2, 1810, and Meigs to Dearborn, July 20, 1810.

[43] *Ibid.*, Retired Classified Files, Meigs to Hawkins, February 25, 1810, and Hawkins to Secretary of War Eustis, December 31, 1810.

[44] Carter, *op. cit.*, VI, 76–77, Secretary of War to Sparks, June 23, 1810.

[45] *Ibid.*, VI, 170, Secretary of War to Hawkins, January 15, 1811; I. O. R., War Department Letter Book C, 58, President to Creek chiefs, January 14, 1811.

[46] I. O. R., Retired Classified Files, Creek Micco to President Madison, May

1811, Hawkins reported that the road through his agency was completed.[47]

In this post-cession period the Chickasaws also had their storms of discontent, all of which seemed to center around George Colbert. After receiving Dearborn's assurance in 1806 on the matter of the Cherokee cession, he had attempted without success to secure a Cherokee recognition of the boundaries claimed by the Chickasaws. As a result, he forwarded to Washington a remonstrance against the purchase of Chickasaw land from the Cherokees. The remonstrance, signed by twenty-nine chiefs, undoubtedly reflected the continuing indignation and apprehension of the nation. The Chickasaws named Meigs as the architect of their troubles, suspecting him of engineering the land purchase and of stimulating the Cherokees against a boundary agreement.[48] Meigs' denial of the accusation was belied by his advice to the Cherokees in November, 1809, to assert their claim to the land between the Shoals and the Tombigbee "while you can remember that you once ceded a road through it."[49] The alacrity with which the Cherokees accepted this advice did not improve Chickasaw relations with the Cherokees nor increase their confidence in the Cherokee agent.[50]

In March, 1809, Colbert complained of white intruders on Chickasaw land, intimating that if this complaint went unheeded, as his others had done, he would himself remove the trespassers. In return for the removal of the intruders, he promised that the Chickasaws would sell to the United States the Cherokee land east of the Elk, which the United States had already bought from both Cherokees and Chickasaws.[51] How well founded was Colbert's complaint was shown when Meigs, after receiving three

---

15, 1811; *ibid.*, War Department Letter Book C, 85–86, 91, Secretary of War to Hawkins, June 27, 1811, and July 20, 1811.

[47] I. O. R., War Department Letter Book C, 105, Secretary of War to Hawkins, December 14, 1811.

[48] *Ibid.*, Retired Classified Files, Meigs to Dearborn, March 1, 1809.

[49] *Ibid.*, Retired Classified Files, Meigs to Cherokee council, November 2, 1809.

[50] *Ibid.*, Retired Classified Files, Cherokee Managers to Meigs, April 11, 1810.

[51] Carter, *op. cit.*, V, 720–22, Freeman to the Secretary of the Treasury, March 4, 1809.

orders, removed 284 trespassing families, requiring fifty-one days to complete the work.[52] Two weeks later the watchful Colbert reported that the intruders were all back again and charged that their return had been with Meigs' connivance and probably at his request; he demanded that someone other than Meigs be in charge of future removals. Meigs retorted that not only had the intruders not returned, but that their original trespass had been on land really belonging to the Cherokees; the Chickasaws, he said, did not even know where their Old Fields were till the Cherokees told them.[53] This interchange of amenities seems to have ended the debate, leaving, as is the habit of debates, the situation unremedied.

In January, 1810, James Neelly, the Chickasaw agent, having been "much teased" by the Chickasaw king and headmen and unable to extract from the Secretary of War any reply to his letters, appealed to Governor Holmes of Mississippi Territory, apparently recalling the almost forgotten fact that the governor of that territory was also superintendent of Southern Indians. The fact that there were now (by unstable Chickasaw counting) four or five thousand intruders, making the Indians a minority party in their own home, stirred the Governor to send Colonel Russell to order their removal.[54] Since the intruders remained impervious to such hints, the War Department in the late spring of 1810 established an army post at Muscle Shoals, from which the Chickasaws, now at the end of their patience, might draw assistance against the intruders overrunning them. The squatters were to be allowed to remain on their illegal holdings until they had harvested their crops and then were to be removed by military force.[55]

The post at Muscle Shoals superseded that at Hiwassee, which

[52] *Ibid.*, V, 739–40 Meigs to Smith (acting secretary of war), June 12, 1809.

[53] I. O. R., Retired Classified Files, Smith to Meigs, July 2, 1809; Meigs to Smith, August 12, 1809.

[54] Carter, *op. cit.*, VI, 44–47, Holmes to Secretary of War, February 7, 1810; *ibid.*, VI, 48, Holmes to Wade Hampton, February 9, 1810. Neelly was appointed Chickasaw agent July 8, 1809, succeeding Thomas Wright, who had died September 20, 1808. The Chickasaws had asked that Neelly be appointed.

[55] *Ibid.*, VI, 70–71, Secretary of War to Wade Hampton, June 15, 1810. The post was placed at Muscle Shoals on the recommendation of Meigs. It was completed about June 1, 1810.

had by 1810 become even more than usually useless. Both the military post and the Cherokee factory had been removed to Hiwassee in the summer of 1807, the former from Southwest Point, the latter from Tellico. General and individual tribulations combined to effect the decay of all the Southern factories except Chickasaw Bluffs in this period. The Napoleonic wars made the securing of factory goods difficult, dangerous, and expensive; the Embargo act made impossible the exportation of peltries, which were the chief reliance of the Southern trade and were little in demand in the United States. By the factory law, apparently designed to embarrass the factories, sales of Indian products were made through auctions held six times a year and only twice in any one state. The Indians, even when not actually hostile to the factories, preferred to deal with the licensed and unlicensed traders, who furnished better goods at lower prices and delivered them in the Indian towns.[56]

The Cherokee factory prospered as little at Hiwassee as at Tellico and was abandoned in 1810, apparently on Meigs' advice. The Creek factory, removed to Fort Hawkins (Macon) in the fall of 1806, continued there the decline it had experienced at Fort Wilkinson; no further supplies were sent it after 1811. No southern factory was so beset by misfortunes as was the Choctaw factory at St. Stephens. Its location was low and unhealthful; Indians could reach it only after a long journey, of which the latter part led through the settlements of objecting white men; supplies could reach it only through Mobile, where the Spanish, deaf to all American arguments concerning the natural privileges of government-owned merchandise and the ameliorating influence of the factory on Indian dispositions, continued to exact their high and customary tolls. The War Department was considering its removal and was trying to find a place accessible both to customers and supplies, without which it could not exert its full influence. In search of such a location Lieutenant E. P. Gaines,

[56] The vicissitudes of the factory system are described in a report by John Mason, superintendent of Indian trade, to the House of Representatives, February 17, 1809 (*Indian Affairs*, I, 756). Mason had succeeded Shea as superintendent in 1807 and had removed the headquarters of the factory system from Philadelphia to Georgetown, D. C.

a brother of the factor, was ordered to explore the region between the Tennessee and the Tombigbee and to investigate the navigation potentialities of the latter stream. Gaines fulfilled this order in the summer of 1807, surveying and marking four routes between the two rivers and thereby incurring the wrath of Colbert, who saw in some of the proposed routes a menace to his lucrative ferry over the Tennessee on the Natchez Trace.[57]

Whether from chronic indecision or out of respect for the feelings of the Chickasaws, already irritated by the Cherokee sale and the invasion of the squatters, the War Department for three years took no further action more positive than complaining, while the factory buildings and business decayed beyond any hope of repair. Finally in August, 1810, Mason, the superintendent of Indian trade, wrongly diagnosing the decay as resulting from Spanish tariffs and Choctaw remoteness, ordered George Gaines, the factor, to visit the Tombigbee, adopt (as a new route to the factory when removed) one of the roads surveyed by his brother three years before, secure from the Chickasaws permission to use such a road through their territory, and then test the feasibility of the route chosen by transporting over it a supply of powder awaiting him at Smithland, Kentucky.[58] In October, Gaines brought the powder to Cotton Gin Port on the Tombigbee over a route which utilized Colbert's Ferry for the crossing of the Tennessee.[59] It may be inferred that his selection of the ferry as the Tennessee terminal of his road influenced the Chickasaws to give their consent. His road, however, did not become permanent, nor did Cotton Gin Port become the site for the factory when it was finally removed after the War of 1812.

[57] Carter, *op. cit.*, V, 558, Dearborn to Gaines, July 31, 1807; *ibid.*, V, 598–602, Gaines to Dearborn, January 29, 1808. The four roads were from Cotton Gin Port on the Tombigbee to the head and foot of Muscle Shoals, to the head of navigation on Bear Creek, and to the mouth of Elk Creek.

George Gaines became factor in 1807, succeeding Chambers, who had been both factor and land agent for the district east of the Pearl. When land sales began in 1807, Chambers resigned as factor in favor of Gaines, who had been his assistant since 1805.

[58] I. O. R., Indian Trade Letter Book B, 187–93, Mason to Gaines, August 28, 1810. Smithland was on the Ohio at the mouth of the Cumberland.

[59] G. S. Gaines, "Reminiscences of Early Times in Mississippi Territory" (MS).

VIII

Tecumseh

1811

ON AUGUST 5, 1811, Tecumseh, the great Shawnee chief, left Vincennes, where he and Governor Harrison had spent an agreeable week in mutual recrimination, and started south on a visit to the Creeks and Choctaws. His announced purpose of uniting these two nations with him in a league of peace was interpreted by the logical Governor as an intention of exciting them to war.[1] The Governor, however, failed even to surmise what practically all later writers have assumed as a fact, that Tecumseh went to secure the Southern Indians as British allies for the War of 1812.

If it is legitimate to substitute contemporary evidence for clairvoyance and patriotic introspection, it would seem clear that Tecumseh went south in response to an invitation, which perhaps had the urgency of an appeal, brought to him in Indiana by Tuscanea (Tusca Heneha), eldest son of Big Warrior (Tustennuge Thlocco), the head chief and speaker of the Creek Nation in succession to Opoie Micco. The invitation was perhaps suggested by some member of John Forbes and Company, was probably endorsed by Big Warrior, and was certainly sponsored by the element of the Creeks that was opposing the civilization program of Benjamin Hawkins.[2] The opposition in its main manifestations

[1] Logan Esarey, ed., *Messages and Letters of William Henry Harrison*, Indiana Historical Collection, VII and VIII, I, Harrison to Secretary of War, August 6, 1811; *ibid.*, I, *idem* to *idem*, August 7, 1811.

[2] Thomas S. Woodward, *Reminiscences of the Creek or Muscogee Indians*, 94, 116.

Mushulatubbee, chief of the Choctaws
*From a Catlin painting in the
Smithsonian Institution*

Photograph courtesy Muriel H. Wright

Tecumseh, Shawnee chief
From Benson Lossing's
The Pictorial Field Book of the War of 1812
(1868)

was so closely similar to that which Tecumseh had for four years been promoting in the Northwest as to suggest that its development may even have inspired, as its origin antedated, the teachings of the Shawnee leader. For Tecumseh himself was of Creek descent; both his father and mother had been born at Sauwanogee, a Shawnee town among the Creeks, and had lived there till about 1790; he had many friends and relatives there; perhaps his grandparents were still living at Sauwanogee in 1811. The retention in peace of that close association with the Shawnees often evidenced in war permitted the Creeks to know, as their own vicissitudes caused them to applaud, the efforts of Tecumseh to prevent the alienation of land and the abandonment of primitive ways. It was so fitting as to be almost inevitable that in the crisis of 1811 they should call their renowned kinsman home for counsel and assistance.

The impetuous summons to Tecumseh in 1811 was apparently an expression of the surge of resentment against the arbitrary seizure of the Coosa Road by the United States in an action which the Creeks, against all assurances, regarded correctly as a threat to their remaining land and liberty. But behind this specific discontent lay a vast reservoir of ill will, which had been accumulating from the time Hawkins had become agent and had begun his reforms. In its early stage, when Bowles was troubling the waters the opposition to these reforms had been more prevalent among the Lower Creeks; the opposition now shifted its strength to the Upper Creeks, among whom Hawkins, who had his agency on the Flint, had fewer opportunities to exert his influence. Twenty-nine of the thirty-four Upper Creek towns were antagonistic; indeed, it was only from the Natchez and Hillaubee people that the agent could expect undeviating support.[3] The malcontents, their numbers increasing and their virulence intensifying with each American encroachment on their land and customs, now comprised probably the larger and certainly the more articulate portion of the nation. Big Warrior, although his political orthodoxy had been validated by Hawkins as a necessary prelude to election, was

[3] *Indian Affairs*, I, 851, Big Warrior to Hawkins, August 4, 1813; Woodward, *op. cit.*, 96.

thought to be in secret sympathy with them. This, if true, was because he was descended from the Piankashaw, a tribe closely associated with the Shawnees, and not because of ratiocination since the chief seems to have gained his name by his physical rather than his intellectual endowment.[4]

It is safe to accept the testimony of Governor Harrison, notwithstanding his tendency to exaggerate the number of his enemies, that Tecumseh's diplomatic entourage, including himself, consisted of twenty men. From the Governor's statement that they descended the Wabash, it may be deduced that they began their journey in canoes. Since no one saw them after they left Vincennes, or if so did not report them until they arrived in the Chickasaw towns, it may be inferred that, instead of following the riparian route to Chickasaw Bluffs, they discarded their canoes after crossing the Ohio, and made the remainder of the trip overland. An anonymous correspondent, who had himself not seen them, wrote that the party consisted of six Shawnees, six Kickapoos, two Creeks, and six of some unknown tribe far to the northwest.[5] If Tecumseh hoped to proselyte the Chickasaws, he displayed neither tact nor intelligence in taking with him a group of their hereditary enemies. It is, indeed, fairly evident that he selected his route not to secure Chickasaw converts but to avoid American observation. His activities among the Chickasaws can be evaluated from testimony that he told them only that he was on his way to the Creeks, from reports that the Shawnees and Kickapoos solicited the aid of the Chickasaw king, or from a tradition that Tecumseh himself appealed to George Colbert.[6] The unidentified six who had come with Tecumseh, not as members of his party or to support his pleas, but on a mission of their own, tendered the Chickasaws a war pipe and solicited an alliance

[4] Woodward, op. cit., 116. Woodward said that Big Warrior was the largest man he ever saw among the Creeks and that he was almost as spotted as a leopard.

[5] Indian Affairs, I, 801, (anonymous) to Secretary of War, September 10, 1811. This letter mentions the fact that there were two Creeks in the party and conjectures that the object of the delegation was to incite Creeks and Cherokees to war. Tecumseh is not mentioned.

[6] Indian Affairs, I, 801, (anonymous) to Secretary of War, September 10, 1811; ibid., I, 802, (anonymous) to Secretary of War, November 29, 1811; H. S. Halbert and T. H. Ball, The Creek War of 1813 and 1814, 41.

with them for a war on the Americans. The opposing counsel of Tecumseh was as earnest as it was unnecessary for securing a Chickasaw rejection.[7]

Agent Neelly, being without recourse to the traditions and retrospections which have been so fruitful for later writing on Tecumseh, apparently failed to notice his passing through the Chickasaws or else considered it too unimportant to report. The agent, to be sure, was perhaps preoccupied, since he had received instructions to "prepare the minds" of the Chickasaws for a cession of their Kentucky and Tennessee lands, and this certainly entailed much preparation. The Chickasaws considered their territory perpetually protected by the talisman of Washington's written guarantee, and to any Chickasaw chief the idea of ceding tribal land held the same potential pleasure as a prospect of personal dismemberment. Neelly was engaged in the delicate but more promising task of securing Chickasaw consent for another Tennessee-Tombigbee road, the War Department having decided that the road selected by George Gaines was unsuitable, presumably because, of all those considered, it was the shortest, most convenient, and possessed the best terminals.[8] This road Neelly obtained, but whatever effort he was exerting in trying to secure an additional road from the Chickasaw agency to the "widow Runnold on the Tennessee" (as the Secretary of War at the behest of Kentucky had instructed him) was apparently labor taken in vain.[9]

[7] I. O. R., War Department Letters Received, Hawkins to Secretary of War, September 21, 1811. Hawkins identified these Indians as members of the "Wappomooka and Too-e-toosh" tribe, who lived high up on the west side of the Mississippi. They were probably Sioux.

[8] Carter, *op. cit.*, VI, 213–14, Secretary of War to Wade Hampton, July 20, 1811. Hampton opened the road—Gaines' Trace—from the Tombigbee to the upper end of Muscle Shoals on the Tennessee. This was the longest of the routes surveyed by Gaines in 1807 and was chosen presumably because its northern terminal was the newly established Fort Hampton on the Tennessee. The best description of the road is G. J. Leftwich, "Cotton Gin Port and Gaines' Trace," *Mississippi Historical Society Publications*, Vol. VII, 263–70.

[9] I. O. R., War Department Letter Book C. 66, Secretary of War to Neelly, March 11, 1811; *ibid.*, C, 91–92, *idem* to *idem*, August 17, 1811. The Chickasaw agency was situated on the headwaters of the Halky, a Tombigbee tributary, near the Tombigbee-Yazoo divide (I. O. R., Letters Received, Long to McKenney, November 5, 1824).

The practically entire absence of contemporary records has permitted conjecture to run even more than usually rampant on Tecumseh's visit to the Choctaws. He went to them from the Chickasaws, and, as he was evidently trying to avoid contact with white men, in all probability followed the old Six Towns trail. Riding now, according to tradition, on black ponies (concerning the obtaining of which tradition gives no details) Tecumseh and his party traversed that region between Macon and Meridian in which the Choctaw towns were concentrated; some of his party, including Seekabo, his kinsman, may have visited the Six Towns. In contrast to his Chickasaw experience, Tecumseh seems to have been received among the Choctaws with honors, treated with consideration, and heard with sympathy. In each of the three districts the chiefs called councils (some half-dozen in all) for him where he explained his mission and delivered his appeals. Tradition is certainly correct in remembering his pleas for intertribal peace, for the sparing of women and children in war, for denying future land cessions, and for a return to those ancient ways from which, in truth, the provincial Choctaws had yet not had much opportunity to depart. These were sermons practically copyrighted by Tecumseh and previously preached by him to many a Northern tribe. But the tradition that he exhorted the Choctaws to war against the United States and to alliance with Great Britain contradicts the entire tenor of his contemporary teaching and must be credited to later imaginings overstimulated by patriotism and consequent prejudice. It is possible that blurred tradition has attributed to Tecumseh not only his own undoubted, and not doubtful, speeches but also those of the Sioux delegates who accompanied (or slightly preceded him) and whose appeals Tecumseh opposed at every opportunity. Tradition is probably correct in remembering that Tecumseh met opposition from Pushmataha, Pitchlynn, and others in the pay of the United States, but their opposition was not to any hypothetical advocacy of war; it was to his appeals for peace and humanity, for a denial of land cessions and a retention of old customs.[10]

[10] The Halbert and Hall report, in *op. cit.*, is the best account of Tecumseh's stay among the Choctaws.

If Tecumseh was preaching war, it was reprehensible that Agent Dinsmoor left it unopposed and apparently unreported. The vacation habit, which Dinsmoor seems to have contracted as soon as he began work, had so increased that he seems to have spent very little time at his agency from 1807 to 1811. To this confirmed absenteeism the War Department, although twice ordering him back to his agency for specific tasks, had shown remarkable indulgence until the fall of 1810 when the West Florida crisis and a memorial from the Mississippi territorial legislature had stirred it to more positive action. To its complaint that Dinsmoor had left the Choctaw country and was living in Washington (Mississippi), the memorial appended a recommendation that all agents be required to live among the Indians to whom they were assigned.[11] Influenced by this memorial and perhaps by complaints from William Simpson that Dinsmoor was speculating with the land cession proceeds instead of paying them to Forbes as the Choctaw treaty of 1805 had provided, the Secretary of War in February, 1811, had directed Dinsmoor to return to his agency and stay there. The harassed Secretary added that if Dinsmoor found this inconvenient, he should notify the Department, which would try to find for him "a successor whose personal views and interests will be consistent with his public duties."[12] Returning to his agency after receiving this ultimatum, Dinsmoor had been displaying his devotion to national interests by a literal execution of his instructions to arrest all travelers without passports on the Natchez Trace. These included some slaves whose masters protested so explosively that shortly after Tecumseh left, Dinsmoor was admonished by the Secretary that his zeal must be tempered by discrimination.[13]

About the middle of September, after a final council at Mushulatubbee's residence, Tecumseh left the Choctaws for the Creek country. The success of his mission among the Choctaws is suggested by the length of his visit and by the addition of nineteen

[11] I. O. R., Retired Classified Files, memorial of the Mississippi legislature, November 30, 1810.
[12] Carter, *op. cit.*, VI, 178, Secretary of War to Dinsmoor, February 22, 1811.
[13] I. O. R., War Department Letter Book C, 103, Secretary of War to Dinsmoor, October 15, 1811.

Choctaws to his party. It was doubtless not a result of chance that his arrival at Tuckabatchee coincided with the regular meeting of the Creek national council on September 20. The presence of five thousand Creeks testified both to the popularity of Tecumseh and to the publicity Big Warrior had given to his visit. The forty-six Cherokees present justified their attendance by the perennial excuse that they had come to arrange with the Creeks an interval of repose from the mutual activities in horse stealing. The aged and ailing Hawkins attended as a matter of course, but seems to have left the routine of business in the hands of his assistant, Christian Limbaugh.

Tecumseh as a visiting notable lodged with Big Warrior and, either by his counsel or from custom, delayed an address until the council had finished transacting the tribal business. In the meantime, notwithstanding his lameness, he joined in the ceremonial dances in the public square, took occasion again to oppose the persistent Sioux who had tendered their war pipe to the Creeks, and talked to Hawkins on the subject of his mission. It seems evident that in his conversation with Hawkins he, from politeness or prudence, stressed only his opposition to war against the Americans and his ambitions for intertribal peace. The departure of Hawkins for the Flint before the Tuckabatchee council ended is an indication amounting to proof that he considered Tecumseh's mission harmless and that he had no apprehensions concerning the coming address of the Shawnee leader.

This address, delayed by council business and not postponed (as has often and fatuously been supposed) until after the departure of the agent, was delivered apparently about September 30 and was duly reported to Hawkins by Big Warrior. He reported that the burden of Tecumseh's talk was his conversation with the Great Spirit concerning Indian affairs, that after the address he (Big Warrior) and some others tried to find out from Tecumseh what he meant, that the result of their efforts was a conviction that Tecumseh was a madman or a great liar, or both, and that they did not understand and would take no notice of his foolish talk.[14] Either Big Warrior in his report was displaying unsuspected

14 The only contemporary accounts of Tecumseh's visit to the Creeks are

powers of dissimilation or was bewildered by the introduction of a spiritual note in Tecumseh's address. The latter is the more probable, for dissembling would have been both dangerous and useless in reporting a speech heard by so many in Hawkins' pay.

There is no contemporary evidence that Tecumseh visited either the Cherokees or the Seminoles, and there is contemporary evidence that his intention was to do neither. It is possible that conversations with the Cherokee delegation at Tuckabatchee convinced him that no co-operation in his program could reasonably be expected from a tribe so divided and so browbeaten. By the election of Pathkiller as head chief, the Cherokees had ended the interregnum resulting from the deposition of Black Fox, but their formal unity and outward harmony covered so many dissensions as to paralyze the tribal will.

In the early spring of 1811, Meigs had been instructed to urge again on the hapless Cherokees the policy, temporarily in abeyance, of mass migration to trans-Mississippi lands for which they should exchange their eastern territory.[15] Individual migration, which had been in progress for two years and had taken some two thousand Cherokees to the White River country, was resulting only in a gradual shifting of Cherokee population without any accompanying cession of Cherokee land. Irritated by this unseemly development, Meigs proposed that the Cherokees, since their inappreciation of United States benevolence prevented any voluntary change in their status as landowners, should either be compelled to remove as a tribe or else be brought under the civil jurisdiction of Georgia and Tennessee. In the latter case the United States should assign their two thousand families 2,000,000 acres in severalty, and appropriate the remaining 11,000,000 for $200,-000. The anticipated reluctance of the Cherokees to surrender either their identity or their lands brought from the agent the

two letters from Hawkins to the Secretary of War on September 21, 1811 and January 7, 1812 (I. O. R., Secretary of War Letters Received). Woodward's account (*op. cit.*, 94–95) is hearsay recalled nearly forty years after the event. A few additional items of Tecumseh's talk are given in a letter from Hawkins to Big Warrior, June 16, 1814 (*Indian Affairs*, I, 845); not to injure Americans, to preserve peace and friendship, not to steal.

[15] I. O. R., War Department Letter Book C, 70, Secretary of War to Meigs, March 27, 1811.

candid and ruthless statement: "I have ever been of the opinion that the Indians have not the right to put their veto on any measure deliberately determined and decreed by the Government."[16] This, however, was a theory that Madison, because of his entanglements and perhaps because of his scruples, could not accept, and Meigs was constrained to limit his promotion of removal to the customary forms of persuasion. Apparently as a method of fitting the prospective *émigrés* for the wild life of Arkansas, he continued to promote their civilization at home; in August, 1811, he reported that the Cherokees possessed 20,000 black cattle, 20,000 hogs, 6,000 horses (presumably their own), and 1,000 sheep.[17]

After the Tuckabatchee council, Tecumseh probably spent some time in the Creek country, going from town to town, visiting his friends and relatives, and doubtless in private conversations urging the views he had publicly expressed. He may have gone to the Seminoles at this time; earlier he could not possibly have gone. Of such a trip, tradition has preserved the details only of his return in October: of coming up the Alabama River and crossing it at Autage, of making a speech there and others at Coosada and the Hickory Grounds.[18] It was probably November when he finally left the Creeks for his long trip home. Seekabo, who had been born among the Creeks, and a few others of the Shawnees remained among the Creeks, presumably to confirm the Creeks in the faith that Tecumseh had preached and to carry the gospel further. Some of the Creeks accompanied Tecumseh on his return. Presumably he visited the Osages as he had intended. In December, 1811, Governor Clark noted his passing through Missouri, his addressing the Shawnees and Delawares there, and his pressing on to the Sac and Fox and to the Sioux.[19] By January 25,

---

[16] I. O. R., Retired Classified Files, Meigs to Secretary of War, April 6, 1811. Meigs' views are given in this letter and two others written to the Secretary of War, April 5 and May 30, 1811 (I. O. R. Retired Classified Files.).

[17] *Ibid.*, Meigs to Secretary of War, August 20, 1811. In 1813 the Cherokees were reported also to have 1500 spinning wheels, 400 looms, and 500 plows (*ibid.*, *idem* to *idem*.) July 30, 1813.

[18] A. J. Pickett, *History of Alabama and Incidentally of Georgia and Mississippi*, II, 240–41.

[19] *Indian Affairs*, I, 807, William Clark to Secretary of War, April 12, 1812.

1812, he, with eight men, had rejoined his brother, the Prophet, in Indiana.[20]

For his contemporaries the visit of Tecumseh to the Southern Indians had no such significance as it has assumed for later writers substituting for direct information a tangled mass of inference, retrospection, and blurred tradition. Hawkins reported it so casually that he did not even mention Tecumseh's name; the Secretary of War considered it too unimportant even for investigation.[21] The visit of Tecumseh, however, did give Governor Harrison an opportunity to gain fame, if not victory, at Tippecanoe, to the resulting political advantage of himself and his descendants. It had no connection with the War of 1812 except to precede it. Although it almost certainly strengthened the hands of those Creeks who opposed Americanization, it is probable that, instead of contributing to, it delayed the imminent Creek civil war. Tecumseh came to the South not to bring war but to bring peace.

[20] *Ibid.*, I, 805, Little Turtle to Harrison, January 25, 1812.
[21] I. O. R., Secretary of War Letters Sent, October 5, 1811.

IX

The Creek War

―――――――――――― 1813-1814 ――――――――

W<small>HEN IN</small> J<small>UNE</small>, 1812, Alexander
Neelly received notice that, because of the hostile disposition of
the Indians, he was being superseded by James Robertson as
Chickasaw agent, he must have experienced a feeling of profound
astonishment.[1] Since the Virginia treaty of 1782 the Chickasaws
had committed against the United States no hostile act graver
than baying at the squatters on their lands. The three other agents
were probably equally mystified, notwithstanding their long connection with the War Department, when shortly after the official
opening of the War of 1812 they were instructed to be vigilant
and keep the Indians quiet.[2] The most active alarmist could im-
pute to the Choctaws no graver misconduct than the possession
of Spanish neighbors, and when Meigs reported that the Cherokees were restless over the approach of a war in which they were
not participants, he was probably attributing to them a state of
mind peculiar to himself.[3]

Among the Creeks, to be sure, there had been in the spring of
1812 a number of routine murders: a Thomas Meredith had been
killed in March by some drunken Autossees (Atasis, Ottosies);
William Lott in May by some Tallassies (as a by-product of rob-

[1] I. O. R., War Department Letter Book C, 134, Secretary of War to Neelly,
June 4, 1812.
[2] *Ibid.*, War Department Letter Book C, 137, Secretary of War to all agents,
June 19, 1812.
[3] *Ibid.*, Retired Classified Files, Meigs to Secretary of War, May 8, 1812.

bery); and a family on Duck River massacred in June by the Hillaubees on a false report that the whites had killed an Indian woman. In every case the Creek council, on the demand of Hawkins, hunted down and killed the murderers: by August 24 they had executed six for murder and whipped seven for theft.[4] In addition to this obliging conduct, a council of the Lower Creeks in May had announced their determination to take no part in the approaching war, and had accepted quietly, if not cheerfully, the deduction of $900 from their annuity in payment for various damages inflicted.[5] Notwithstanding Hawkins' insistence that Creek affairs were normal, Governor Holmes of Mississippi Territory and Governor Willie Blount of Tennessee professed to the War Department their conviction that the Creeks were restless and hostile and that only an invading army could restore them to their proper serenity; the Governor of Georgia, also, as was the gubernatorial custom in that state, took a very gloomy view of Creek conduct.[6] The unanimous declaration of the Creek national council on October 30 for peace with the United States only confirmed the governors in their opinion of Creek duplicity.[7]

The Creek war was, in its beginning at least, a civil war, having its cause neither in Tecumseh's visit in 1811 nor in British seductions in 1812, but in a long-gathering dissatisfaction with the civilization program instituted by Hawkins and officially countenanced by the tribal government. Although the tension between the two Creek factions had been measurably increased by the death penalties of 1812, all of which had been inflicted on members of the opposition, war between them became inevitable only after February, 1813. At that time a band of Creeks led by Little Warrior, returning from a visit to the Shawnees, were informed by some guileful or mistaken Chickasaws that a Creek-American war had begun, and promptly made their contribution to it by

[4] The details of these murders and their punishment are given in *Indian Affairs*, I, 809ff.

[5] *Ibid.*, I, 809, Hawkins to Secretary of War, May 11, 1812.

[6] Carter, *op. cit.*, VI, 297, Holmes to Secretary of War, June 29, 1812; *Indian Affairs*, I, 813, Blount to *idem*, June 25, 1812.

[7] *Indian Affairs*, I, 813, Hawkins to Secretary of War, November 2, 1812. At this meeting the Creeks finally came to terms with John Forbes and Company and agreed to pay the remainder of their debt.

murdering seven families settled near the mouth of the Ohio.[8] Acting on garbled report from Robertson, Hawkins demanded that the murderers be punished, and the complaisant council voted the death penalty. In April, 1812, eight of the condemned men were killed by the warriors sent after them; all resisted arrest and all died fighting and defiant.[9]

The opposition faction was in no mood to accept calmly these further executions of its members as a normal operation of the due process of law. While the example of the Northern Indians encouraged them to resist their subservient, and certainly unrepresentative, tribal government, the frenzied exhortations of the "prophets" among them incited them continuously to a war of revenge. Limiting their program to vengeance, they set themselves to the task of killing everyone concerned in the recent executions (including Big Warrior, McIntosh, and Hawkins), of destroying Tuckabatchee and Coweta, and of eliminating from the tribe all traces of the hated civilization which Hawkins had been fostering. By July, 1813, they had successfully inaugurated their program by the killing of nine of the executioners, the burning of several villages friendly to Hawkins, and the slaughter of all cattle, hogs, horses, sheep, goats, and other evidences of civilization they could find.[10]

The leaders in this reform movement were Menauway (Ogillio Heneha), chief of Okfuskee, Hopoie Tustanugga, a warrior of Tuskegee, Peter McQueen, Hossa Yaholo, and the Tame King of Tallassie, now bowed down with age but as virulent as in the time of Bowles; the heart and soul of it were the "prophets," of whom Josiah Francis was the chief. The order of the prophets was perhaps instituted by Seekabo (who had been living with the Creeks since Tecumseh's visit), following the example set by

[8] *Ibid.*, I, 839, Hawkins to Cornell, March 25, 1813, and to Big Warrior March 29, 1813; Woodward, *op. cit.*, 36. On his return to the Creeks, Little Warrior presented to the council a Shawnee exhortation for war, but was reprimanded and excluded from the council.

[9] *Ibid.*, I, 843, Report of Nimrod Doyell; Woodward, in *op. cit.*, 37, implies that Little Warrior and his party were convicted on the testimony of Captain Isaacs (son-in-law of McGillivray), who had taken part in the murder but secured his safety by turning state's evidence.

[10] *Ibid.*, I, 847, Talosee Fixico to Hawkins, July 15, 1813.

Tecumseh's brother among the Shawnees. They claimed supernatural powers, including a command of lightning and earthquakes. To these handy possessions they added (so they claimed) an ability to convert dry ground into swamps, to divert the course of bullets, and to make magic rings which would bring death to everyone entering them. They practiced the same arts and acquired the same influence over the Creeks as the religious orators among their white neighbors. They prayed, exhorted, prophesied, and, when the spirit moved them, danced the impassioned Dance of the Lakes, which the Shawnees had taught them. Such Creeks as could withstand their eloquence, or resist the contagion of their passion, were constrained by terror of their magical powers to accept their direction. The prophetic movement seems to have been inaugurated among the Creeks in December, 1812, and to have been confined, for the most part, to the Alabama towns, which were the most primitive and unprogressive of the Creek confederacy. The tribal councilors at first evaluated the prophets only as a source of amusement or an object of ridicule. In June, 1813, they sent a messenger to them with a derisive invitation to come to Tuckabatchee for a public exhibition of their magical powers. Derision changed to something like consternation when the prophets killed the messenger, swept up the Alabama River murdering and burning, and announced they were on their way to the destruction of Tuckabatchee. The surprised chiefs of Tuckabatchee at once called in all their people, summoned the neighboring towns to help, and, upon their refusal to oppose the prophets, sent Alexander Cornell, the deputy agent, to the Lower Creeks for assistance.[11]

The revolting Creeks, in fact, having completed their program of private vengeance, were now inclined to carry out their plans for public retribution. But needing more arms and ammunition, the only products of civilization they were willing to retain, in July they sent Peter McQueen and Jim Boy (High Head Jim) with a force—100 by Indian account, 350 according to Hawkins— to Pensacola to obtain them. While awaiting the return of this party, the revolutionists maintained a loose siege of Tuckabatchee,

[11] *Ibid.,* I, 845, Cornell to Hawkins, June 22, 1813.

which, for lack of ammunition, they were unable to storm. Tucka-batchee itself was in need not only of ammunition but of food, and sent out lusty cries to the Lower Creeks for deliverance. The Lower Creeks showed no great enthusiasm for intervention, but finally the Cusseta Micco started a force of two hundred well-armed men to the relief of the beleaguered town. Apparently these warriors managed to enter Tuckabatchee without a fight, found the people there in great distress, took them away under guard, and by July 26 had them all safe at Cusseta, which now became the official "capital" of the nation. Hawkins had sent with the relieving force a letter of remonstrance to the Alabamas, and on their refusal to accept it tried to send a direct message but desisted from his efforts on the advice of the returning warriors.[12]

Meanwhile, McQueen's party on its way to Pensacola plundered the house of James Cornell, a half-blood who, like the majority of the half-bloods, was in opposition to the prophets, severely beat a Negro slave and a white man, and carried off Cornell's wife to be sold as a slave at Pensacola. On their return with one hundred horses laden with ammunition, they were met on Burnt Corn Creek by Cornell with a considerable force of half-bloods and white men whom he had collected in the neighborhood. In the ensuing "battle" on July 27, McQueen drove off the half-bloods and white men. The latter admirably combined thrift and prudence by tightly retaining in their headlong flight that portion of the ammunition they had siezed in their first attack.[13]

Since by the time McQueen arrived in the Creek country Tuckabatchee had already fallen by evacuation, the chiefs sent out a call for an attack on Coweta, but while the broken days were running, the families of the warriors slain at Burnt Corn Creek forced a change of the objective to Fort Mims, where the hated half-bloods had congregated. Thirteen of the Upper Creek towns participated in this attack, while three others aided by a feint toward Coweta.[14] If the Indians in attacking Fort Mims meant

[12] *Ibid.*, I, 849, Cusseta Micco to Hawkins, July 10, 1813, and Hawkins to Secretary of War, July 26, 1813; *ibid.*, I, 849–50, Hawkins to Secretary of War, July 28, 1813.
[13] Woodward, *op. cit.*, 97–98; *Indian Affairs*, I, 851, Big Warrior to Hawkins, August 4, 1813.

only to punish the half-bloods, they either forgot their good intentions in the fury of battle or else exercised very poor powers of discrimination. The massacre there of some five hundred men, women, and children changed the character of the conflict from a civil war to a war (perhaps neither desired nor anticipated) against the United States.

As a matter of fact, the Creeks, had they considered themselves at war against the United States, might have justified their course as a response to the act of the United States in July, 1813, authorizing the governors of Georgia and Tennessee to raise fifteen hundred men each and move them against the Creeks "as circumstances may direct, either separately or together."[15] The circumstances directing this step were certainly not any advices from Hawkins, who still regarded the Creek conflict as a civil war, nor the appeals of Tuckabatchee in June for white help in exchange for a cession of their opponent's territory.[16] The United States acted in acceptance of representations from the governors of Tennessee, Georgia, and Mississippi Territory, who, with powers of diagnosis apparently sharpened by remoteness, alleged that Hawkins' talk about Creek divisions was a subterfuge and that the entire Creek Nation was united in a war against the United States; they advocated a war that would result in both private and public profits by the confiscation of the entire Creek territory and the subsequent seizure of all Spanish Florida. From intuition unassisted by evidence, they recognized the Creek troubles as originating in British machinations and encouraged by covert Spanish aid.[17]

While the war, from the Indian (and therefore unhistorical) point of view, still remained a civil war, each of the Creek op-

[14] *Indian Affairs*, I, 855, Hawkins to Floyd, September 30, 1813. The participating towns were Hoithlewaula, Fooschatchge, Coolooma, Ecanhutke, Sawanogee, Mooklausa, Alabama, Hookchoioochee, Ocheubofa, Wewocau, Purceuntallahassee, Woccocau, and Pochusehatche. The towns making the Coweta diversion were Okfuskee, Tallassie, and Autossee. Three towns—Kialije, Eufaula, and Tjlotlogulgau—took no part in either operation.

[15] I. O. R., War Department Letter Book C, Secretary of War to Hawkins, July 22, 1813.

[16] See n. 10 above.

[17] The views of Blount are repeated at length in a letter to Flournoy, October 18, 1813 (*Indian Affairs*, I, 855).

ponents had vainly sought assistance from the neighboring tribes, the government from them all, and the revolutionists from the Choctaws and Cherokees.[18] Both Choctaws and Cherokees were divided on the same lines as the Creeks, and any intervention in the affairs of their neighbor would possibly result in civil war at home. But when the United States entered the war, it became safe for those Cherokees and Choctaws under the influence of the United States to go boldly to the aid of their Creek brethren enjoying a similar distinction. Early in September the Cherokee national council declared for action following a talk (accompanied by a piece of tobacco decorated with colored beads) sent by Big Warrior from Coweta, where he was exercising *in absentia* his amputated authority. The Cherokee council was opposed to intervention but yielded to the threats of Ridge, who was acting from motives unknown.[19] Meigs, ever since the beginning of the War of 1812, had been urging an unresponsive War Department to recruit the Cherokees, at first against the British and finally against the Creeks, whom he, faithfully adhering to the views of his superiors, considered British partisans.[20]

Whether because the wooing of Dinsmoor was less ardent or their own minds undetermined, the Choctaws showed even more restraint than did the Cherokees in espousing the cause of the United States. As late as August, 1813, Dinsmoor, evidently yet uninstructed, was inquiring of the War Department, apparently indifferent, if it wished to have Choctaw recruits, while Mushulatubbee was advising Governor Holmes that a faction of the Choctaws was disposed to join the Creek revolutionists.[21] The Gover-

[18] Halbert and Ball, *op. cit.*, 120–21; *Indian Affairs*, I, 847, Talosee Fixico to Hawkins, July 15, 1813. Halbert and Ball represent the Creek-Choctaw conference as being held in July at Pushmataha's residence at Causeyville, about ten miles southeast of Meridian, with Pushmataha, Mushulatubbee, and Huanna Mingo negotiating for the Choctaws. Who the Creeks were is not known, but at approximately the same time Weatherford and Ochillie Haujo are represented as conferring with Mushulatubbee.

[19] McKenney and Hall, *op. cit.*, II, 96–97. At the time of the attack on Fort Mims, McIntosh of Coweta was visiting the Cherokees apparently to urge intervention. Ridge and some others, by order of the chiefs, escorted him home, where they found the Creek national council in session. Ridge took Big Warrior's talk to the Cherokees.

[20] I. O. R., Retired Classified Files, Meigs to Secretary of War, August 6, 1813.

nor suspected that Mushulatubbee's information was gained from personal membership in the faction itself. In the same month Brigadier General F. L. Claiborne, commanding the Mississippi militia and chafing under Flournoy's inability to detect a connection between the Creek uprising and the British war, sent a Major Ballinger into the Choctaw country to confer with Pushmataha. Until September 29, Pushmataha apparently continued to maintain a rigid control over his inclination to assist the United States, but on that date went to Gaines at St. Stephens and offered his services, explaining that he had just then heard of the Fort Mims massacre.

Since the agent was again absent, the factor accompanied the chief to Mobile (recently come into American possession) to see General Flournoy, commander of the southern district since the transfer of Wilkinson to the Canadian front. Flournoy, still unconvinced that the Creeks, or any part of them, were at war with the United States, followed an oral rejection with a written acceptance of his services and sent him, with Gaines and Colonel McGraw, back to the Choctaws to secure recruits. At the home of John Pitchlynn (on the Tombigbee near the mouth of the Octibbeha) they met the ubiquitous John McKee, whom Andrew Jackson, commanding the embattled Tennesseans, had sent down to promote a combined Choctaw and Chickasaw diversionary attack on a Creek village at the falls of the Black Warrior. Pitchlynn and McKee in the northern district enlisted six hundred Choctaws for the Black Warrior expedition, which on January 7, 1814, reached its objective, found the Creek village deserted, burned it, and returned home without casualties and without glory.[22] The doubtful participation of the Chickasaws in this useless enterprise constituted, apparently, their only contribution to the American cause during the war.

Gaines and Pushmataha held a conference in the southern district, where they harangued the assembled five thousand Choctaws (not including Mushulatubbee), and returned to St. Steph-

[21] Carter, *op. cit.*, VI, 391–92, Dinsmoor to Secretary of War, August 4, 1813; *ibid.*, 390–91, Holmes to *idem*, August 3, 1813.

[22] I. O. R., Retired Classified Files, McKee to Secretary of War, July 1, 1816. (This letter is also in *Indian Affairs*, II, 118–19).

ens with a declaration of war and a few recruits. Subsequently, Mushulatubbee hesitatingly brought in some warriors, and finally Chief Puskshenubbee with a few men came out of the West. All were, for the time being, immobilized at Mobile for lack of arms.[23]

In the winter of 1812 the Creek revolutionists, generally called the Red Sticks, were menaced by forays from Georgia and Mississippi and an invasion from Tennessee. While the Georgia militia slowly mobilized and moved to the Chattahoochee, the Lower Creek towns remained for the most part inactive, constrained by courtesy as well as prudence from anticipating by any self-assertion the American aid they had solicited. Since their larder was sagging seriously under the accumulated gastronomic attacks of the refugees, they probably welcomed the defection of Yuchee which gave them an excuse for confiscating their crops. They kept their patrols out toward the Tallapoosa and prevented a Miccosukee force from joining the prophets, but otherwise stood on the defensive, reluctant to begin a struggle that, however resulting, would certainly leave the nation weak and helpless.[24] The Red Sticks in their headquarters at Autossee seemed content to await, rather than to launch, an attack. They were without ammunition, having practically exhausted what they had salvaged at Burnt Corn Creek and being unable to utilize the imaginary supplies which they were hypothetically receiving from supposed British and Spanish sources. The thoroughgoing destruction of such hated symbols of civilization as cattle, hogs, sheep, goats, and chickens, while doubtless contributing to their spiritual uplift, had seriously diminished their food supply. Lacking both food and arms, they retained only their fanaticism upon which to feed and fight.

The Georgia militia under General Floyd reached the Flint

[23] G. S. Gaines, "Reminiscenses of Early Times" (MS); Halbert and Ball, *op. cit.*, II, 290–92; J. S. Bassett, ed., *Correspondence of Andrew Jackson*, I, 380–81, Jackson to Pinckney, December 10, 1813. Mashulatubbee early in December sent out a war party which took some scalps and provoked a Creek retaliatory raid at Christmas. Then Mushulatubbee summoned his district to meet January 11, 1814, to go to war (Carter, *op. cit.*, VI, 440–44, McKee to Secretary of War James Monroe, June 29, 1814).

[24] *Indian Affairs*, I, 849, 852, Hawkins to Secretary of War John Armstrong, July 28 and August 23, 1813.

agency on October 18, 1813, and after considerable delay marched on over the Federal Road into the Upper Creek country. The force was ill-disciplined, disinclined to accept from the Lower Creeks help that would have to be remembered in dictating terms of peace, and contemptuous of Hawkins, whose offer of maps, guides, and interpreters they disdainfully rejected. Under such circumstances the 450 refugees and Lower Creeks who accompanied the expedition did so more as spectators than as combatants. Floyd halted on the Chattahoochee to build Fort Mitchell and then struggled on to Autossee, where the Red Sticks attacked him and inflicted such losses on him that, although he succeeded in burning the flimsy houses of Autossee and Tallassie and killing 200 warriors, he was compelled to retreat to Fort Mitchell. When he again advanced in January, 1813, he was defeated on Caleebe Creek by Red Sticks, armed chiefly with bows and arrows, and again forced back to Fort Mitchell.[25]

Between the first and second coming of Floyd from Georgia, the Red Sticks had received a visitation by General Claiborne from Mississippi Territory. Claiborne came up the Alabama River in December, commanding an army of 1,000 white men with an auxiliary of Choctaws under Lieutenant Colonel Pushmataha. The volunteering of only 135 men from a nation with a population of perhaps 20,000 indicates that the Choctaws were more ardent in declaring war than in waging it.[26] The objective of Claiborne's expedition was Ecunchate, which the Americans called the Holy Ground, a camp-meeting site which the prophets, after the massacre at Fort Mims, had established on the left bank of the Alabama River, near the present Benton in Lowndes county. Here they were accustomed to hold high revel, perform their magical rites, and send out objurgatory defiance to their enemies. Drawn by these attractions, a considerable number of the Red Sticks could generally be found camping here with their women and children and attending the religious services at such times as the business of fighting had grown slack. To this objective, ideal for

---

[25] Woodward, *op. cit.*, 101-102; Mooney, *Myths of the Cherokee*, pp. 92, 93; *Indian Affairs*, I, 858, Hawkins to Secretary of War, June 7, 1814.

[26] The 135 Choctaws under Pushmataha were divided into four companies of 51, 22, 40, and 12 men respectively (Halbert and Ball, *op. cit.*, 215).

attack since it was unfortified and encumbered with women and children, Claiborne was guided by the half-blood, Sam Monroe, reaching it on December 23. The warriors and prophets stood their ground until the women and children had crossed the Alabama to safety, when with the loss of a few bowmen they scattered in the neighboring swamps. Claiborne assigned to Lieutenant Colonel Pushmataha the essential task of destroying the service sheds and religious relics and then, having celebrated Christmas with a banquet of parched corn and boiled acorns, returned home with his troops, whom he described as lacking shoes, blankets, shirts, and pay, but "still devoted to their country and properly impressed with the justice and the necessity of the war."[27]

The expeditions of Floyd and Claiborne had been mere forays, which, because of their speedy withdrawals, rather encouraged than damaged the Red Sticks; the penetration of Creek territory by Andrew Jackson from Tennessee, on the other hand, aimed not merely at invasion but conquest. Jackson's army included some six hundred Cherokees organized in nineteen companies, thirteen of which were commanded by half-bloods.[28] It is probable that the proportion of half-bloods among the men was about the same as among the officers. There are many indications that the full-blood Cherokees were as apathetic to the war as were the full-blood Choctaws. The Cherokees serving in the first campaign were almost all in the East Tennessee force of General White, which co-operated but did not merge with Jackson's army.

No amount of rhetoric can disguise the fact that Jackson, although leading in overwhelming force a well-armed and equipped army against a foe reduced to a dependence on bows and arrows, was twice beaten back by his fanatical adversaries. On his first campaign in the fall of 1813, Jackson struck for the Coosa, which

[27] It is impossible to reconcile the description of the Holy Ground and the account of the battle as given in Woodward, *op. cit.*, 100–101, with that given in Mrs. Dunbar Rowland, *Andrew Jackson's Campaign against the British, or the Mississippi Territory in the War of 1812*, 171–81.

[28] I. O. R., Retired Classified Files, estimate of pay due to Cherokee warriors, October 7, 1813, to April 11, 1814. Only nine of these companies were with the army on its 1813 campaign. Ridge was a major in the Cherokee force, Gideon Morgan, and John Lowry, colonels.

Andrew Jackson
From an engraving by Charles Phillips
after a painting by John Wesley Jarvis in 1815

Courtesy Library of Congress

Major Ridge, Cherokee
From McKenney and Hall's
History of the Indian Tribes of North America
(1838)

was as inevitable a highway into the Creek country from the north as the Alabama was from the south or the Federal Road from the east. The first exploit of the army was the slaughter of the entire force of two hundred Creek bowmen at Tallassiehatchee, at which place they had rallied after being driven by White from the beleaguerment of Pathkiller in Turkeytown; three hundred more victims were added at Talladega, after which the martial career of the army culminated on November 18 in the butchery by White of sixty unarmed and unresisting warriors at Hillaubee after the town had surrendered to Jackson. The Creeks were so impressed by this unique reward of submission that they did not again propose surrender during the course of the war.

After the Hillaubee episode Jackson was forced by desertion, mutiny, service expirals, and a balky commissary to retire up the Coosa to Fort Strother, from which place, garrisoned by the Cherokees, he sent out lusty and successful calls for reinforcements. His second campaign, beginning in January, 1814, carried him down the Coosa almost to its junction with the Tallapoosa before the gathering Creeks on January 24 checked him on Emuckfaw Creek and by another attack at Hillaubee drove him, in something resembling a rout, back to Fort Strother. Only the supposition that they had completely exhausted their scanty supply of ammunition explains the uncharacteristic decision of the Red Sticks to stay on the defensive against the third attack in the spring of 1814. Tohopeka was a death trap, but even so it fell, not to Jackson's inept and storming frontal attack, but to the infiltration of the Cherokee half-bloods from the rear. The loss of one thousand warriors here on March 27 did not break the spirit of the hostile Creeks, for the towns on the Alabama, uninvolved in the recent defeat, were still defiant and wanting to continue the war.[29]

The Lower Creek chiefs wanted to continue the punishment of their brethren, but Hawkins, remarking that enough blood had been shed, exerted himself to bring to the broken Upper towns an invitation, extended by General Pinckney, to surrender and consequent peace. To Pinckney, the nominal superior of Jackson

[29] *Indian Affairs*, I, 858, Hawkins to Pinckney, April 25, 1814.

and Floyd, the War Department had entrusted the mission of making peace on terms including a land cession sufficient only to indemnify the United States for the cost of the war.[30] But pressure from Tennessee, fearful of losing the full fruits of victory, compelled the Department to replace him with Jackson, who promptly declared that he would not limit himself to the peace terms of his predecessor.[31] Jackson wanted not an indemnifying but a political cession that would separate both Upper and Lower Creeks from Florida, unite the settlements of Georgia with those of Mississippi, and establish a corridor from Tennessee to the Spanish boundary; unmindful of Cherokee help and Chickasaw friendship, he urged that the United States should, while it had its troops in the field, force a cession of all the Cherokee and Chickasaw territory in Tennessee.[32]

On August 9, 1814, Jackson exacted from a motley array of Creek chiefs at his newly erected Fort Jackson the cession upon which he had determined. No reputable chief was present from an Upper Creek town, for eight of the Tallapoosa and Alabama towns, led by Peter McQueen, Hossa Yohola, Savannah Jack, the Prophet Josiah Francis, the Durants, and the youthful Osceola, had escaped to the Seminoles, Menauway was in hiding, and most of the others were dead.[33] Big Warrior signed the treaty as "Speaker of the Upper Creeks" and Tustanuga Hopoie as "Speaker of the Lower Creeks"; half-bloods Timpoocha Barnard of Yuchee, William McIntosh of Cusseta, Noble Kinnaird of Hitchitee, John O'Kelly of Coosa, John Carr of Tuskegee, and Alexander Grayson of Hillaubee signed for their respective towns. The territory ceded comprised over twenty million acres of land west of the Coosa and north to the undefined Cherokee boundary, and a wide strip of both Upper and Lower Creek land along the Florida bor-

[30] *Ibid.*, I, 836, Secretary of War to Pinckney, March 17, 1814; Bassett, *op. cit.*, I, 508, Jackson to Secretary of War, April 25, 1814.

[31] *Indian Affairs*, I, 857, Pinckney to Hawkins, April 23, 1814.

[32] Bassett, *op. cit.*, I, 497, n. 11, Jackson to Pinckney, May 18, 1814. Jackson wrote Pinckney that a cession was justified from the Chickasaws because that tribe had failed to protect white travelers on its roads and had let the enemies of the United States pass through its territory to plunder and make war.

[33] Woodward, *op. cit.*, 42–43; *Indian Affairs*, I, 860, Hawkins to Secretary of War, July 19, 1814.

der from the Tombigbee almost to the St. Marys in Georgia. Big Warrior, protesting against the taking of Lower Creek land for political purposes, signed the treaty, Hawkins and Meigs witnessed it, and then Andrew Jackson, having despoiled both his friends and his enemies, departed for Mobile.[34] To Hawkins the treaty of Fort Jackson must have brought great bitterness of spirit. The war had demonstrated that his long efforts to civilize the Creeks had failed, and he found himself now a mere spectator while others took the direction of the Creeks out of his hands, where it had rested for twenty years. On April 25, 1814, he had asked to be relieved of his agency and had been informed on June 30 that he might retire as soon as his successor could be selected; on December 17 he was instructed to turn over his agency to his assistant, Christian Limbaugh.[35]

After the happy conclusion of the Creek war, Jackson, wishing to have Indian help in his further campaign against the British and Spaniards, directed all agents to enroll the warriors and place them on the payroll.[36] The Cherokees, apparently satiated by the slaughter at Tohopeka, evaded the call by deferring the matter until the payment of their annuities.[37] Among the Lower Creeks, who had not received any annuities for three years, McIntosh raised four or five hundred men and started with them to Mobile on September 23.[38] The prospects for further help from the Choctaws was dimmed by tribal resentment aroused by Flournoy's refusal to permit a pursuit of the Creeks into Florida, and by tribal confusion incident to a change of agents. Dinsmoor had been dis-

---

[34] The scanty preliminary negotiations of this treaty are given in *Indian Affairs*, I, 837ff.; the text of the treaty with an interesting list of signers is in Kappler, *op. cit.*, II, 108–109; maps of the cession are in Royce, *Indian Land Cessions*, plates CVIII and CXXII.

[35] I. O. R., War Department Letter Book C, 173, 187, 188. Hawkins' opinion of the Fort Jackson treaty is given in *Indian Affairs*, II, 493, Hawkins to Graham, August 1, 1815. Hawkins had been much criticized during the war because he had failed to detect the alleged hostility of the Upper Creeks to the United States.

[36] Bassett, *op. cit.*, II, 30–31, Jackson to the Secretary of War, August 5, 1814.

[37] *Ibid.*, II, 31–33, 41–42, Jackson to Butler, August 27 and September 4, 1814; I. O. R., Retired Classified Files, Butler to Meigs, September 10, 1814, and Pathkiller *et al.* to *idem*, September 14, 1814.

[38] *Indian Affairs*, I, 861, Hawkins to Acting Secretary of War Monroe, October 5, 1814.

missed as a result of forged letters of complaint allegedly written by Pushmataha and Mushulatubbee, and John McKee had taken over the agency as his successor on June 28, 1814.[39] The vigorous efforts of Jackson and McKee to remove the Choctaw disaffection were powerfully aided by Dinsmoor on his return to the Choctaws.

Persuasive as these men undoubtedly were, there can be little doubt that the 750 Choctaws, who by November 1 had enlisted for further service with Jackson, had been induced to do so not by white exhortations, but by the more domestic influence of Pushmataha, for 600 of the number came from the Six Towns, which made up the most belligerent, as well as the most subservient, portion of his district.[40] The Chickasaws seemed as little disposed to fight the British and the Spanish as they had been to face the Creeks. None had enlisted by November 1, but Jackson was hopeful that Coffee's march through Mississippi would stimulate their martial ardor. When this attraction proved inadequate Jackson felt constrained to appeal directly to Levi Colbert.[41] Chickasaw apathy was due partly to the fact that Agent James Robertson was dead and the tribe was apprehensive about his successor. Their appeal to the War Department for an agent from the Northern states had been blandly ignored when, on September 28, the appointment had been given to William Cocke.[42]

[39] Carter, *op. cit.*, VI, 440–42, McKee to Secretary of War, June 29, 1814; I. O. R., War Department Letter Book C, 167, Secretary of War to McKee, April 30, 1814. McKee detected the forgery when he took over the agency and at once informed the War Department. Dinsmoor attributed his dismissal entirely to the forged letters. An entirely different story attributing his dismissal to the enmity of Jackson is given in James Parton's *Life of Andrew Jackson*, I, 349–56, 576–81.

[40] Bassett, *op. cit.*, II, 73–74, 85, Jackson to Secretary of War, October 14 and October 31, 1814.

[41] *Ibid.*, II, 82–83, Jackson to Secretary of War, October 26, 1814; I. O. R., Retired Classified Files, *idem* to Colbert, February 7, 1815.

[42] I. O. R., Retired Classified Files, Colbert *et al.* to Secretary of War, September 9, 1814; I. O. R., War Department Letter Book C, 180, Secretary of War to Cocke, September 28, 1914. The Chickasaws declared they would not receive King (the forger of the Dinsmoor letters).

X

Boundaries and Removal

—————1815-1820—————

THE TERRITORY ceded at Fort
Jackson, after "an unprovoked, inhuman and sanguinary war
waged by the hostile Creeks against the United States hath been
repelled, prosecuted and determined successfully on the part of
the said states in conformity with the principles of national justice
and honorable warfare," extended north and west to Cherokee,
Chickasaw, and Choctaw boundaries which no man knew. The
determination of these limits, a necessary prerequisite to the complete enjoyment by the United States of the domain thus charac-
teristically acquired, was complicated by a boundary dispute
between Cherokees and Chickasaws, each of whom claimed much
of the land on the northern border of the Creek cession.

Since the cession, once made, was United States property,
the Creeks deftly removed themselves from the boundary con-
troversies as something no longer concerning them.[1] Meigs, always ready to demand justice for his charges from everyone except the United States, presented the Cherokee case. The Cherokees claimed considerable land south of the Tennessee, since by
three successive wars they had driven the Creeks more than a degree of latitude south of Turkey Town on the Coosa, had expelled
the Chickasaws from their Old Fields, and had been in actual occupation of the country since.[2] These, the Cherokees acknowl-

[1] I. O. R., Retired Classified Files, Hawkins to Meigs, September 18, 1815.
[2] Ibid., Meigs to Hawkins, September 19, 1815; Indian Affairs, II, 146, Richard Riley to President Monroe, November 22, 1817.

edged, were traditional things, but the Cherokee claims south of the Tennessee had been recognized by the United States in the Hopewell treaty of 1785 and the Dearborn convention of January, 1806. Against these arguments were opposed the Creek statement that after the Sevier raid of 1782 the homeless Cherokees had applied to the Upper Creeks and had been lent the Creek territory only in the angle of the Coosa, Will's Creek, and Coosada Island in the Tennessee,[3] and the Chickasaw possession of Washington's written guarantee of Chickasaw claims south of the Tennessee.

Compared to the wild tangle of conflicting claims on the north, the dispute over the western boundary of the cession was so mild as almost to constitute an agreement. The Creeks had claimed land west to the Tombigbee and Black Warrior, the Choctaws east to the Tombigbee–Cahaba divide. By one of the little ironies of history, the United States in exacting the Choctaw cession of 1805 over Creek protests had effectually estopped itself from contesting the Choctaw claims and so, because of its avidity in seeking a cheap cession from the Choctaws then, had now to resign a free one from the Creeks. The Choctaw claims extended north only to the Oktibbeha, which by an agreement in 1807 had been recognized by both Choctaws and Chickasaws as the boundary between them.[4]

The United States had long realized the danger for the Indians and, possibly, the embarrassment for itself inherent in conflicting tribal boundaries. In the administration of John Adams, Hawkins and Dinsmoor, on instructions from Secretary of War McHenry, had endeavored to promote a Cherokee-Creek agreement, but had been thwarted by the opposition of the Creeks, who at that time apparently regarded, with some justification, the Cherokees as merely auxiliaries of the Creek confederacy.[5] In

---

[3] Bassett, *op. cit.*, II, 226, statement of Creek chiefs and Headmen, January 22, 1816; *Indian Affairs*, 153–54, questions to Shoe Boots and answers, October 19, 1817.

[4] I. O. R., Retired Classified Files, Cocke to Secretary of War Calhoun, 1817. By this agreement, made at the house of the Chickasaw king, the Choctaw-Chickasaw boundary was the Oktibbeha, and a line from its source to the mouth of the St. Francis on the Mississippi.

[5] See n. 1 above.

May, 1811, the agents had been instructed to appoint commissioners in each tribe to resolve the boundary conflicts, but the plan would have become impracticable, because of the Creek uprising, even had it not been forgotten in the excitement of the British war.[6] In an effort to secure a definite northern limit for his prospective Creek cession, Jackson in 1814 had invited Meigs to bring a delegation of Cherokee chiefs to Fort Jackson to confer with the Creeks. The conference, after the air had been cleared by an interchange of vituperation, resulted in an agreement on a line to run from the Coosa, at the crossing of the military road, to Flat Rock on what the Cherokees called Long-leafed Pine Creek. Jackson, knowing intuitively that the Tennessee was the proper boundary, refused to incorporate in the treaty a line which left in Cherokee possession so much land that he considered he had conquered from the Creeks.[7]

The eastern line of the cession presented no difficulties, since it was defined in the treaty and involved nothing more serious than a Creek amputation. For the performance of this surgical operation the commissioners appointed by President Madison (in accordance with a Congressional act of March 3) met in June, 1815, on the Upper Coosa, where Meigs had been instructed to join them and show them the Cherokee-Creek corner.[8] The non-attendance of Commissioner John Sevier and of the promised Creeks forced a postponement of the survey, whereupon Commissioner Kershaw returned at once to South Carolina and resigned. The Creeks' respite endured until the last of September, when the appointment of Hawkins, by filling the commission, permitted the survey to proceed. The commissioners, beginning at Fort Strother, moved down the Coosa accompanied by Meigs, Big Warrior, McIntosh, Alexander Cornell (wearing his wife's Iroquois coat), and others. The commissioners' progress was in-

[6] Royce, *The Cherokee Nation*, 205.

[7] Bassett, *op. cit.*, II, 214–15, Jackson to Hawkins, August 14, 1815; *ibid.*, II, 246–49, Jackson to Secretary of War Crawford, June 13, 1816; I. O. R., Retired Classified Files, Creek-Cherokee agreement, August 9, 1814.

[8] I. O. R., War Department Letter Book C, 256, Secretary of War to Meigs, August 5, 1815. Letting Meigs determine the corner was, of course, equivalent to accepting the Cherokee contentions.

terrupted by the death of the aged Sevier in October and the subsequent illness or ill will which forced first Hawkins and then Barnett, one of the original commissioners, to leave the line. E. P. Gaines, appointed to succeed Sevier, finished the survey in late December, 1815.

An increasing crowd of Creeks followed the surveyors, sullen and protesting as they saw the great part of their country passing out of their possession, but offering no opposition until the line reached the Chattahoochee. The Creeks, both Upper and Lower, were on the verge of starvation, for the United States had not delivered the supplies promised at the treaty, had not paid for the property destroyed in the Lower towns by the Georgia troops, had not paid the wages of the Creek soldiers allied with the Americans in the Creek war, and for three years had not paid the Creek annuities. At the Chattahoochee the Indians declared the line should go no farther, but their fragile resolution faded in the presence of the eight hundred Americans assembled at Fort Mitchell and finally dissipated in a threat to prevent the settlement of the land ceded in southern Georgia.[9] It may be that this shadowy resurgence of spirit was occasioned not merely by the proddings of poverty, hunger, and patriotism, but by the assurances given the Creek by Colonel Edward Nicolls from Florida that England considered the enforced cession a violation of the Ghent treaty and would guarantee freedom and independence to the Creek Nation.[10]

The commissioners, of course, had no instructions or authority for surveying the northern boundary of the cession, because the location of such a boundary had not yet been decided by the United States with the Cherokees and Chickasaws. What the United States had not authorized and the commissioners had not thought to attempt, General Coffee, in evident collusion with Gaines and Jackson, brazenly and illegally undertook. Coffee, who had failed to be selected in succession to Kershaw only because of the tardiness of Jackson's recommendation, secured his

[9] Heloise Abel, *The History of Events Resulting in Indian Consolidation West of the Mississippi*, 278; Bassett, *op. cit.*, II, 210 n.; Woodward, *op. cit.*, 10.

[10] Bassett, *op. cit.*, II, 211, n. 3.

opportunity when Gaines, authorized by the Secretary of War William Crawford to appoint Coffee in case of Hawkins' death or resignation, appointed him at once without waiting for either of these anticipated events.[11]

The pseudo commissioner went to Fort Strother the middle of January and, after waiting a week for the other commissioners who, he alleged with evident falsity, had promised to meet him there, proceeded to run the line where certain "Creek chiefs and Headmen," collected by himself, told him it should be. His line from the mouth of Will's Creek on the Coosa to Coosada Island in the Tennessee, down the Tennessee to Caney Creek, fifteen miles below the Shoals, and thence by Gaines' Trace to Cotton Gin Port on the Tombigbee, enclosed in the ceded territory practically all the land claimed by the Cherokees and Chickasaws south of the Tennessee and was therefore highly pleasing to Jackson, who encouraged, as he no doubt instigated, the entire proceeding. Coffee attempted by "Dick Brown and his clan" to obviate the anticipated objection of the Cherokees to his illegal procedure and appealed to Jackson to prevent Chickasaw opposition. Jackson, in his capacity of major general commanding the southern district, responded loyally by sending a stern warning to Colbert not to interfere with Coffee, whose enclosure of alleged Chickasaw land could be remedied only by presenting, after the line was run, satisfactory proofs of ownership. With Colbert's reply that neither he nor any other Chickasaws had ever heard of Coffee's being a line commissioner, the matter rested until the Secretary of War had the grace to interpose his authority.[12]

The Secretary of War had shown his antipathy to Jackson's spoliation schemes by permitting Meigs to determine the Cherokee-Creek corner on the Coosa and by instructing him in November, 1815, to collect testimony supporting Cherokee rights.[13]

[11] I. O. R., War Department Letter Book C, 268, Secretary of War Crawford to Gaines, October 24, 1815; Bassett, *op. cit.*, II, 222, Gaines to Jackson, December 12, 1815.

[12] The activities and collaborations of Coffee and Jackson are revealed in letters interchanged by them in January and February, 1816 (Bassett, *op. cit.*, II, 225–26, 228–29, 230–31, and 231–33). The Jackson-Colbert interchange came on February 13 and March 1 (*ibid.*, II, 233–34).

[13] I. O. R., War Department Letter Book C, 277–78, November 22, 1815.

These instructions Meigs had anticipated by going, on an invitation from Big Warrior, to Tuckabatchee in September to consult with the Creeks, but, finding them disposed to assert extreme claims, he appealed to Hawkins. Hawkins explained the Creek attitude as emanating from Big Warrior's ambition to be chief of all Southern Indians and advised him, in effect, to disregard the Creeks and deal only with the United States.[14] Meigs had an opportunity to heed this advice when in March, 1816, he arrived in Washington with a Cherokee delegation to confer with the Secretary concerning a cession of their South Carolina lands.[15] In the two resulting treaties of March 22, 1816, the Cherokees, with real or pretended reluctance, ceded for $500 their remote and practically uninhabited lands in South Carolina and received (undoubtedly in exchange) a recognition of their land claims south of the Tennessee.[16]

The news of this treaty brought speedy and violent protests from the governor of Tennessee, from the people of Davidson County, and from Andrew Jackson. The memorial of the citizens of Davidson County and the protest of Jackson, differing only in the superior vituperation of the latter, asserted that the land confirmed to the Cherokees had always belonged to the Creeks until conquered by Jackson, and intimated that Meigs had hoodwinked Congress into its surrender. Both protestants denounced the slur on the Tennessee militia implied in the provision of the treaty providing for a payment of $25,500 to the Cherokees for damages inflicted upon them by the Tennessee militia in 1813 and 1814.[17] The Secretary of War, disregarding

[14] The correspondence between Meigs and Hawkins (both of whom were at Tuckabatchee) is in I. O. R., Retired Classified Files, under the dates September 17, 18, and 19, 1815; Meigs addressed Hawkins as "agent for Indian Affairs in the Southern Department." In the Retired Classified Files is a letter (unsigned and dated only 1815), addressed to Philemon Hawkins, elaborately setting forth the Cherokee boundary contentions.

[15] Royce, *The Cherokee Nation*, 204–205. South Carolina in December, 1810, had asked President Madison to extinguish Indian titles in the state and in March, 1811, had received assurances this would be done if possible. The War of 1812 intervened, but in December, 1814, Meigs had been named commissioner to negotiate for the lands. Failing, he was instructed in November to bring a Cherokee delegation to Washington.

[16] Kappler, *op. cit.*, II, 124–26; Royce, *Indian Land Cessions*, plate CLXI.

[17] *Indian Affairs*, II, 99, Memorial of Tennessee senators and representa-

the protests, applied salt to Jackson's psychical wounds by requiring him to remove from the Cherokee land the numbers of squatters previously encouraged by Coffee and Jackson to settle there, and this requirement Jackson finally began to fulfill after vainly representing that the militia would refuse to support him. The Chickasaws, part of whose land guaranteed by Washington had been recognized by the treaty as belonging to the Cherokees, sent a delegation to Washington in June in double protest against the treaty and their agent. Agent Cocke was accused of letting his relatives settle on Indian lands, of taking Indian money to buy furniture for himself, of selling blacksmith iron and pocketing the money, and of running a tavern to the neglect of his agency.[18]

Disregarding all protests with novel firmness, the Secretary of War instructed the commissioners (Barnett, Hawkins, and Gaines) to proceed with the running of the Cherokee line as described in the treaty just concluded; after this line was run, they were to mark the Chickasaw and Choctaw lines as soon as these highly volatile objects could be located.[19] No trouble was anticipated from the Choctaws, to whom the United States meant to concede the boundaries it had recognized in the treaty of 1805 and then buy from them everything east of the Tombigbee; in May, 1816, commissioners were named and instructed to this end.[20] But the Chickasaw claims, repeatedly guaranteed and contravened, could neither be conceded nor denied. Since the only possible way out of the dilemma was to compromise or purchase

tives, April 17, 1816; *ibid.*, II, 89–91, Davidson County memorial (no date); *ibid.*, II, 110–11, Jackson to Secretary of War, June 10, 1816. In a letter to Coffee, July 21, 1816 (Bassett, *op. cit.*, II, 254–55), Jackson denounced the treaty as a "wanton, hasty, useless thing" which it was the "hight" of his diplomatic ambition to undo. The Governor of Tennessee sent his protest with Jackson's.

[18] I. O. R., War Department Letter Book C, 387, Secretary of War to Cocke, June 26, 1816.

[19] *Indian Affairs*, II, 109–10, Secretary of War to commissioners, April 16, 1816. Gaines resigned from the commission early in June, and the Department ruled that Coffee automatically succeeded him. Hawkins died June 6, 1816 (Merret B. Pound, "Colonel Benjamin Hawkins of North Carolina, Benefactor of the Southern Indians" *The North Carolina Historical Review*, Vol. XIX, 1–21, 168–86).

[20] I. O. R., War Department Letter Book C, 326–27. Secretary of War to McKee, April 16, 1816; *Indian Affairs*, II, 118, Secretary of War to McKee, Coffee, and John Rhea, May 20, 1816.

the conflicting claims, the Secretary sponsored, or approved, a four-nation conference to attempt an adjustment, negotiated for the Chickasaw land with the Chickasaw delegation then at Washington, and instructed Meigs to buy the Cherokee land. All failed.

The all-Indian council, composed of the head men and warriors of the four tribes and attended by Barnett, met on May 29 and agreed on everything except essentials. The Creeks and Choctaws agreed that the Black Warrior–Cahaba divide was the Choctaw eastern boundary; the Creeks and Cherokees agreed to pool their land for occupation by both tribes; the Cherokees and Chickasaws could reach no agreement at all.[21] The Cherokees refused to sell either south of the Tennessee or north of it, as Meigs had with overoptimism asked,[22] and the Chickasaw delegation refused to negotiate.

Influenced by these untoward developments, the persistent Secretary called for a conference on September 1 at the Chickasaw council house to be attended by delegates from the four tribes, by the Choctaw commissioners, and by Jackson, David Meriwether, and Jesse Franklin as United States commissioners in charge of the proceedings. At the conference, represented to the Indians as one for the adjustment of boundaries only, the commissioners were instructed to secure all the land in dispute between the Cherokees and Chickasaws south of the Tennessee, all the Cherokee land north of the Tennessee, and all Chickasaw land in Tennessee and Kentucky.[23] Instructions to suspend the removal of intruders pending the outcome of the conference convinced Jackson that the recent Cherokee treaty had, as he had hoped, no "reality" and could be virtually, if not formally, abrogated.

For securing this abrogation, now to him a question of personal honor, Jackson wrote (with no results) scathing letters to Meigs and attempted to undermine Cherokee resolution by bribing (through Coffee) their chiefs—Brown, Lowry, Pathkiller, Ridge,

[21] Royce, *The Cherokee Nation*, 207–208; Charles Hicks to Meigs, July 4, 1816. Barnett of the line commissioners attended the conference.
[22] *Indian Affairs*, II, 112, 113–14, Secretary of War to Meigs, June 24, 1816 and Meigs to Secretary of War August 9, 1816.
[23] I. O. R., War Department Letter Book C, 395–403, Secretary of War to Jackson, Meriwether, and Franklin, July 5, 1815; *Indian Affairs*, 102–103.

and Ratcliffe—by threatening prosecution for allegedly false damage claims, and by collecting Creek affidavits affirming former Creek ownership of all land south of the Tennessee.[24] He supplemented these diplomatic efforts by writing to James Colbert, demanding a Chickasaw cession of their land claims south of the Tennessee. The wary Chickasaws refused not only the cession but even a conference unless it were held in the center of their nation.[25] The Cherokees showed themselves as obdurate as the Chickasaws by rejecting the demands of Governor McMinn when he visited them the latter part of July to urge a cession.[26]

The Chickasaw conference began at the Chickasaw council house (the home of George Colbert) on September 8, having been delayed for a week by the tardiness of the Cherokee delegates. Franklin, to Jackson's relief, was unable to be present until late in the proceedings,[27] but Jackson, Meriwether, Governor McMinn, Colonel Lawrence, the Choctaw commissioners, delegates from the Cherokees, Choctaws, and, of course, the Chickasaws were at hand for the opening. Instead of a Creek delegation there was a message from Big Warrior expressing regrets and, in evident expectation that the Chickasaw conference would fail, inviting all four tribes to meet at Turkey Town on October 1. Judging that Big Warrior had sent this message in collusion with the Cherokees in order to defeat the Chickasaw conference, Jackson sent out runners to bring in the Creeks. The Cherokee delegation headed by Tuckasee had been chosen at Willstown, August 20, and given positive instructions to cede no land. Jackson seems to have made no effort to exceed his instructions, although he undoubtedly sympathized with McMinn's logical statement that no Indians, however friendly, were justified in owning 8,000,000 acres of Tennessee land. Declaring that the south-of-the-Tennessee lands in dispute between the Chickasaws and the Cherokees

[24] *Indian Affairs*, II, 113–14, Meigs to Secretary of War, August 9, 1816; Bassett, *op. cit.*, II, 253–56, Jackson to Coffee, July 19, 21, and 26, 1816; *ibid.*, II, 255–56, *idem*, to Secretary of War, July 24, 1816.

[25] *Indian Affairs*, II, 102–103, James Colbert to Jackson, July 17, 1816.

[26] *Ibid.*, II, 115, McMinn to Secretary of War, October 25, 1816.

[27] Bassett, *op. cit.*, II, 260–61, Jackson to Coffee, September 19, 1816. Commenting on Franklin, Jackson wrote: "He is butting at everything, his horns are getting sore, and I believe he will be docile and butt no more."

were shown by the affidavits of the Creeks themselves to have belonged to neither Cherokees nor Chickasaws but to the Creeks, Jackson on September 12 offered to buy the claims of the two now contending parties. After two days' deliberation the Cherokee delegation, in violation of its instructions, accepted. The reasons inducing the Cherokees to this decision are plainly stated by Jackson in his report: "In concluding the treaty with the Cherokees, it was found both well and polite to make a few presents to the chiefs and interpreters." Jackson's assent to the Cherokee contention that the treaty must be subject to ratification by the Cherokee council sprang perhaps from his confidence that the council would be as amenable to reason as the delegation had been.

The Chickasaws, irritated by the Cherokee treaty, distracted by the death of a principal chief (the Factor), and aware of their strong position behind Washington's explicit guarantee, were more obdurate than the Cherokees. The Jacksonian formula for gaining a position he was forbidden to storm is revealed in his report: "It was soon found that a favorable result to the negotiation was not to be anticipated unless we addressed ourselves feelingly to the predominant and governing passions of all Indian tribes, i.e., their avarice or fear. Our instructions pointed to the former and forbade the latter: we therefore were compelled, not from choice, but from instructions, to apply the sole remedy in our power. It was applied and presents offered to the influential chiefs, amounting to $4,500, to be paid on the success of the negotiations. This measure seemed to produce some sensible effect." Jackson added that these expenditures could not be mentioned in the treaty since such publicity would destroy the influence of chiefs whom the United States might need again. The treaties, thus secured, gave to the Cherokee Nation $5,000 and a ten-year annuity of $6,000, to the Chickasaw Nation $4,500 and a ten-year annuity of $12,000.[28] The Cherokee treaty was signed

[28] *Indian Affairs*, II, 104–105, Jackson, Meriwether, and Franklin to the Secretary of War, September 20, 1816; Kappler, *op. cit.*, II, 133–34, 135–37. Meigs did not attend the conference and Cocke was present only as a spectator. Jackson, instructed to investigate the charges against Cocke, recommended his removal, and he was finally removed on December 6, 1817, after repeated demands by

by the twelve members of the delegation; the Chickasaw by twenty-three chiefs, including James, Levi, William, and George Colbert.

The trail of perfidy led from the Chickasaws to Turkey Town, where on September 28, 1816, the Cherokees held a meeting with the commissioners to consider ratification of the treaty into which they had been betrayed by their suborned delegation at the Chickasaw council house. The strong opposition to the treaty was reflected in the delay of ratification for a week while Jackson plied the diplomatic arts he had rehearsed among the Chickasaws. On October 4 the treaty was declared ratified with the signatures of eight chiefs. The Cherokees later charged that the "ratification" was done in meeting late at night and that only four of the chiefs voted in favor of it.[29]

The Choctaw negotiations, suspended while the Choctaw commissioners and chiefs, for reasons not clearly evident, attended the Chickasaw conference, were resumed in the fall of 1816. The only difficulty was not about the righteousness of Choctaw claims, which the Creeks had affirmed, but about the disgruntlement of the Choctaw chiefs. Although they had secured the removal of the factory in 1816 to old Fort Confederation, it profited them little because of the depletion of their game. They wanted the agency removed to the eastern part of the nation, they were none too well pleased with the military road that was being cut through their nation to Lake Pontchartrain, and they had not yet been paid either for their services against the Creeks and the British or for the supplies they had furnished to the Kentucky and Tennessee militia going to New Orleans in 1814.[30]

the Chickasaws. Cocke had defended himself against the Chickasaw charges by ascribing the enmity of Colbert and Tishomingo to his interference with their monopoly of annuities and trade. The treaty provision that there should be no more licenses given for trade among the Chickasaws tends to confirm his claims (*Indian Affairs*, II, 106–107, Cocke to Secretary of War, September 22, 1816). Cocke was succeeded by Colonel Henry Sherburne.

[29] *Indian Affairs*, II, 117, Jackson to Secretary of War, November 12, 1816; *ibid.*, II, 145, instructions to Cherokee deputation, September 19, 1817. The chiefs whose names appear on the treaty were Pathkiller, Glass, Sour Mush, Chulioa, Dick Justice, Richard Brown, Boat, and Chickasautchee. Meigs' name is attached as a witness.

[30] I. O. R., Retired Classified Files, McKee to Secretary of War, July 1 and November 18, 1816; conference between Coffee and the Choctaws, August 27, 1816.

These dissatisfactions having been dispelled by a judicious distribution of presents and promises, the Choctaws on October 4 signed a treaty ceding all their remaining land east of the Tombigbee, receiving therefor $10,000 and an annuity of $16,000 for twenty years.[31]

The four cessions of 1816 exhausted the possibilities open to the United States of despoiling, on the pretext of boundary rectification, its recent comrades in arms. There remained, however, the pretext of removal. It was, indeed, his expectation of obtaining on the removal issue the Cherokee and Chickasaw Tennessee lands that had prevented Jackson from demanding them at the Chickasaw conference.[32] McMinn, who was Jackson's alter ego, urged the plan on the War Department in October; in November, Meigs contributed the same advice; in December, North Carolina requested removal at least from that state; and in that month the Secretary of War, apparently oppressed by these multiple importunities, instructed Meigs to acquire another cession from the Cherokees.[33] When the Cherokees, although still dazed from the October ratification proceeding, refused, the War Department, now under the direction of Calhoun, named Jackson, Meriwether, and McMinn to negotiate an exchange of western land for eastern.[34] With such unscrupulous Indian-baiters as these, the Cherokees were utterly unable to cope. They were still divided on the subject of removal, with Tuckasee and Richard Brown favoring it, while the great majority of the tribe was opposed. Their government, by their own testimony, was corrupt, and many of the chiefs were willing to take, and even to solicit, bribes. They were vulnerable on the question of removal because

[31] Kappler, op. cit., II, 137. For the military road see W. A. Love, "General Jackson's Military Road," Publications of the Mississippi Historical Society, Vol. XI, 403–17.

[32] Indian Affairs, II, 115, McMinn to the Secretary of War, October 25, 1816. McMinn suggested that the nonemigrating Cherokees might be given lands in severalty and have the status of free Negroes.

[33] Ibid., II, 116–17, Meigs to Secretary of War, November 8, 1816; I. O. R., War Department Letter Book C, 447, Secretary of War to Meigs, December 9, 1816.

[34] I. O. R., War Department Letter Book D, 30, Secretary of War Calhoun to Governor Miller (North Carolina), April 1, 1817; ibid., 36–37, Secretary of War to Jackson, May 14, 1817.

a portion of the tribe was living in Arkansas on lands for which they had given no compensation.

When Jackson and Meriwether opened the treaty convention on June 20, 1817, at the new agency, called Calhoun, up the Hiwassee River, there were present only fifteen chiefs, and these composed an Arkansas delegation which had stopped off on its way to Washington. Evidently the Cherokees were seeking by a boycott to avoid the cession which experience taught them invariably followed a conference. Their stratagem won nothing but a week of grace, for by June 28 all members of the council had been gathered at Calhoun, where, in unwilling audience, they were forced to hear Jackson's demands. These demands were, first, a cession compensating the United States for the western land already occupied by emigrating Cherokees, whose number Jackson, perhaps sincerely, estimated at 3,700; and second, a removal to Arkansas of the entire tribe to land to be given them in exchange for their territory thus vacated. When the stunned council refused even to place these inordinate demands before the chiefs, Jackson himself called the chiefs together and addressed them. Thereupon the council presented a remonstrance, signed by sixty-seven chiefs, against the whole policy of emigration as originating in fraud and continuing contrary to tribal will.

Outraged by receiving a remonstrance where he had asked only for acquiescence, Jackson called on the signers of the document to repudiate it and when only two, Tuckasee and Glass, did so, announced that he would make a treaty with the Arkansas delegation alone. Had the Cherokee remained firm, it is possible that Jackson would not have dared carry out his threat, and even had he done so, he could only have treated for lands in compensation. But the council, having exhausted by the remonstrance its last reserve of temerity, yielded and on July 8 joined the Arkansas delegation in a treaty ceding two tracts of land in Georgia and Tennessee. For neither of these did the tribe receive any compensation, since it was assumed that compensation had already been given in the Arkansas lands.[35]

[35] Bassett, *op. cit.*, II, 291, note 1; *ibid.*, 298, Jackson to Coffee, June 21, 1817; *ibid.*, 300–305, Commissioners to Secretary of War, July 8 and 9, 1817; *Indian*

It is clear that Jackson in securing this treaty supplemented open intimidation with wholesale hidden bribery, for secret articles provided for the payment of $4,225 to certain eastern chiefs, and even Chisholm, of the western delegation, received $1,000 to "stop his mouth and attain his consent." It was so evident, from the report of the commissioners themselves, that the treaty had been fraudulently obtained from an illegal minority that Graham, the acting secretary of war, expressed doubts of its acceptance.[36] He had, however, underestimated the capacity of the Senate for condoning profitable fraud.

Apparently recovering some measure of spirits after Jackson had left the nation, the Cherokee council in a meeting at Amoha (Amoyee) in September attempted to lock the doors against further thefts by forming a committee of thirteen that would manage their affairs subject to the unanimous consent of the council of chiefs. This committee formed, they sent, as an offset to the Arkansas delegation, a delegation of six to the "new President" to declare their opposition to removal and to protest the iniquities perpetrated against them at the Chickasaw council house, at Turkey Town, and at Calhoun. The delegation presented its memorial to President Monroe on November 22: on December 26 the new President proclaimed the Calhoun treaty in force.[37]

Although during the course of negotiations at Calhoun the Cherokees had made evident the tribal opposition to emigration and had made no commitment in the treaty itself, they found in the ensuing months that the United States was apparently de-

Affairs, II, 142–43, Cherokee chiefs to Commissioners, July 2, 1817; Kappler, *op. cit.*, II, 140–44; Royce, *Indian Land Cessions*, plates CXII and CLXI.

[36] *Indian Affairs*, II, 143, Graham to Commissioners, August 1, 1817. To this, Jackson replied August 19 that the treaty had been freely signed by all the Cherokee chiefs except Pathkiller, who was sick (Bassett, *op. cit.*, II, 232).

[37] *Indian Affairs*, II, 145–46, instructions to Cherokee deputation, September 19, 1817; Pathkiller and Hicks to Secretary of War, October 28, 1817; Cherokee deputation to the President, and Richard Riley to *idem*, November 22, 1817. The instructions to this deputation were signed by Pathkiller and Charles Hicks as principal chiefs and sixteen others, including Ridge, Sour Mush, and Richard Brown. The deputation at Washington did not ask the abrogation of the treaties, but only an increase of annuity (because of their "inability in negotiation") and an equitable division of annuities with the Arkansas Cherokees.

termined to bring emigration about. The nation looked on, sullen and helpless, while the War Department contracted for boats to transport the prospective emigrants to Chickasaw Bluffs, a ferry-boat to take them across the Mississippi, and keelboats for the Arkansas, while it delivered to the agency rifles, lead, powder, kettles, blankets, and traps for their use; and, on Jackson's insistence, appointed Sam Houston as assistant to Meigs, specially assigned to promote their removal.[38] A significant number of them succumbed to the threats, persuasion, and bribery of Governor McMinn, who had been placed in charge of emigration, and were seduced into enrolling for the trans-Mississippi journey.

By McMinn's report 6,000, by Cherokee count 3,500, went west during 1818 and the latter half of 1817. To prevent the threatened disruption of their nation, the Cherokees, using the only weapon still remaining to them, resorted to the persecution of those who enrolled. The resulting disturbance was both a sectional and a class war, since the emigrants were generally from the poorer population of the hill districts relatively untouched by civilization, while the chiefs opposing removal were from the river towns and had, thanks to United States tutelage, accumulated property, which they were now asked by the United States to abandon.[39]

Meanwhile, the Cherokee annuities remained unpaid, since McMinn, ostensibly because of the persecution, refused to take the census which was to determine its division between eastern and Arkansas Cherokees. In an effort to end the stalemate the Cherokee council early in 1819 appointed a delegation to confer with Secretary of War John C. Calhoun. Although the members of the delegation were promptly bribed by McMinn, they proceeded to Washington and convinced Calhoun (already penitent, per-haps, of following in the wake of Jackson's chariot) if not of the

[38] *Ibid.*, II, 144, Secretary of War to Meigs, August 9, 1817; I. O. R., Retired Classified Files, Secretary of War to Meigs, September 29, 1817, and Meigs to Secretary of War, September 9, 1817.

[39] I. O. R., Retired Classified Files, Meigs to Secretary of War, December 30, 1817. Meigs characterized the Cherokee government as a mild aristocracy which because of the number of chiefs was really a democracy.

justice of their cause, at least of the reality of their woes and their wishes.[40] In the resulting treaty of February 27, 1819, Calhoun accepted a cession of their peripheral land as a compensation for past and future emigration and agreed on a division of annuities at the ratio of two to one.[41] Since there was no reason for further promoting an emigration for which payment had already been received, McMinn was instructed to discontinue the various forms of encouragement he had been extending emigration. At the price of three cessions the badgered Cherokees had finally purchased a decade of peace.

The program of removal could, of course, be applied to the other tribes as well as to the Cherokees, provided commissioners could be found with the capacity for the necessary chicanery and intimidation. Fortunately, Andrew Jackson again became available in 1818 after his return from his weird adventures in Florida. In May of that year, Calhoun, apparently judging that a man for whom he was recommending a court-martial for his invasion of Florida was a proper person to deal with the Indians, appointed Jackson to treat with the Chickasaws; as a fellow commissioner he was given former Governor Shelby, whose docility was taken for granted because of his age and the benefit to Kentucky from a Chickasaw cession. At the same time and for the same purpose McKee, Carroll, and Burnett were named to treat with the Choctaws.[42]

The last of July, Jackson went to the Chickasaw country to arrange with James Colbert a time and place for the meeting. When Colbert, with an unexpected blindness to the attractions of emigration, seemed inclined to refuse even a meeting, Jackson bluntly informed him that the land in question rightfully be-

[40] *Ibid.*, McMinn to Calhoun, January 24, 1819. McMinn gave Walker and Taylor $500 each, Harlen $250, and Adair $150; agreed to enlarge the reservations of Starr, McNair, and Spear; bribed Morgan (with a sum not stated); and tried with only partial success to bribe Lowry and Brown. Lowry, Brown, Martin, Walker, and Morgan were on the delegation.

[41] *Indian Affairs*, II, 187–90, Secretary of War to Cherokee delegation, February 11, 1819; Kappler, *op. cit.*, II, 177–79; Royce, *Indian Land Cessions*, plate CLXI. After the treaty, 837 Cherokees withdrew their names from the enrollment for emigration.

[42] *Indian Affairs*, II, 173–74, Secretary of War to Shelby and Jackson, May 2, 1818; *ibid.*, 151–52, *idem* to McKee, Carroll, and Burnett.

longed to the United States, the citizens of which were now determined to have it, and if the Chickasaws refused to cede, the United States would seize it by virtue of the Hopewell treaty.[43] The reference to the Hopewell treaty was apparently an improvisation made necessary by Monroe's deafness to his earlier contention (March, 1817) that Indians should be dealt with by legislation instead of treaties. It is unlikely that Colbert was converted to this novel interpretation of the Hopewell treaty; he consented to a conference, but only at the Chickasaw Old Town and not at Nashville, where Jackson, on the pretext of Shelby's health, wished it to be held.

On September 29, 1818, the two commissioners, apparently prepared, as Jackson insisted, to take firm ground with the Chickasaws and overcome the Colberts by touching their interest and "avarace," arrived at the Old Town and, finding the Indians still uncollected, busied themselves in sending to Nashville for money to pay the annuities promised for the 1816 cession. The Secretary had suggested to Jackson in July that a payment at this time might have its advantages. When the money arrived, the negotiations began, on October 12, with a demand by the commissioners for the Tennessee and Kentucky land, for the reason that it had been "sold by North Carolina and Virginia about 35 years ago to pay the debt of the Revolutionary War." This somewhat precarious legal foundation for American rights the commissioners proceeded to strengthen by the economic argument that the land in question was barren of game and therefore useless for Indian purposes. If the Chickasaws would neither sell nor exchange this land, the United States felt itself unable any longer to restrain its settlers from taking possession of it.

Finding the Chickasaws impervious to this logic, the commissioners resorted to the customary bribery: $20,000 was given to the three Colberts and two other leaders under pretext of paying for the reservations secured to them by the treaty of 1816. The reservation deeds were made out to James Jackson. After this

[43] *Ibid.*, II, 178, Jackson to Secretary of War, July 13, 1818, and Sherburne to *idem*, July 29, 1818; Bassett, *op. cit.*, II, 387–88; Jackson to Shelby, August 11, 1818.

measure of high finance the commissioners on October 19 persuaded the nation to cede the Kentucky and Tennessee land outright for a sum ultimately fixed at $300,000, to be paid in twenty installments. In addition, the commissioners agreed to pay the debts of certain leading men. The journal of the commissioners was kept secret, since it would have been injudicious to reveal to the Chickasaws the corruption of their chiefs.[44]

The Choctaw mission of 1818 failed because (so it was explained) McKee was unpopular and the other two were lacking in the qualifications necessary for obtaining an Indian cession.[45] The following March, Calhoun replaced Commissioner Carroll with Andrew Jackson, who had recently displayed such signal qualifications in negotiating with the Cherokees and Chickasaws. In June, 1819, McKee sent Pitchlynn to the Lower Towns and Six Towns, where, by arguments not preserved in the records, he induced the chiefs, including Mushulatubbe and Pushmataha, to agree to a conference. But at the Choctaw council in August both of these head chiefs expressed their opposition to an exchange of land, assigning the double reason that Mississippi was their old home and that the promised land in Arkansas was inferior.[46] So opposed to emigration was the tribe that in the fall of 1819 it sent a protesting delegation to Washington, displaying its earnestness by paying its expenses itself when McKee refused to furnish the money.

After this the negotiations languished until October, 1820, when the chiefs were finally induced to meet a reconstructed commission of Jackson and Thomas Hinds at Doak's Stand. Puckshenubbee, head chief of the western district was the leading opponent of the treaty, displaying his opposition in an extreme form

[44] The journal of the commissioners and the text of the treaty are in Williams, *Beginnings of West Tennessee*, appendices A and B. For the Indian side of the negotiations see Gideon Linceum, "Life of Apushimataha," *Publications* of the Mississippi Historical Society, Vol. IX, 415–85.

[45] Bassett, *op. cit.*, II, 406–407, James Pitchlynn to Jackson, December, 1818. James Pitchlynn was the leader of an Arkansas delegation, which, like the Arkansas Cherokees, worked hand in hand with Jackson.

[46] *Indian Affairs*, II, 231, James Pitchlynn to Jackson, June 22, 1819; *ibid.*, II, 230, Choctaw Council, August 12, 1819. McKee wrote Jackson the day after the council meeting that the Six Towns had been willing to emigrate but that a few half-bloods had misrepresented Arkansas land (*ibid.*).

by refusing to accept rations during the negotiations. His opposition was perhaps inevitable to a cession which would all but
extinguish the district of which he was chief. The half-bloods
throughout the nation were opposed to emigration, since, like the
Cherokee half-bloods, they were the element that had prospered
most from Americanization and had accumulated property which
they were unwilling to leave.

Jackson demanded from the tribe a cession of land on the
Mississippi in exchange for land between the Arkansas-Canadian
and the Red. This cession the Mississippi Choctaws opposed since
the Arkansas land would be useless to them unless they emigrated,
while the Arkansas Choctaws favored it because it would give
them land where now they legally had none. When the opposition continued, Jackson finally resorted to the threat he had used
so effectively against the Cherokees: he would deal with the
Arkansas band alone. His somewhat tenuous justification for this
action was that the Arkansas Choctaws were living on United
States land for which no payment had been made. At this threat
of Jackson's the alarmed Choctaws appointed a committee of the
head chiefs and some delegates from the three districts to arrange
a treaty. This treaty, signed on October 18, made the exchange
Jackson had demanded.[47]

From this era apparently consecrated to Indian spoliation the
Creeks emerged relatively unscathed. They were not vulnerable
to victimization on the plea either of rectifying a boundary or of
providing for their western emigrants, and the huge cession of
1814 seemed momentarily to satisfy Georgia that the Compact
of 1802 was being respected. The slaughter of the Red Sticks and
the Florida migration of the survivors removed from Creek society its hunting element, on which the existence of the factory
depended, and consequently the removal of that institution to
Fort Mitchell in 1816 failed to restore its vitality. Both factory
and fort were abandoned in 1819. On January 22, 1818, D. B.
Mitchell, who had succeeded Hawkins as agent the preceding
year, obtained without difficulty from the complaisant Lower

[47] Kappler, *op. cit.*, II, 192–94; Royce, *Indian Land Cessions*, plate CLXIII.
The journal of the negotiations is in *Indian Affairs*, II, 239–43.

Creeks a cession of two small tracts: one south of the Altamaha-Ocmulgee, the other between the Upper Ocmulgee and the Cherokee boundary.[48] Upon the acquisition of Florida by the United States, the Creeks promptly put forth a claim to the Seminole lands. The United States as promptly refused to admit this claim and countered with a proposal that the Creeks receive the Seminoles into their own land in return for a compensation from the United States.[49]

[48] *Indian Affairs*, II, 153, Mitchell to Secretary of War, January 28, 1818; Royce, *Indian Land Cessions*, plate CLXII.

[49] I. O. R., War Department Letter Book D, 278–80, talk to Creek delegation, March 28, 1819; *ibid.*, D, 312–13, Secretary of War to Mitchell, August 23, 1819.

XI

The Shadow of Georgia

1820-1825

D URING THE YEARS 1820–25 the Chickasaws and Choctaws, having been thoroughly plucked in the previous decade, lived quietly, if not contentedly, on their diminished domains. They quarreled, as a matter of routine, with their agents—Nicholas, who had aroused the wrath of the Chickasaw Colberts, and Ward, whom the Choctaws accused of such eccentricities as appropriating their annuities and exchanging whiskey for Choctaw property on terms highly advantageous to himself.[1] It is not likely that the Choctaws displayed any jubilation over the removal of their agency to the Noxubee River in 1822 or indulged in any grief when their factory was closed in the general abolition of the factory system the same year. After its removal to Fort Confederation in 1816, the factory had prospered briefly, serving both Chickasaws and Choctaws until the huge cessions of 1818 and 1820 had forced both tribes, unwillingly, into agriculture, the fruits of which were unacceptable at the government store. When it closed in 1822, it possessed merchandise valued at $16,451, peltry valued at $12,400, and debts due it of $12,402, valued correctly at nothing at all.[2] In 1819 the Chicka-

[1] I. O. R., War Department Letter Book E, 231–32, 285–86, Secretary of War to Nicholas, March 18, 1822, and June 20, 1822; *ibid.*, 177–78, 207–208, *idem* to Ward, October 25, and December 21, 1821. Nicholas had succeeded Sherburne, who had resigned in 1820. Nicholas resigned in 1822 and was succeeded by B. F. Smith. Ward was the successor of John McKee, who had resigned in 1821 to enter Alabama politics.
[2] *Indian Affairs*, II, 5.

THE SOUTHERN INDIANS

saw Bluffs factory had been removed, amid Chickasaw rejoicing, to Arkansas.

In contrast to the humdrum existence of Choctaws and Chickasaws, the current of events among Cherokees and Creeks was running swift and dangerous. By the treaty of 1819 the Cherokees had bought, at a heavy price and at almost the moment of extreme unction, a respite from oncoming doom. The narrowness of their escape and the remembrance of their bitter humiliations in 1818 seemed to shock them into a realization of their social faults and weaknesses. After the return of the delegation from Washington, the hundred chiefs of the nation, taking counsel of their fears, had the grace to end the dissensions which had been paralyzing them and sought to reorganize their government in such a manner as to carry out better, and better reflect, the tribal will.[3] Retaining the principal chief as the titular head of the tribe, they created an elective bicameral legislature by making their national committee co-ordinate with the national council. Intent less on legislation than on justice, they divided the nation into eight judicial districts, in each of which a judge, a marshal, and a local council, meeting in spring and fall, were to apply the laws. For every two districts there was a circuit judge who was accompanied on his rounds by a company of light-horsemen to execute his decision, and, perhaps, to protect his life. The marshal collected, on commission, the taxes, the principal of which was a poll tax of fifty cents levied on each head of a family and on each single man under sixty.[4] To support the dignity of their government, they built a new capital at the junction of the Conasauga and

[3] I. O. R., Retired Classified Files, Meigs to Secretary of War, November 22, 1822. Meigs said that the Cherokees had about one hundred chiefs and that these were controlled by some twenty "speculating individuals," some of whom were making fortunes by selling whiskey. Not all Cherokee dissensions disappeared at this time. In January, 1821, Lower Cherokee chiefs representing eighty families appealed to the United States for a reservation south of the Tennessee and in November, 1822, proposed to sell their share of Cherokee land and emigrate. Both proposals were rejected (Indian Affairs, II, 502–506).

[4] Ayers Collection No. 689, John Howard Payne Papers concerning the Cherokee Indians, II, 10; Indian Affairs, II, 279–83, laws of the Cherokee nation; Mooney, Myths of the Cherokee, 106–107. In 1820, Pathkiller was the principal chief, John Ross, president of the national council, Alexander McCoy and Elijah Hicks, clerks of the committee and council. The Cherokee treasury was at Fortville (I. O. R., Retired Classified Files, Hicks to McMinn, May 20, 1823).

Oostanaula rivers; to this capital they gave the name New Echota, but commonly referred to it as Newtown.[5] Finally, on December 11, 1821, they closed their only open boundary by agreeing with the Creeks on a dividing line from Buzzard Roost on the Chattahoochee to the mouth of Will's Creek on the Coosa, and thence down the Coosa to Fort Strother.[6]

At the time the treaty was made, it appeared that this line would soon be a division, not between Cherokees and Creeks, but between Cherokees and Georgia. Georgia in 1820 was loudly clamoring for the execution of the Compact, and on August 8 of that year the President, yielding without apparent reluctance to the state's insistence, had appointed commissioners to treat with the Creeks for a land cession.[7] The commissioners had been instructed, on the suggestion of Georgia, to secure a cession separating Creeks and Cherokees; failing to do so, they were to accept one farther south. When they met the Creeks at Indian Springs early in January, 1821, both they and the Creeks were appalled by a Georgia presentation of claims for $450,000 allegedly due under the ancient treaties of Augusta, Galphinton, and Shoulderbone. The Creeks rightly and vainly protested that these claims had been outlawed at the treaties of New York and Colerain; the only concession they could gain was a reference of the matter to the President for determination.[8] The chiefs in attendance at the treaty were few in number and representing only Lower Creek towns. They preferred to make, and the commissioners were willing to accept, a cession, not of the lands along the Cherokee border, but of the territory between the Ocmulgee and the Flint. For this they were to receive $200,000 and the payment of their al-

[5] I. O. R., Retired Classified Files, Meigs to Secretary of War, December 15, 1819.

[6] *Ibid.*, treaty made between Creeks and Cherokees at William McIntosh's, December 11, 1821.

[7] The commissioners appointed were Andrew Pickens and Thomas Flournoy. Both resigned, their place being filled by D. M. Forney and David Meriwether. Before resigning (as a result of friction with the governor of Georgia), Flournoy made the arrangements for a treaty.

[8] These claims were audited later by a commission, which allotted Georgia $25,000. In their report the commissioners expressed the opinion that the Georgia claims were excessive by $350,000.

leged obligations to Georgia.[9] It will be noticed that in the negotiation of this treaty the commissioners had no help and asked none from Agent Mitchell. Mitchell, as the result of one of the amenities of Georgia politics, had been accused by the governor of running slaves from Africa and was now busy trying to refute the charges. In February, 1821, the Secretary of War, sensitive about misconduct of Indian agents outside their own field, dismissed him from the service.[10]

While the United States and Georgia were combining for the further undoing of the Creeks, the United States was locking horns with the rejuvenated Cherokee government about the removal of the agency, the payment of the Cherokee light-horse, and the taxing of licensed traders.

Since the War Department, on the questionable assumption that agents could exert more influence over Indians by living among them, had always insisted on keeping its agencies on Indian ground, frequent removals became necessary to prevent the agent from losing contact with his receding clients. Meigs had moved his agency up the Hiwassee early in 1817, but at the request of the Cherokees had returned to his former location. In the spring of 1820 the Secretary of War decided that the agency must be moved to ground (as yet) unceded, and after consulting all interested parties except the Cherokees themselves fixed on a location up the Hiwassee near Calhoun. The Cherokee council, with the understandable desire of keeping the agency as far away as possible, at once protested this move and, when Meigs persisted, refused to grant lands for the necessary buildings on the Cherokee (south) side of the river. They finally agreed, in 1823, that, although they would not make a cession, they would not obstruct the agency if established on unceded land.[11]

To the organization of the Cherokee light-horse the Sec-

9 *Indian Affairs*, II, 249–55; Kappler, *op. cit.*, II, 195–96; Royce, *Indian Land Cessions*, plate CXXII.

10 The correspondence concerning Mitchell's slave-running activities is in I. O. R., War Department Letter Book D, 377–88, 391, 401–402, and in *ibid.*, Retired Classified Files, December 4 and 25, 1817, and January 1, 1818.

11 The correspondence concerning the removal is in *ibid.*, War Department Letter Book D, 405–408, 449, and *ibid.*, Retired Classified Files, under dates of May 18, 1820, August 14, 1820, and October 6, 1823.

retary had given a grudging approval accompanied by the stipulation that it should not be used against intruders except with Meigs' permission. The Cherokees' demand that the United States pay for such services rested on the logical premise that the prevention of encroachment was an obligation imposed on the United States by treaty. However, in November, 1820, the Secretary of War, vulnerable only to his own logic, refused to pay, and there the matter rested for the time being.[12] The Cherokee law of October 28, 1819, placing a tax of $80 on licensed traders was less a revenue measure than a tariff for the protection of local industry. Irrespective of its nature, the traders refused to pay, and Meigs suspended the law while he referred the matter to the Secretary. Eventually the issue went to the attorney general, who, on the theory (at that time believed in) that the power to tax was the power to destroy, decided against the Cherokees.[13]

The Cherokee sallies into political science were viewed with undisguised hostility by the Georgians, who wished to see the Cherokees not improve but depart. It did not escape their watchful and suspicious notice that this departure, promised in the Compact of 1802, had remained almost wholly unaccelerated from Georgia, while Kentucky, Tennessee, and Alabama had, entirely or in large part, been relieved of the Cherokee incubus. Their rising indignation over this fact was intensified by those clauses in the treaty of 1819 which apparently foreshadowed Cherokee citizenship and permanent residence. In 1820 the governor and legislature of Georgia presented to Congress a memorial protesting against these treaty provisions and won the approval of a sympathetic House committee. In June, 1822, President Monroe, impressed by this flank attack, appointed commissioners to treat with the Cherokees for a cession of their Georgia land.[14]

12 *Ibid.*, War Department Letter Book E, 30–31, Secretary of War to Meigs, November 14, 1820; *ibid.*, Retired Classified Files, Pathkiller to McMinn, October 11, 1823.

13 *Ibid.*, Retired Classified Files, Cherokee delegation to Secretary of War, February 25, 1824; Decision of Attorney General Wirt, April 2, 1824.

14 The commissioners appointed were John Floyd, Freeman Walker, and J. A. Cuthbert; Walker and Cuthbert declined, and D. G. Campbell and David Meriwether were named to succeed them; David Meriwether died, and James Meriwether succeeded; finally Floyd resigned, and his place was not filled.

By the time the commission, delayed by deaths and resignation, which wholly changed its personnel, arranged a meeting with the Cherokees, the tribe had a new agent. Meigs died January 28, 1823, after twenty-three years of service as Cherokee agent. A Cherokee petition to the President asking for Silas Dinsmoor as Meigs' successor was promptly answered by the appointment of McMinn, apparently on the theory that the more obnoxious an agent was to his charges the more effective he would be.[15] In August, 1822, the Cherokees had refused Meigs' invitation to a conference, but the legislature at its fall session in October, 1822, voted to meet the commissioners, provided the conference be held at New Echota, and at the same time informed the Secretary that the tribe would never again make a land cession. When in February, 1823, McMinn (then acting agent) charged them with disrespect to the President by presuming to name the place for the conference, the Cherokees disclaimed all lack of respect, but remained resolute to negotiate only in their capital, saying that this was the custom of all nations. To this application of international law the astonished McMinn was forced to consent and in July, 1823, advised the commissioners to go to New Echota.[16]

When the conference opened on October 6, the Cherokees, remembering certain misrepresentations in the past, successfully insisted that the negotiations should be carried on in writing. The commissioners asked for a cession on the ground that the Cherokee holdings were out of proportion to their numbers and that the Great Father of the Universe had never intended the earth to be so unequally divided. To this the Cherokees gravely replied that they did not know the intention of the Supreme Father in this particular, but that evidently the principle had never been observed or respected by nations or individuals. The commission-

[15] Meigs had been in very poor health for two years before his death. In 1821 the Secretary of War had asked McMinn to take charge of the agency in case of Meigs' death, and this McMinn did in February, 1823, before his formal appointment in March.

[16] I. O. R., Retired Classified Files, John Ross *et al.* to Secretary of War, August 23–24, 1822; Meigs to *idem*, November 22, 1822; Cherokee chiefs to McMinn, April 25, 1823.

ers then argued that the Hopewell treaty made the Cherokees mere tenants at will, holding their land only by the forbearance of the United States. Apparently doubting the efficacy of these religious and legal arguments, the commissioners had recourse to bribery, having doubtless been informed by McMinn how susceptible in the past the Cherokees had shown themselves to persuasions of this sort. In this effort they employed the Creek chief William McIntosh, who, after betraying his own tribe at Indian Springs, had now come to New Echota to perform a similar service for the Cherokees. On October 21, 1823, he wrote to John Ross, president of the national committee:

"My Friend, I am going to inform you a few lines as a friend, I want you to give me your opinion of the treaty, whether the chiefs will be willing or not. If the chiefs feel disposed to let the United States have the land part of it, I want you to let me know. I will make the United States commissioners give you two thousand dollars, A. McKoy the same and Charles Hicks $3,000 for present, and nobody shall know it. And if you think the land wouldn't sold. I will be satisfied. If the lands should be sold I will get you the amount before the treaty sign, and if you got any friend you want him to received they shall received the same amount. Nothing more to inform you at present I remain your affectionate friend. N. B. The whole amount is $12,000. You can divide among your friends, exclusive $7,000. An answer return."[17]

Two days later the Cherokees definitely refused to make a cession and adhered to their decision in the face of menaces and threats until October 27, when they declared the conference closed.[18]

Notwithstanding their firmness in parrying the clumsy thrusts of the commissioners, the Cherokees were worried by the American discovery of the Compact and anxious to have their cause

[17] *Ibid.*, McIntosh to Ross, October 21, 1823.

[18] *Indian Affairs*, II, 465–72, correspondence between the commissioners and the Cherokee council, October 4–27, 1823; I. O. R., Retired Classified Files, commissioners to Cherokee council, October 25, 1823; Georgia had two agents at this conference, and they took an active part in the proceedings.

presented more accurately than they had any reason to believe would be done by the commissioners or by McMinn. Accordingly, in January, 1823, they sent Ross, Ridge, Hicks, and George Lowry to Washington to see the President. They were met with a recital of the Compact and a reiteration of the demand that they cede their land and remove to Arkansas. In the course of their refusal the Cherokees said:

"Sir, to these remarks we beg leave to observe and to remind you that the Cherokee are not foreigners but original inhabitants of America, and that they now inhabit and stand on the soil of their own territory and that the limits of this territory are defined by the treaties which they have made with the government of the United States, and that the states by which they are now surrounded have been created out of land which was once theirs, and that they cannot recognize the sovereignty of any state within the limits of their territory."[19]

They asked the President to abrogate the Compact, suggesting that Georgia be given Florida as compensation for the Indian lands which the United States had promised but would never be able to deliver. They requested the removal of McMinn because of misrepresentation and misconduct of various kinds, asked that the light-horse be paid, that the agency be located according to their wishes, and that their tax on traders be upheld. Their request that the United States begin paying the $1,000 annuity promised in the treaty of 1804 brought from the startled Secretary of War a denial that there had ever been any such treaty. But the Cherokees produced their duplicates, which Jefferson and John McKee had guaranteed, and a little later a thorough hunt through the Indian records revealed the original.[20]

After the conference had arrived at its inevitable stalemate, the Secretary of War advised Governor Troup of Georgia of

[19] I. O. R., Retired Classified Files, Cherokee delegation to Secretary of War, February 11, 1824; *Indian Affairs,* II, 474.
[20] I. O. R., Retired Classified Files, *idem* to *idem,* February 25, 1824; *Indian Affairs,* II, 473–74, *idem* to President, January 19, 1824. McMinn died November 17, 1824.

the inability of the United States to secure the desired Cherokee cession. This drew from the militant Governor a denunciation of Cherokee "effrontery" and a renewed demand that the Compact be carried out. The Georgia Congressional delegation loyally and intemperately supported their Governor in a protest to Monroe against the bad faith of the United States. Apparently stung by this charge of bad faith, the normally serene President sent a special message to Congress recounting the amount of Georgia territory cleared of Indian title since 1802 and contending, quite accurately, that the Compact did not commit the United States to the use of force.[21]

Since both the President and the Secretary of War were in favor of Indian removal, it is unnecessary to consider their further efforts to secure Indian cessions as political strategy in a presidential election year. Whatever their motive or justification, they seem to have owed their opportunity and their success to the invaluable William McIntosh, who at the New Echota conference had hinted to the disconsolate commissioners that they might secure a cession from the Creeks in compensation for that refused by the Cherokees.[22] In accord with, if not as a result of, this hint, the President in July, 1824, appointed Campbell and Meriwether commissioners to treat with the Creeks for a minimum cession of their remaining land in Georgia; a cession of the Alabama land also would be acceptable.

If the commissioners at the time of their appointment did not know, they quickly learned that certain developments among the Creeks since the New Echota meeting threatened the defeat of their intended negotiations. On its return from its extended stay in Washington, the Cherokee delegation revealed to the Creeks the collaboration of McIntosh with the Americans and proposed that the two tribes take concerted action to protect themselves against his treachery. As a result, a Creek council at Tuckabatchee in May, 1824, followed the Cherokee example by

[21] Richardson, *Messages and Papers*, II, 234–37, Monroe to Congress, March 30, 1824; *Indian Affairs*, II, 475–76, Troup to Secretary of War, February 28, 1824. The Cherokee delegation, still in Washington, replied to the Georgia protest on April 16.

[22] *Indian Affairs*, II, 464, Campbell to Secretary of War, November 28, 1823.

adopting a resolution never again to cede land and to punish with death any chief or chiefs negotiating such a cession. Since the council had apparently been composed mostly of Upper Creeks, the resolution was sent to the Lower Creek chiefs, who assembled at Broken Arrow and, with only McIntosh dissenting, approved. The most active champion of the Creek resolution was Big Warrior, whose attitude reflected not only his patriotism but also his enmity toward McIntosh, who, by his influence among the Lower Creeks, was a rival for leadership. Uninfluenced by the Creek resolution, except to promise McIntosh protection in his expected collaboration, the commissioners proceeded with their arrangements, and in due season summoned the Creeks to a conference at Broken Arrow in December, 1824.

Presumably as a measure for strengthening their spirits for the coming ordeal, eighteen chiefs, including Big Warrior, Little Prince of Broken Arrow, and the Coweta Chief, met at the home of Sub-agent Walker (son-in-law of Big Warrior) at Pole Cat Springs and re-enacted their resolution against land cessions.

The negotiations began at Broken Arrow, December 1, with two hundred chiefs and ten thousand Americans (by commissioners' estimate) present. After the usual opening preliminaries, the commissioners declared to the Creeks that they had been conquered in the Revolution and had since held their lands as tenants at will and demanded a cession of the said lands in exchange for territory in the West. Referring to the Tuckabatchee and Pole Cat Springs resolutions, they observed that the Upper Creeks had once before, in 1813, defied the wishes of the United States and had thereby brought condign punishment on themselves. Following this address the Creeks held a council, as usual, and on December 14 returned a refusal to make any cession at all. For four days they remained firm, returning quick negatives to the repeated demands of the commissioners until on December 18 the commissioners adjourned the meeting so that Campbell might go to Washington to consult the President. To Campbell's request for authority to negotiate with the Lower Creeks alone for a cession of the Creek lands in Georgia, the President gave a prompt refusal but, either unsuspecting or indifferent to the opportunities for fraud, gave him permission to accept such a cession if approved by the entire nation. The President also agreed that Agent Crowell should be reprimanded for not aiding the commissioners and that Sub-agent Walker should be dismissed for complicity in the opposition to them.

Armed with these new weapons, Campbell returned to Georgia and summoned a Creek meeting at Indian Springs for February 7, 1825. Either because the Upper Creeks were not notified or because they boycotted the meeting, only the Lower Creek chiefs appeared at Indian Springs; of the fifty-six Creek towns then existing, only eight were represented at the conference, which the commissioners spoke of as a general assembly of the nation. Four of these towns in January had sent a petition to the President for the removal of Big Warrior and had authorized McIntosh and seven others to go to Washington for the purpose of ceding the lands desired. From an assembly so composed Campbell had no difficulty securing all he asked. In the treaty of February 12, 1825, the partial representation of the Lower Creeks ceded to the United States not only the Georgia lands but practically all of the Alabama territory inhabited by the Upper Creeks; in return, the United States promised an equal acreage between the Arkansas and Canadian rivers. McIntosh received for his collaboration his expected reward in the form of a payment of $25,-000 for his small reservation.[23]

When the Senate ratified and the President John Quincy Adams promulgated this measure of iniquity over the protests of the Creeks and their agents, the outraged nation finally took the law into its own hands. On May 1 a company of warriors, sent down from Tuckabatchee, surrounded the house of McIntosh, set fire to it, and killed both McIntosh and another of the treaty makers as they fled from the burning building. They also killed one son-in-law of McIntosh and tried to kill another. These executions were ordered by a council meeting at Tuckabatchee, but whether this was a national council or (as is likely) one of the Upper Creeks alone, it is impossible to say. In all probability, even had there been no council action, McIntosh would have

[23] *Ibid.*, II, 568–84.

been killed. For Big Warrior had died just as the treaty was being signed, and his death had inflamed the indignation aroused by the treaty. The Creek council declared that while it would not oppose the United States in war, it would neither carry out the treaty nor emigrate.

McIntosh's son hurried to Washington, where he demanded vengeance and the Creek annuities. His outcries attracted the attention and aroused the suspicion of the Puritan President who after investigation refused to execute a treaty so fraudulently obtained. In the fall of 1825 an authorized Creek delegation, stabilized by two Cherokee secretaries, went to Washington, where in January, 1826, it secured an abrogation of the treaty of 1825, ceding in return all the Creek lands (so the delegation thought) in Georgia. For this cession the Creeks received $247,600 in cash, and a perpetual annuity of $20,000.

XII

After Half a Century

THE ENFORCED SHRINKING of their domain in the half-century between 1775 and 1825 had brought to the Southern Indians more spiritual anguish than physical inconvenience. The land ceded, except by the Cherokees, had been hunting grounds that had lost their utility because the hunters had changed their occupation when the hunted disappeared. The game reserve of the South, as of the North, which had been redundant as long as the Indians hunted merely for subsistence, had rapidly vanished in the mass slaughter when they became hunters for trade. Not the loss of their hunting ground but the extinction of the game limited the Southern Indians to an agriculture which had once been only a partial means of support. For a livelihood by farming the twenty-five million acres remaining to the four tribes in 1825 were as sufficient as their vast possessions in 1775 had been for hunting.

In the course of fifty years the Indians had changed their habits but not greatly their habitations. The Cherokees, forced to move many of their towns in Tennessee, most of those in North Carolina, and all in South Carolina, had gradually shifted their homes and their capital to Georgia. But the Creeks still lived on the Coosa, the Tallapoosa, and the Chattahoochee; the Choctaw towns still lay along the upper waters of the Pearl and the Chickasawhay; the Chickasaws clung still to their high divide between the Yazoo and the Tombigbee.[1] The Indian towns were as constant in numbers as in location, and, although the Creeks had lost appreciably in the uprising of 1813 and the consequent migration to Florida, the Southern Indian population in 1825 was probably about the same as it had been fifty years before. Of this population the full-bloods, retaining their ancient gregariousness, generally preferred the village life with its social amenities, while the half-bloods were more inclined to "settle out" in search of individual betterment.

In all the four tribes the half-bloods had both multiplied and prospered. Not with superior intelligence, but with fuller understanding, they were better able to cope with and to profit from the chicanery of the white men. They were the chief patrons of the schools, the best farmers, where few were good, lived in the best houses, accumulated the most property, professed the loudest religion, and exhibited the worst morality in the entire Indian country. There was no apparent prejudice against mestizos and none against zambos among any of the Southern Indians except the Cherokees, among whom marriages between Negroes and Indians were prohibited, perhaps as a measure of avoiding the criticism of their white neighbors. Among the Chickasaws, the Colberts; among the Choctaws, the Folsoms and Le Flores; among the Creeks, the McIntoshes, Taitts, and McGillivrays; and among the Cherokees, the Rosses, Vanns, Hickses, Lowrys, and McCoys, were the actual rulers of the tribes. With the passing of Tinebe (1820), Pushmataha (1825), Big Warrior (1825), and Pathkiller (1827), they became the nominal rulers as well.

Only the Cherokees had made any appreciable change in their form of government since 1775. The Cherokees and the Creeks still had their head chiefs; the Chickasaws, their "king." The change of the Choctaws early in the century from head chief to district chiefs was not an innovation but a relapse. Only the Chero-

[1] C. W. Long, acting sub-agent of the Chickasaws, in the course of a ten-page description of Chickasaw conditions in 1824, said that the Chickasaws lived in four districts: Pontatock, ten miles north of the agency, where the old town was abandoned; Chesafaliah, ten miles northeast of the agency; Chuquafalia, four miles east of Chesafaliah; and Big Town (where the whole nation had lived till 1789), four miles from Chuquafalia (I. O. R., Retired Classified Files, Long to McKenney, November 5, 1824).

kees had changed the ancient council into a legislature, and even there the making of laws was little more than the recording of customs. In 1825, little less than in 1775, the Indians were still governed by customs rather than by laws, for the carrying out of which no tribe, except the Cherokees, had been able, or inclined, to devise the adequate machinery. There is little indication that in the half-century the Southern Indian had become less individualistic or more tolerant of authority than in 1775. But if the governments had not grown strong, neither had they grown expensive, and except for the Cherokees the Indians lived a life enviably free from taxation. The few costs of administration were paid from the annuities which all tribes were receiving in return for surrendered land. In 1825 the Cherokees were receiving from the United States $15,000 a year, of which $9,000 was a permanent annuity and $6,000 due to expire the next year; the Chickasaws, the plutocrats of the South, were drawing $35,000 a year, of which, however, only $3,000 was permanent, while $10,000 expired in 1828 and $20,000 in 1833; the Choctaws were receiving $11,400, of which $5,400 was permanent and $6,000 expired in 1826; and the Creeks were receiving $14,500, of which $4,500 was permanent and $10,000 was to expire in 1829.[2] In addition to these sums, some of the leading chiefs received small individual annuities and many more had earned bribes of various amounts. By 1825 the annuities were generally in the form of specie, sent to the different agencies and there distributed to the head chiefs, with whom (so it was often charged) it frequently remained. The Cherokees, after they reformed their government in 1819, received their annuity at the agency and then carried it under guard to their treasury at Fortville.

It is possible that the idea of civilizing the Indians originated in altruism and that only as an afterthought did it occur to its originators that Indian civilization could be used not only to improve the recipient but also to benefit the sponsor. Logically beginning as a proposition for fitting the Indians for a life in the East, it was continued illogically to promote their removal to the West.

[2] I. O. R., Retired Classified Files, statement of annuities by William Lee, second auditor, October 14, 1800.

As a matter of fact, the government of the United States committed itself almost simultaneously to the support of these mutually inconsistent, if not contradictory, policies: in March, 1802, it authorized the spending of $15,000 a year to civilize the Indians *in situ*, and a month later signed the Georgia Compact foreshadowing removal. The Congress, however, did not hamper the president by actually appropriating any part of the sum it authorized him to spend, thus leaving him free to furnish domestic animals, implements of husbandry, merchandise, and instruction agents to whatever extent he could find the funds.

On March 3, 1819, the Congress of the United States essayed to supplement these activities by authorizing and actually appropriating $10,000 for the employment of capable persons, always of good moral character, to instruct the Indians (both Northern and Southern) in the mode of agriculture suited to their situation, and to teach the Indian children reading, writing, and arithmetic. This cautious appropriation, the President decided, could be best utilized in the support of schools already established and to be established by the various religious denominations and benevolent societies.[3]

The Indians of the South, while willing to have their children educated to an understanding of the white man's way, were intolerant of the white man's religion, which they considered uselessly encumbered with morality. They were persuaded to accept the missions as the only practicable method of securing the teaching. The first of these Southern Indian missions was that begun among the Cherokees in December, 1801, at Spring Place under the sponsorship of the Society of United Brethren, known generally as Moravians. Spring Place was near the Conasauga River and on the Georgia Road. Close by was the home of Joseph Vann, who, with a reputation yet unsullied, was and remained the chief sponsor of the school. Until 1817, Spring Place was the only school in existence among the Southern Indians,[4] but in that

[3] The government undertook to pay two-thirds of the cost of the buildings in these schools, and to give them an annual appropriation proportioned to the number of students (I. O. R., Letter Book D, 378; 48 Cong., 2 sess., II, pt. 2, *Sen. Doc. No. 95*).

[4] In 1803 the Presbyterian missionary with money collected from the north-

year the American Board of Foreign Missions established a second at Brainerd among the Cherokees and the next year a third at Eliot for the Choctaws. Permission to establish Brainerd was secured by Cyrus Kingsbury from the chiefs at Turkey Town, in 1816, where they had assembled in the vain hope of rejecting the treaty to which their untrustworthy delegation had consented at the Chickasaw council house. For the proposed school the United States bought from John McDonald 160 acres of ground on Chickamauga Creek in the eastern outskirts of the present Chattanooga, and there in January, 1817, the missionaries began erecting their buildings: a mission house, a schoolhouse, a dining hall and kitchen, a gristmill, sawmill, barn, stable, and (for the boys) five log cabins. By May 18, Brainerd had forty-seven pupils and fifty acres of ground under cultivation.[5]

Eliot was located about three miles south of the Yalobusha River, some thirty miles above its junction with the Yazoo. It was named for the noted Massachusetts apostle to the Indians. By 1820 it had sixty acres of cleared land, a horse mill, a joiner-and-blacksmith shop, 22 other buildings, a wagon, 2 carts, 2 plows, 7 horses, a yoke of oxen, 220 cattle, 60 hogs, and a keelboat, all valued at $11,478.[6] From these statistics it becomes evident that whatever difficulties the missionaries had in spreading religion or teaching the three R's, they were successfully setting the unemulating Choctaws an example of thrift.

Anyone cynically inclined would not fail to notice the great increase in missionary ardor after the President's decision to subsidize the missions. Three missions were established before 1820; eighteen were added by 1826. It would appear from the statistics available that the Choctaws most approved, or least resisted, the missions, having among them nearly half of the entire number;[7]

ern churches established two schools, on Sale Creek and on the Hiwassee. Both died in 1810 (Brown, *op. cit.*, 468).

[5] Jedidiah Morse, *Report to the Secretary of War on Indian Affairs*, 159. Brown, *op. cit.*, 480; Marion L. Starkey, *The Cherokee Nation*, 34. Brainers was named for Rev. David Brainerd.

[6] Morse, *op. cit.*, 185.

[7] Of the nine Choctaw schools, only Eliot and Mayhew were of any considerable size. Mayhew, established in 1822 by the American Board of Foreign Missions, possessed a frame dining room, four log houses, four cabins, three

that the Creeks were the last and the most reluctant to admit either teaching or preaching as was shown by the precarious existence among them of but one school;[8] that the small Chickasaw nation was perhaps academically overstocked with two schools;[9] that the Cherokee schools were the best equipped in the Indian South;[10] that at the close of 1825 the schools had ninety-six teachers ministering to some six hundred "scholars"; and that the United States was underwriting their efforts to the extent of $7,280 a year.

What access of civilization resulted from this vigorous plowing of the vineyard is problematical. The Indians in 1825 were certainly more agriculturally inclined, but this oblique approach to civilization resulted less from propaganda and formal instruction than from the exhaustion of their game supply. There is little evidence that the missionaries were qualified to give, and still less that the Indian children were inclined to accept, an agricultural training which they were required to exemplify by work at the missions themselves.

It seems clear that the missions were much more successful in teaching weaving, sewing, and other household arts to the girls than in imparting a knowledge of farming and mechanics to the boys. Moreover, the "scholars" of both sexes had as noticeable a tendency to backslide in education as their white neighbors had in religion. But whatever their lack of enthusiasm for vocational training, they preferred it to the cultural education in reading, writing, and arithmetic. The teachers, being without knowledge of the Indian languages and, with rare exception, devoid of any

---

storehouses, a joiner-and-blacksmith shop, three stables, and two cribs (Morse, *op. cit.*, 192; W. A. Love, "The Mayhew Mission to the Choctaws," *Publications of the Mississippi Historical Society*, Vol. XI, 363–402).

[8] Withington, the only Creek school, was established in 1823 by the Baptist General Convention.

[9] The two Chickasaw schools were Monroe, established by the Synod of South Carolina and Georgia in 1821, and Charity Hall, established by the Cumberland Missionary Society in 1822. The former was suspended in 1829.

[10] Of the eight Cherokee schools at the close of 1825, Brainerd was the largest, the Valley Towns second, and Spring Place third. The Valley towns school was established (in the southwest corner of North Carolina) by the Baptist General Convention in 1820. An excellent account of the Cherokee missions is R. S. Walker, *Torchlights to the Cherokees*. The Cherokee schools were distributed thus: four in Georgia and two each in Alabama and Tennessee.

wish to learn them, taught only in English pupils who rarely knew any English at all. Under such conditions reading became a matter of memory without meaning; writing, of copying without comprehension; and arithmetic, an exercise in misunderstanding. Small wonder that the "scholars" were addicted to running away from school.

In October, 1820, the Cherokee legislature enacted that "whereas much inconvenience and expense have devolved on the missionaries from the scholars running away from school," they should be paid in such cases for the clothing, board, and tuition of the absentees. One of the "inconveniences" resulting from truancy was that it left the teachers to do all the mission work themselves. A considerable part of the avidity with which the Cherokee children learned the alphabet which Sequoyah invented (1822) was due to the release it brought them from the hideous and almost hopeless task of learning to read and write English.[11]

Practically all the half-bloods *spoke* English, but the language they used showed few traces of missionary influence. The linguistic knowledge of the full-bloods was generally limited to the fields of profanity and obscenity, in both of which they revealed to the astonished and embarrassed missionaries a remarkable virtuosity. To this ability to speak English, if such be considered an evidence of advancing civilization, may be added other indications of Indian improvement. They had adopted the American dress, although their manner of combining the various items was not always orthodox and in the summer they often relapsed into their ancient approach to nudity; the clothing of the women conformed to white standards better than did that of the men. In comparison with their condition fifty years earlier, they lived in better houses, log cabins for the masses, quite often frame houses for the half-bloods, and an occasional brick for the well-to-do. They had more constant food, more furniture, more implements and utensils, and more creature comforts of various kinds. All these material things they had gained from the Americans, and the gain was not small. Perhaps their greatest intangible gain, whether result-

[11] Probably the best account of this "Cherokee Cadmus" is Grant Foreman's *Sequoyah*.

ing from American pressure or from their own improved understanding, had been the total abandonment of intertribal war.

On two vital points they had remained unchanged and, it may be, unimproved. They had not accepted the white man's religion or his idea of holding land in severalty. Many of the half-bloods, perhaps the greater part of them, were affiliated with the frontier religious denominations, but the full-bloods remained almost to a man skeptical and intolerant. The Indians, especially the elders, were glad to receive teachers for their children, provided the teacher did not turn preacher. The Creeks, indeed, in their one school at Withington refused any religious instruction or exhortation.[12] In 1825 the Southern Indians were as strongly communistic as in 1775; the development of agriculture among them had not altered their conception of land as a tribal possession or inclined them to the acceptance of any private ownership thereof. Tribal ownership permitted private utilization and private control but forbade private alienation. Among the Cherokees by positive law, and in the other tribes by equally positive custom, an occupant of land could transfer his holdings only with tribal consent. To the Southern Indians, tribal ownership of land seemed to be the foundation of tribal unity; private ownership an evidence, if not a cause, of tribal disintegration. Their tribal land was to them not a property but a home. This home they were unwilling by private ownership to exploit, by cession to divide, or by emigration to abandon.

[12] I. O. R., Retired Classified Files, Webb to Capers, May 25, 1823; *ibid.*, Smith to———, September 20, 1825.

XIII

Epilogue: The Last Stand

1825-1830

Aᴀ1825 the history of the Southern Indians is limited to the epic and tragic theme of removal. The constant and unrelenting pressure by the United States warped all Indian relations; Indian resistance to removal determined practically all tribal actions. Their leaders were chosen because of their attitude toward removal, their councils deliberated only on the subject of removal. Removal was the focus of their thoughts, and the dread of it virtually paralyzed their lives.

From his predecessor, President Adams inherited not only the old problem of Cherokees, Creeks, Choctaws, and Chickasaws, but also the new problem of the Seminoles. These were the only Florida Indians remaining in 1821, the other tribes having gradually attained extinction in the normal course of contact with the Spanish and British. The first of the Seminoles were Lower Creeks who in late colonial times had moved in to occupy the region left vacant since the involuntary departure therefrom of such Apalachees as had survived the Moore raid of 1704. Without loss of ancient identity they gained a new name and were called Seminoles because they were frontiersmen. Miccosukee was their principal town, and to its chief the Seminoles usually paid that small measure of allegiance consonant with Creek practice. The Seminoles considered themselves a part of the Creek people, invariably supported them in war, usually attended their councils, and acknowledged, if they did not always respect, the authority of the Creek head chief. To their geographical detachment from the other Creeks had been added, in 1795, a political cleavage, with the result of so increasing their already considerable spirit of independence that they became practically a separate tribe. As frontiersmen they gave sympathy, and some assistance, to the Red Sticks in the Creek war of 1814, and after the war gave refuge to those who had survived the onslaught of American craftiness and Cherokee valor. The virtue of this act was not divorced from necessity since the newcomers outnumbered the older Seminoles two to one. The entire tribe now numbered some five thousand people divided among fifteen or eighteen villages located for the most part between the Apalachicola and the Suwannee rivers. Miccosukee retained its primacy as the largest and most important town, but the head chief of the tribe was Neamothla, a Red Stick, whose residence was at Cohowofooche, near the present Tallahassee.[1]

Because Florida was so vast, the Indian population so scanty, and white immigration so small, it would seem that there was little need for either removal or concentration. Nevertheless, Andrew Jackson, acting as governor, urged the United States to return the Red Sticks to Alabama and to concentrate the remainder of the tribe along the Apalachicola. Investigation, however, convinced the War Department that the Red Sticks would not return without war, and that the Apalachicola region, because of its fertility, was unsuitable for Indian occupancy. On September 18, 1823, the Seminole chiefs were induced, by a liberal application of the customary methods of persuasion, to accept a reservation in central Florida between Lake Okechobee and the Withlacoochee River.[2] In representing this region to the Seminoles as a place where they would be free from white encroachment, the commissioners spoke with complete, if unintentional, accuracy,

---

[1] *Indian Affairs*, II, 408–16.

[2] *Ibid.*, 429–30. The journal of the commissioners makes the interesting suggestion that the predecessors of the Seminoles were Yemassees. It names the Seminole towns and their chiefs. Neamothla's town was twenty-three miles northwest of St. Marks. Neamothla appears in Angie Debo's *The Road to Disappearance* as Eneah Amarthla. Both forms are titles and not personal names.

since it was barren of game, swampy, frequently inundated, and incapable of cultivation.

Neamothla, after denouncing the reservation, signed the treaty which consigned his tribe to destruction, but permitted him and five other chiefs to remain on reservations along the Apalachicola. Government inefficiency and Indian reluctance combined to postpone for a year the removal of the Seminoles to their reservation. Whether from old habit or in illogical protest against the treaty he had signed, Neamothla permitted and perhaps encouraged his followers to drive off or kill the cattle and burn the houses of his white neighbors. An end was put to this pastime when Governor Duval in the summer of 1824 called out the militia, marched on Neamothla's town, overawed the Indians, and ordered the entire tribe to meet him at St. Marks the last of July. In a conference with the six hundred who actually came, Duval deposed Neamothla as head chief, appointed John Hicks in his place, and fixed October 1 as the date for beginning the removal.[3]

Before the rear guard of the Seminoles reached the reservation, the vanguard began leaving it, having convinced themselves by actual inspection that their new home could profitably be utilized only as a cemetery. Promised government supplies failed to reach them, nothing edible could be gleaned from the reservation, and the starving Seminoles could maintain a feeble vitality only by breaking out of the reservation and subsisting on the cattle they could steal from the scanty white population of Florida. In these enterprises the Miccosukees, it is interesting to note, took a vigorous lead and by so doing regained the moral ascendancy they had previously lost to the Red Sticks. For the four years of Adams' administration the Seminoles continued to roam, hungry and desperate, over North Florida, returning to their reservation only when threatened by overwhelming force or allured by the infrequent arrival of government supplies.

While the Seminoles were engaged in mitigating, after their fashion, the misdemeanors of the Monroe Indian policy in Florida,

[3] *Ibid.*, 619. Duval to Secretary of War, July 12, 1824. After his deposition as head chief of the Seminoles, Neamothla returned to Alabama and took an active part in Creek resistance.

their Creek kinsmen were intent on undoing the felony committed against them at Indian Springs. Only after President Adams had sent the treaty to the Senate and had seen it ratified did the evidence of its iniquity reach him in the form of condemning reports from Agent Crowell and General Gadsden, and indignant protests from the Creeks.[4] Unwilling either to condone a fraud or to exasperate the Georgians, the President undertook to obtain from the Creeks in a fair treaty the Georgia territory of which they had recently been so unfairly deprived. To this the Creeks, apparently prizing their property less than their pride, agreed; and in the treaty of Washington, January 24, 1826, they supposed they were surrendering, as Adams supposed he was obtaining, all the Creek land in Georgia. When it became evident that both were mistaken, an amendment to the treaty was adopted (March 3, 1826) to repair the error, but the new line still lay east of the Alabama boundary; and a third treaty, November 15, 1827, was required before the Creeks could divest themselves of the last remnant of those Georgia lands to which, since the time of Alexander McGillivray, they had so tenaciously clung.

The Creek dissensions resulting from the treaty of Indian Springs were lessened by Adams' policy of recognizing the Upper Creeks as the legal, because the largest, faction, and disappeared with the consequent migration of the McIntosh faction west of the Mississippi. But the now spiritually united nation experienced fresh exasperation from Alabama and Georgia, both of which insisted that the Indian Springs treaty was valid inasmuch as it had received Senate ratification. The Alabama legislature on January 11, 1827, extended the state jurisdiction over the Alabama region ceded in that treaty and forbade hunting and trapping therein by the Indians; the Georgia legislature authorized the survey of the entire Indian Springs cession even before the date fixed in the treaty. The Alabama courts, recognizing the validity of the Washington treaty, invalidated the legislative act,

[4] Telamon Cuyler MSS. (University of Georgia) Indian Affairs, 1800-, Apothla Yahola and others to Secretary of War, December 16, 1825. These letters were probably composed and written by John Ridge, the Cherokee secretary of the Creek delegation.

but Georgia persisted in her surveys in complete disregard of both Creek protests and Presidential prohibitions. The last public act of Little Prince, the aged head chief of the Creeks, was to drive off a party of Georgia surveyors.[5]

While the United States was preoccupied with the Seminoles and Georgia with the Creeks, the Cherokees had experienced, if they had not enjoyed, a brief respite from troubles. The death in January, 1827, of Pathkiller, the head chief with a penchant for appeasement, left the tribal government in the hands of resolute, if not always judicious, men.[6] In March, 1827, they denied a cession of their North Carolina land and a right of way for a Georgian-projected canal to connect the waters of the Tennessee and the Coosa. Naïvely thinking they could forestall further demands for removal by presenting evidence of civilization, they decided to adopt a written constitution and to establish a national newspaper. On July 26, 1827, delegates from the various Cherokee towns in the four states met at New Echota and adopted a written constitution modeled closely upon that of the United States; the newspaper, the *Cherokee Phoenix*, issued its first number (in English and Cherokee) at New Echota on February 2, 1828.[7]

The first effect of these cultural forays was a domestic rebellion; the second, a revival, or at least an intensification, of the controversy with Georgia. The first was a protest against the imitation of white civilization; the second, an answer to its alleged defiance. The rebellion was sponsored by Whitepath, a full-blood Cherokee councilor, who demanded the rejection of all white culture, Christianity included, and a return to primitive ways. It was, therefore, a feeble and belated echo of the Creek movement

[5] Creek Indian Letters, 1813–1829, pt. 3, 1110, 1111; *ibid.*, 1112, Little Prince to Georgia Surveyors, January 12, 1827; *ibid.*, 1115 *id.* to Troup, January 22, 18, 27; *ibid.*, 1782–1839, 109, Barbour to Troup, January 29, 1827.

[6] Rachel Caroline Eaton, *John Ross and the Cherokee Indians*, 54–55. Pathkiller was succeeded by C. R. Hicks, who died about two weeks after Pathkiller's death. Then the government was administered by Major Ridge and John Ross until the meeting of the council, which made William Hicks principal chief with John Ross as second chief.

[7] For an account of the constitution making and the establishment of the newspaper, see Mooney, *Myths of the Cherokee*, 112.

of 1814. John Ross, now head chief under the constitution, made short work of the uprising, which ended with the submission of Whitepath and the restoration of his forfeited seat on the council.[8]

The horror expressed, and doubtless felt, by Governor Forsyth over the new Cherokee constitution was lacking in logic, since the Cherokees were no more of an entity under their constitution than before. But he sent the President a copy of the constitution with an accompanying protest from the Georgia legislature. To this Adams responded by instructing Agent Montgomery to secure, if possible, the removal of the Cherokees from Georgia, and by sending two commissioners to assist him in his efforts to promote the emigration of Cherokee individuals.[9]

President Adams, notwithstanding his opposition to Georgia practices, did not disapprove the principle of Indian removal. In October, 1826, he sent a three-man commission to the South to negotiate removal treaties with the Choctaws and Chickasaws. The Choctaws, regarding a visit from a federal commission as somewhat in the nature of a hostile invasion, prepared their defenses by replacing their old chiefs with younger and more resolute men. Pushmataha, chief of the southern district, had died some years before and had been succeeded by Tupeau Homa. On the eve of the conference, the Choctaws of the northeastern and northwestern districts took the unprecedented action of deposing their old chiefs, Mushulatubbe and Robert Cole, and of electing in their place David Folsom and Greenwood LeFlore. These men were half-bloods well acquainted with white ways and wiles.

Instead of bringing to the conference the rank and file, who were all too susceptible to bribery and corruption, the new chiefs entrusted the conduct of the negotiations to a committee of thirteen whom they thought invulnerable to American pressure. To the commissioners' offer of $1,000,000 for their Mississippi territory, transportation to the West, and reservations in Mississippi for all preferring to remain under state jurisdiction, the committee of thirteen gave a firm, although not a unanimous, rejection, commenting that if they could not trust to an American guarantee of

[8] *Ibid.*, 113; Eaton, *op. cit.*, 113.
[9] Royce, *The Cherokee Nation*, 241–42, 258, 259.

Chief John Ross of the Cherokees
From a painting by John Neagle, 1846

Courtesy Philbrook Art Center

David Folsom, Mushulatubbe's successor

Courtesy Oklahoma Historical Society

their present territory, they could not have faith in a guarantee of new lands. They also refused a cession of a small tract on the Tombigbee that the commissioners had been instructed to get in case their larger demands were refused. The commissioners, after deploring the absence of the Choctaw rank and file and expressing their amazement at Choctaw ingratitude, departed for the Chickasaws.

The Chickasaws laid the groundwork for their reception by decreeing that no Chickasaws could accept a private reservation and by successfully insisting that the conference be held not at the agency but at the tribal council house. In the conference held after these precautions had been taken, they refused either to cede their lands or to send an exploring party to the West.[10]

It was only by honoring his professions and completely ignoring his practices that the Southern Indians could expect from Jackson the justice they had experienced under Adams. Whatever may have been the hopes of the Indians, the advocates of removal felt that with the election of President Jackson in November, 1828, their hour of triumph had arrived. In order to render the Cherokees more receptive to the anticipated actions of the incoming President, the Georgia legislature on December 20, 1828, extended the state jurisdiction over all the land within the Georgia limits; in order to give Jackson time to act, the enforcement of the law was deferred until June 1, 1830.[11] Jackson justified the faith of Georgia by informing a delegation of protesting Cherokees through Secretary Eaton that he could not protect them against the Georgia laws and that their only course was submission or removal.

When the Cherokees returned home firm in their determination to do neither, the President on May 27 commissioned William Carroll, a special agent, to travel through the Cherokee and Creek country with the double objective of securing tribal cessions and individual migration.[12] Cherokee officials refused to treat with Carroll and also refused a second bid for their North

[10] *Indian Affairs*, II, 709–27, journal of the commissioners William Clark, Thomas Hinds, and John Coffee.
[11] Mooney, *Myths of the Cherokee*, 117.
[12] Royce, *The Cherokee Nation*, 259.

Carolina lands. They likewise refused to accept the Georgia interpretation of a northern boundary for the Creek cession and had the unusual satisfaction of seeing their stand supported by Jackson's line commissioner, John Coffee.[13] These were Pyrrhic victories, for both Jackson and Georgia were determined on removal. Jackson in his annual message to Congress, December 8, 1829, asked that body to give removal the same legislative sanction it had long had from the executive. Eleven days later the Georgia legislature upheld his hands by enacting the first of a series of laws annulling all Cherokee laws, forbidding further meetings of their council or other assemblies within Georgia limits, declaring all contracts between white men and Indians invalid unless witnessed by two white men, making an Indian incapable of being a witness against a white man, providing for the survey and distribution of Cherokee land, and excluding the Cherokees from digging gold in the newly discovered gold fields in the Cherokee country.[14]

The example set by the Georgia Act of 1828 was followed by Mississippi in February, 1829, with the enactment of a law declaring the Indian territory in the state subject to legal process. In September, 1829, the Choctaw agent, Ward, interrupted his embezzlement of Choctaw annuities long enough to urge the Choctaws to cede their lands and remove west. In November a special and less malodorous envoy, Major David Haley, was sent down with the same demand. Both propositions were promptly rejected by Folsom, chief of the northeastern district, speaking for the tribe. A break in the tribal will became evident in the winter of 1829, when LeFlore of the northwestern district visited Nashville on Jackson's invitation and, for reasons unrecorded, became a convert to the policy of removal.[15]

On May 28, 1830, President Jackson approved a law of Congress providing for the removal of the Indians. The law had re-

[13] Telamon Cuyler MSS, Indian Affairs, 1780–1830, Coffee to Gilmer, November 26, 1829; *idem* to Eaton, December 30, 1829.

[14] Mooney, *Myths of the Cherokee*, 117. Gold was discovered in northern Georgia in 1828. For the resulting gold rush, see F. M. Green's "Georgia's Forgotten Industry: Gold Mining, *Georgia Historical Quarterly*, Vol. XIX, 93–111, 210–28.

[15] Abel, *op. cit.*, 370–72.

ceived only a bare majority over the strenuous opposition of Northern Congressmen whose solicitude for the Southern Indians was perhaps not divorced from an inclination to throttle the increase of a Southern white electorate. The law made removal inevitable; it marked the end of the trail for the Indians in the Southeast. To be sure, the law did not provide for compulsory removal; the Indians had the alternative of remaining in their homes on individual reservations, without tribal organization, subject to state jurisdiction. The governor of Georgia on July 3 declared in force the state laws previously made and deferred; Alabama in 1829 had annexed the Indian territory within the state limits and placed the Indians themselves under state jurisdiction; Mississippi in March, 1830, enacted a law providing that Indian chiefs presuming to perform their functions be subject to a fine of $1,000 and imprisonment for a year.[16]

All the tribes except the Cherokees soon ceased to struggle. The badgered Creeks, bereft of leadership by the death of Little Prince, and seeing their lands increasingly appropriated by white intruders whom they were powerless to remove, sent to Washington a delegation which, on March 24, 1832, signed an agreement to remove. The Seminoles yielded on the following May 9. The Choctaws, after their other chiefs had resigned in fear of the Mississippi law, were influenced by LeFlore to accept removal in the infamous treaty of Dancing Rabbit Creek, October 28. The Chickasaws agreed on October 20. The Cherokees alone continued the contest, driving the intruders off their lands, removing their capital to Tennessee, and appealing to the Supreme Court of the United States for protection. These measures postponed but did not avert the final doom. On December 29, 1835, at New Echota in the absence of John Ross and other tribal officials, a few dissident chiefs were corrupted into signing a treaty of removal, which Jackson shamelessly utilized as an expression of tribal consent.

[16] *Ibid.*, 371; Debo, *op. cit.*, 97.

BIBLIOGRAPHY

MANUSCRIPTS

United States Archives, Washington, D. C.

The Indian Office Records are by far the most extensive and the most valuable single source of information on the Southern Indians and are the foundation of this account. The writer used them before they were collected in the Archives and consequently retains in his annotation the classification of that time. The most important part of these records for the present study were the Retired Classified Files consisting chiefly of letters received from Indian agents in the field. The letter books of the secretary of war and of the superintendent of Indian trade give the outgoing letters. The records of the various factories are invaluable for Indian trade.

Library of Congress, Washington, D. C.

Colonial Office Records, British Transcripts.

These have been utilized for the Revolutionary period. The correspondence of Stuart and Browne with the home authorities throws much light on the part of the Indians in the Revolution.

Papers of the Continental Congress are utilized for the Revolutionary and Confederation periods.

The Newberry Library, Chicago, Ill.

The Ayer Collection contains the John Howard Payne Papers (Cherokee) and many transcripts from the Archivo Nacional de Cuba, including Indian Trade Documents, 1783–1821.

Wisconsin Historical Society, Madison, Wisconsin.
> The Tennessee Papers of the Draper Manuscripts were useful for the Revolutionary and Confederation Period.

Department of Archives and History, Atlanta, Georgia.
> The most rewarding of these records are the Creek Indian Letters and Cherokee Indians, Talks and Treaties.

The Lawson McGhee Library, Knoxville, Tennessee.
> In addition to a wealth of other material in the McClung Collection the Library contains the Henley Papers and an extensive collection of British Transcripts for the Revolutionary period.

The Filson Club, Louisville, Kentucky.
> The Ballard Thruston transcripts of the George Rogers Clark Papers were used for the history of Fort Jefferson and the Virginia-Chickasaw Treaty of 1783.

Department of Archives and History, Jackson, Mississippi.
> The Mississippi Provincial Archives, Spanish Dominion, were used for the period 1793-98. These are Spanish documents drawn from the archives of Spain and Cuba bearing on the history of Mississippi.

Florida Historical Society Library, University of Florida, Gainesville.
> The Panton, Leslie and Company Papers consist of the Cruzat and Greenslade Papers. They are largely concerned with domestic matters but have much incidental material on Indian trade.

Alabama Department of Archives and History.
> G. S. Gaines, "Reminiscences of Early Times in Mississippi Territory." Gaines was for many years Factor at St. Stephens and had an influential part in enlisting Indian support in the War of 1812.

University of Georgia
> Telamon Cuyler MSS, Indian Affairs, University of Georgia.

BOOKS

Abel, Heloise. *The History of Events Resulting in Indian Consolidation West of the Mississippi*. The American Historical Association *Annual Report*. Washington, 1906.

Abernethy, T. P. *Western Lands and the American Revolution*. New York, 1937.

Alden, J. R. *John Stuart and the Southern Colonial Frontier*. Ann Arbor, 1944.

American State Papers, Indian Affairs, 2 vols.; *Foreign Relations,* 6 vols.; *Public Lands,* 8 vols. Washington, 1832–61.

Annals of Congress, 1789–1824, 42 vols. Washington, 1834–56.

Bartram, William. *Travels through North and South Carolina, Georgia, East and West Florida, the Cherokee Country, the Extensive Territories of the Muscogulgees or Creek Confederacy, and the Country of the Choctaws,* 1773–1778. Philadelphia, 1791.

Bassett, J. S., ed. *The Correspondence of Andrew Jackson.* 6 vols. Washington, 1924–33.

Brown, John P. *Old Frontiers.* Kingsport, 1938.

Calendar of Virginia State Papers, 1652–1869. 11 vols. Richmond, 1875–93.

Candler, Allen D., ed. *Colonial Records of Georgia.* 26 vols. Atlanta, 1904–16.

Carter, C. E., ed. *Territorial Papers of the United States:* Territory South of the River Ohio, and Mississippi Territory. Vols. II, V, and VI. Washington, 1934——.

Caughey, J. W. *McGillivray of the Creeks.* Norman, 1938.

——. *Bernardo de Gálvez in Louisiana, 1776–1783.* Berkeley, 1934.

Clark, Walter, ed. *North Carolina State Records.* 15 vols. Winston-Salem, 1895–96.

Collins, Lewis and Richard. *History of Kentucky.* Reprint, Louisville, 1924.

Crane, Verner W. *The Southern Frontier, 1670–1732.* Durham, 1928.

Cushman, H. B. *History of the Choctaw, Chickasaw and Natchez Indians.* Greenville, Texas, 1899.

Debo, Angie. *The Road to Disappearance.* Norman, 1941.

Eaton, Rachel Caroline. *John Ross and the Cherokee Indians.* Menasha, Wisconsin, 1914.

Ellicott, Andrew. *The Journal of Andrew Ellicott.* Philadelphia, 1803.

Esarey, Logan, ed. *Messages and Letters of William Henry Harrison.* Indiana Historical Collection. Vols. VII and VIII. Indianapolis, 1922.

Ford, W. C., and Gaillard Hunt, eds. *Journals of the Continental Congress, 1774–1789.* 27 vols. Washington, 1904–28.

Foreman, Grant. *Sequoyah.* Norman, 1937.

Halbert, H. S., and T. H. Ball. *The Creek War of 1813 and 1814.* Chicago, 1895.

Hamilton, Peter J. *Colonial Mobile.* Boston, 1910.

Hanna, Charles A. *The Wilderness Trail.* 2 vols. New York, 1911.

Hawkins, Benjamin. *Letters of Benjamin Hawkins, 1796–1806.* Collections of the Georgia Historical Society. Vol. IX. Savannah, 1916.

———. *A Sketch of the Creek Country in the Years 1798 and 1799.* Publications of the Georgia Historical Society. Vol. III. Americus, Georgia, 1938.

Haywood, John. *The Civil and Political History of the State of Tennessee.* Nashville, 1915.

Hodge, F. W., ed. *Handbook of American Indians North of Mexico.* Bureau of American Ethnology *Bulletin No. 30.* 2 vols. Washington, 1910–11.

Kappler, Charles J. *Indian Affairs, Laws and Treaties.* 3 vols. Washington, 1892–1913.

Lester, W. S. *The Transylvania Company.* Spencer, Indiana, 1935.

McKenney, Thomas L., and James Hall. *A History of the Indian Tribes of North America.* 3 vols. Philadelphia, 1838–44.

McLendon, S. G. *History of the Public Domain of Georgia.* Atlanta, 1924.

Milfort, Louis (Le Clerc). *Mémoire ou coup d'oeil rapide sur mes différens voyages et mon séjour dans la nation Crëck.* Paris, 1802.

Miller, Hunter. *Treaties and other International Acts of the United States of North America.* 8 vols. Washington, 1931–48.

Milling, Chapman J. *Red Carolinians.* Chapel Hill, 1940.

Mooney, James. *Myths of the Cherokee.* Bureau of American Ethnology *Nineteenth Annual Report,* Part I. Washington, 1900.

———. *The Siouan Tribes of the East.* Bureau of American Ethnology *Bulletin No. 22.* Washington, 1894.

Morse, Jedidiah. *Report to the Secretary of War on Indian Affairs.* New Haven, 1822.

Parton, James. *Life of Andrew Jackson.* 3 vols. New York, 1887–88.

Pickett, A. J. *History of Alabama and Incidentally of Georgia and Mississippi.* 2 vols. Birmingham, 1900.

Pope, John. *Tour through the Southern States and Western Territories of North America.* Richmond, 1792.

Putnam, A. W. *History of Middle Tennessee.* Nashville, 1859.

Ramsey, J. G. M. *The Annals of Tennessee to the End of the Eighteenth Century.* Kingsport, Tennessee, 1926.

Richardson, James D., ed. *Messages and Papers of the President, 1789–1897.* 10 vols. Washington, 1896–99.

Roosevelt, Theodore. *Winning of the West.* New York, 1889.

Rowland, Dunbar, ed. *Mississippi Provincial Archives, English Dominion.* Nashville, 1911.

———, ed. *The Mississippi Territorial Archives, 1798–1803.* Nashville, 1905.

———, ed. *Official Letter Books of W. C. C. Claiborne,* 1801–1816. 6 vols. (Mississippi Department of Archives and History.) Jackson, 1917.

———, and A. G. Sanders, eds. *Mississippi Provincial Archives, French Dominion.* 3 vols. (Mississippi Department of Archives and History.) Jackson, 1927–32.

Rowland, Mrs. Dunbar. *Andrew Jackson's Campaign against the British or the Mississippi Territory in the War of 1812.* New York, 1926.

Royce, Charles C. *Indian Land Cessions in the United States.* Bureau of American Ethnology *Eighteenth Annual Report,* Part II. Washington, 1889.

———. *The Cherokee Nation of Indians.* Bureau of American Ethnology *Fifth Annual Report.* Washington, 1887.

Saunders, William L., ed. *The Colonial Records of North Carolina.* 10 vols. Raleigh, North Carolina, 1886–90.

Schoolcraft, Henry R. *Historical and Statistical Information Regarding the History, Condition and the Prospects of the Indian Tribes of the United States.* 6 vols. Philadelphia, 1851–57.

Serrano y Sanz, Manuel. *España y Los Indios Cherokis y Chactas en la Segunda Mitad del Siglo XVIII.* Seville, 1916.

Shaw, Helen Louise. *British Administration of the Southern Indians, 1756–1783.* Lancaster, Pennsylvania, 1931.

Smith, W. H., ed. *The St. Clair Papers.* 2 vols. Cincinnati, 1882.

Starkey, Marion L. *The Cherokee Nation.* New York, 1946.

Swanton, John R. *Early History of the Creek Indians and Their Neighbors.* Bureau of American Ethnology *Bulletin No. 73.* Washington, 1922.

———. *Source Material for the Social and Ceremonial Life of the Choctaw Indians.* Bureau of American Ethnology *Bulletin No. 103.* Washington, 1931.

———. *Social Organization and Social Usages of the Indians of the Creek Confederacy.* Bureau of American Ethnology *Forty-second Annual Report.* Washington, 1928.

———. *Indian Tribes of the Lower Mississippi Valley and Adjacent*

Coast of the Gulf of Mexico. Bureau of American Ethnology *Bulletin No. 43.* Washington, 1911.

――――. *Social Beliefs and Usages of the Chickasaw Indians.* Bureau of American Ethnology *Forty-fourth Annual Report.* Washington, 1928.

Thomas, Cyrus. *The Cherokees in Pre-Columbian Times.* New York, 1890.

U. S. Supreme Court. Report of Cases Argued and Adjudged . . . . 12 Wheaton, *Harcourt v. Gaillard*, 716.

Walker, R. S. *Torchlight to the Cherokees.* New York, 1932.

Whitaker, A. P. *Spanish-American Frontier, 1783–1795.* Boston, 1927.

Willett, William Marinus. *A Narrative of the Military Activities of Colonel Marinus Willett.* New York, 1831.

Williams, Samuel C. *Beginnings of West Tennessee in the Land of the Chickasaws, 1541–1841.* Johnson City, Tennessee, 1930.

――――. *The Lost State of Franklin.* New York, 1933.

――――. *Dawn of Tennessee Valley and Tennessee History.* Johnson City, Tennessee, 1939.

――――, ed. *Early Travels in the Tennessee Country, 1541–1800.* Johnson City, Tennessee, 1928.

――――, ed. *Adair's History of the American Indians.* Johnson City, Tennessee, 1930.

Woodward, Thomas S. *Reminiscences of the Creek or Muscogee Indians.* Reprint, Tuscaloosa, Alabama, 1929.

Wright, Muriel H. *A Guide to the Indian Tribes of Oklahoma.* Norman, 1951.

ARTICLES

Beckner, Lucien. "Eskippakithiki: The Last Indian Town in Kentucky," *The Filson Club History Quarterly*, Vol. VI, 355–82.

Burnett, E. C., ed. "Documents Relating to Bourbon County, Georgia, 1785–1786," *American Historical Review*, Vol. XV, 66–111, 297–353.

Caughey, J. W. "Willing's Expedition down the Mississippi," *Louisiana Historical Quarterly*, Vol. XV, 5–36.

Corbitt, D. C. "James Colbert and the Spanish Claim to the East Bank of the Mississippi," *Mississippi Valley Historical Review*, Vol. XXIV, 457–72.

――――, ed. and trans. "Papers Relating to the Georgia-Florida Frontier, 1784–1800," *Georgia Historical Quarterly*, Vols. XX–XXV.

——, and Roberta, eds. "Papers from the Spanish Archives Relating to Tennessee and the Old Southwest," *East Tennessee Historical Society Publications*, Vols. IX–XXIII.

——, and Lanning, J. T. "A Letter of Marque Issued by William Augustus Bowles as Director-General of the State of Muscogee," *Journal of Southern History*, Vol. XI, 246–61.

Cotterill, R. S. "The Virginia-Chickasaw Treaty of 1783," *Journal of Southern History*, Vol. VII, 483–96.

——. "A Chapter of Panton, Leslie and Company," *Journal of Southern History*, Vol. X, 275–92.

Cox, I. J. ed. "Documents Relating to Zachariah Cox," *Quarterly Publication* of the Historical and Philosophical Society of Ohio, Vol. VIII, 31–114.

Crane, Verner W. "The Origin of the Name of the Creek Indians," *Mississippi Valley Historical Review*, Vol. V, 339–42.

——. "The Southern Frontier in Queen Anne's War," *American Historical Review*, Vol. XXIV, 379–95.

Cruzat, Heloise H. trans. "Journal of an Indian Talk," *Florida Historical Society Quarterly*, Vol. VIII, 131–42.

Downes, R. C. "Creek–American Relations, 1782–1790," *Georgia Historical Quarterly*, Vol. XXI, 142–84.

Franklin, Neil. "Virginia and the Cherokee Indian Trade, 1673–1752," *East Tennessee Historical Society Publications*, Vol. IV, 3–21.

Goodpasture, A. V. "Indian Wars and Warriors of the Old Southwest, 1720–1807," *Tennessee Historical Magazine*, Vol. IV, 3–49, 106–11.

Green, F. M. "Georgia's Forgotten Industry: Gold Mining," *Georgia Historical Quarterly*, Vol. XIX, 93–111, 210–28.

Greenslade, Mrs. J. W., transcriber, "A Journal of John Forbes," *Florida Historical Society Quarterly*, Vol. IX, 279–89.

Griffin, James B. "On the Historical Location of the Totero and the Mohetan in the Ohio Valley," *American Anthropologist*, New Series, Vol. XLIV, 275–80.

Halbert, Henry S. "Nanih Waiya, the Sacred Mount of the Choctaws," *Publications* of the Mississippi Historical Society, Vol. II, 228–34.

——. "Funeral Customs of the Mississippi Choctaws," *Publications* of the Mississippi Historical Society, Vol. III, 353–66.

——. "The Choctaw Creation Legend," *Publications* of the Mississippi Historical Society, Vol. IV, 267–70.

———. "District Divisions of the Choctaw Nation," *Publications* of the Alabama Historical Society, Miscellaneous Collections, Vol. I, 375–85.

Hamer, P. M. "The Wataugans and the Cherokee Indians in 1776," East Tennessee Historical Society *Publications*, Vol. III, 108–26.

———. "John Stuart's Indian Policy During the Early Months of the American Revolution," *Mississippi Valley Historical Review*, Vol. XVII (December, 1930), 351–67.

———. "The British in Canada and the Southern Indians," East Tennessee Historical Society *Publications*, Vol. II, 107–34.

———, ed. "Letters of William Blount," East Tennessee Historical Society *Publications*, Vol. IV, 122–33.

Haskins, C. H. "The Yazoo Land Companies," *Papers* of the American Historical Association, Vol. V, 395–437.

Henderson, Archibald. "The Treaty of Long Island of Holston, July, 1777," *North Carolina Historical Review*, Vol. VIII, 55–116.

Kinnaird, Lawrence. "The Significance of William Augustus Bowles' Seizure of Panton's Apalachee Store in 1792," *Florida Historical Society Quarterly*, Vol. IX, 156–92.

———. "International Rivalry in the Creek Country," *Florida Historical Society Quarterly*, Vol. X, 59–85.

Leftwich, G. J. "Cotton Gin Port and Gaines' Trace," Mississippi Historical Society *Publications*, Vol. VII, 263–70.

Linecum, Gideon. "Life of Apushimataha," *Publications* of the Mississippi Historical Society, Vol. IX, 415–85.

Love, W. A. "The Mayhew Mission to the Choctaws," *Publications* of the Mississippi Historical Society, Vol. XI, 363–402.

———. "General Jackson's Military Road," *Publications* of the Mississippi Historical Society, Vol. XI, 403–17.

McMurry, Donald L. "The Indian Policy of the Federal Government and the Economic Development of the Southwest, 1789–1801," *Tennessee Historical Magazine*, Vol. I, 21–39 and 106–19.

Myer, W. E. "Indian Trails of the Southeast," Bureau of American Ethnology *Forty-second Annual Report*, 1928. pp. 727–857.

Parish, J. C. "The Intrigues of Dr. James O'Fallon," *Mississippi Valley Historical Review*, Vol. XVII, 230–63.

Pound, Merret B. "Colonel Benjamin Hawkins of North Carolina, Benefactor of the Southern Indians," *North Carolina Historical Review*, Vol. XIX, 1–21, 168–86.

Robertson, James. "Correspondence of James Robertson," *American Historical Magazine*, Vol. IV, 89–94.

Storm, Colton, ed. "Up the Tennessee in 1790: The Report of Major John Doughty to the Secretary of War," The East Tennessee Historical Society *Publications*, Vol. XVII, 119–32.

Street, Oliver D. "Houston County in the Great Bend of the Tennessee," *Alabama Historical Quarterly*, Vol. VI, 50–59.

———. "Cherokee Towns and Villages in Alabama," *Publications* of the Alabama Historical Society, Vol. I, 416–21.

Swan, Caleb. "Position and State of Manners and Arts in the Creek or Muscogee Nation in 1791," H. R. Schoolcraft, *Indian Tribes*, Vol. V, 251–83., *q. v.*

Swanton, John R. "Siouan Tribes in the Ohio Valley," *American Anthropologist*, New Series, Vol. XLV, 49–66.

———. "Aboriginal Culture of the Southeast," Bureau of American Ethnology *Forty-second Annual Report*, (1928). pp. 673–728.

Thompson, Isabel. "The Blount Conspiracy," East Tennessee Historical Society *Publications*, Vol. II, 3–21.

Turner, F. J., ed. "Documents on the Blount Conspiracy, 1795–1797," *American Historical Review*, Vol. X, 574–606.

Warren, Harry. "Some Chickasaw Chiefs and Prominent Men," *Publications* of the Mississippi Historical Society, Vol. VIII, 555–70.

Weeks, S. B. "General Joseph Martin and the War of the Revolution in the West," American Historical Association *Annual Report* (1893). pp. 401–27.

Whitaker, A. P. "Alexander McGillivray, 1783–1789," *North Carolina Historical Review*, Vol. V, 181–203, 289–309.

———. "The Muscle Shoals Speculation, 1783–1789," *Mississippi Valley Historical Review*, Vol. XIII, 365–86.

———. "Spain and the Cherokee Indians, 1783–1796," *North Carolina Historical Review*, Vol. IV, 85–98, 252–69.

White, Kate. "John Chisholm, a Soldier of Fortune," East Tennessee Historical Society *Publications*, Vol. I, 60–66.

INDEX

of which *The Southern Indians* is the thirty-eighth volume, was inaugurated in 1932 by the University of Oklahoma Press, and has as its purpose the reconstruction of American Indian civilization by presenting aboriginal, historical, and contemporary Indian life. The following list is complete as of the date of the printing of this volume:

1. Alfred Barnaby Thomas. *Forgotten Frontiers:* A Study of the Spanish Indian Policy of Don Juan Bautista de Anza, Governor of New Mexico, 1777–1787.
2. Grant Foreman. *Indian Removal:* The Emigration of the Five Civilized Tribes of Indians.
3. John Joseph Mathews. *Wah'Kon-Tah:* The Osage and the White Man's Road.
4. Grant Foreman. *Advancing the Frontier, 1830–1860.*
5. John Homer Seger. *Early Days among the Cheyenne and Arapahoe Indians.* Edited by Stanley Vestal. Out of print.
6. Angie Debo. *The Rise and Fall of the Choctaw Republic.*
7. Stanley Vestal (ed.). *New Sources of Indian History, 1850–1891.* Out of print.
8. Grant Foreman. *The Five Civilized Tribes.*
9. Alfred Barnaby Thomas. *After Coronado:* Spanish Exploration Northeast of New Mexico, 1696–1727.
10. Frank B. Speck. *Naskapi:* The Savage Hunters of the Labrador Peninsula. Out of print.
11. Elaine Goodale Eastman. *Pratt:* The Red Man's Moses.
12. Althea Bass. *Cherokee Messenger:* A Life of Samuel Austin Worcester.
13. Thomas Wildcat Alford. *Civilization.* As told to Florence Drake. Out of print.
14. Grant Foreman. *Indians and Pioneers:* The Story of the American Southwest before 1830.
15. George E. Hyde. *Red Cloud's Folk:* A History of the Oglala Sioux Indians.
16. Grant Foreman. *Sequoyah.*
17. Morris L. Wardell. *A Political History of the Cherokee Nation. 1838–1907.* Out of print.
18. John Walton Caughey. *McGillivray of the Creeks.*
19. Edward Everett Dale and Gaston Litton. *Cherokee Cavaliers:* Forty Years of Cherokee History as Told in the Correspondence of the Ridge-Watie-Boudinot Family.
20. Ralph Henry Gabriel. *Elias Boudinot, Cherokee, and His America.* Out of print.

97. Georgiana C. Nammack. *Fraud, Politics, and Dispossession of the Indians:* The Iroquois Land Frontier in the Colonial Period.

98. *The Chronicles of Michoacán.* Translated and edited by Eugene R. Craine and Reginald C. Reindorp.

99. J. Eric S. Thompson. *Maya History and Religion.*

100. Peter J. Powell. *Sweet Medicine:* The Continuing Role of the Sacred Arrows, the Sun Dance, and the Sacred Buffalo Hat in Northern Cheyenne History.

101. Karen Daniels Petersen. *Plains Indian Art from Fort Marion.*

102. Fray Diego Durán. *Book of the Gods and Rites and The Ancient Calendar.* Translated and edited by Fernando Horcasitas and Doris Heyden. Foreword by Miguel León-Portilla.

103. Bert Anson. *The Miami Indians:* Sovereigns of the Wabash-Maumee.

104. Robert H. Ruby and John A. Brown. *The Spokane Indians:* Children of the Sun. Foreword by Robert L. Bennett.

105. Virginia Cole Trenholm. *The Arapahoes, Our People.*

106. Angie Debo, *Indians of the United States:* A General History.

107. Herman Grey, *Tales from the Mohaves.*

108. Stephen Dow Beckham. *Requiem for a People:* The Rogue Indians and the Frontiersmen.

109. Arrell M. Gibson. *The Chickasaws.*

110. *Indian Oratory:* A Collection of Famous Speeches by Noted Indian Chieftains. Compiled by W. C. Vanderwerth.

111. *The Sioux of the Rosebud:* A History in Pictures. Photographs by John A. Anderson, text by Henry W. Hamilton and Jean Tyree Hamilton.